Play for Java

Play for Java

COVERS PLAY 2

NICOLAS LEROUX
SIETSE DE KAPER

MANNING

SHELTER ISLAND

For online information and ordering of this and other Manning books, please visit www.manning.com. The publisher offers discounts on this book when ordered in quantity. For more information, please contact

Special Sales Department
Manning Publications Co.
20 Baldwin Road
PO Box 261
Shelter Island, NY 11964
Email: orders@manning.com

Manning Publications Co.   Development editor: Karen Miller
20 Baldwin Road   Copyeditors: Benjamin Berg, Melinda Rankin
PO Box 261   Proofreader: Andy Carroll
Shelter Island, NY 11964   Typesetter: Dottie Marsico
                                 Cover designer: Marija Tudor

ISBN 9781617290909
Printed in the United States of America
1 2 3 4 5 6 7 8 9 10 – EBM – 19 18 17 16 15 14

brief contents

contents

foreword

Before Struts existed I wrote an entire Java web application inside a single Servlet method because that is basically how I'd done things in Perl. Back then web apps were simple and the tools were immature. As the web evolved, dozens of Java web frameworks emerged which were all built on the same Servlet foundation. Being over 15 years old, the Servlet foundation is showing its age. The traditional Java web frameworks haven't kept up with the modern needs for higher developer productivity and emerging web techniques like RESTful JSON services, WebSockets, asset compilers, and reactive architectures.

Play Framework was created to revolutionize Java web application development. Play is built for modern web needs and puts developer productivity at the core of the framework. I love that with Play I just hit Refresh in my browser and I instantly see my changes, whether they're Java, JavaScript, or CSS. There is no container to redeploy into or restart. If there are compile errors I see them in a helpful way in my browser. Things like testing tools, persistence libraries, JSON support, and other commonly needed pieces come out-of-the-box with Play. By being RESTful by default, supporting push channels, and utilizing non-blocking connections, Play provides a solid foundation for scalable reactive applications.

When I made the transition from Perl to object-oriented Java web apps, I needed some help to get me over the hurdles of figuring out new ways to do things. Luckily books like *Thinking in Java* (Bruce Eckel) and *Java Servlet Programming* (Jason Hunter) helped me move into a new way of thinking which allowed me to quickly and easily make the transition to something new and better. I have no doubt that the book you're reading now will do the same for you. Nicolas and Sietse have been using Play from its early days. They're experts who haven't just played with the framework, they've built numerous production applications using Play. They've experienced the challenge of adopting something new and know the pains you can avoid.

Web programming has changed dramatically since the early Servlet days. Play has revolutionized the development experience for building modern Java web applications. This book will help you quickly make the transition to more productive ways to build modern web apps. I'm confident that down the road you will look back on this book like I look back on Eckel's and Hunter's books. I just wish this book had existed when I learned Play.

JAMES WARD
PRODUCT OWNER OF PLAY FRAMEWORK AT TYPESAFE
@_JAMESWARD | WWW.JAMESWARD.COM

preface

Back in 2009, I discovered Play by chance while surfing the web. I was surprised at how easy it was to get started with the framework. At the time, I was doing most of my web development using the Seam web framework. Play was a game changer then, and I started to build all my applications using it. Soon enough, I joined Guillaume Bort, the founder of Play, and contributed to the framework.

The framework started to gain more and more traction, though mostly in Europe. Time passed, and we released Play 1.1 and then Play 1.2. Then Guillaume started to envision a complete rewrite of Play using Scala as a core language, giving Play extra power. The goal was to empower Play's users while keeping the main success ingredients: Play's simplicity and rapidity. Guillaume soon joined forces with Sadek Drobi. Sadek put his functional programming knowledge into the mix and Play 2 was born! Though the Play 2 core uses advanced Scala features, Play 2 focuses on simplicity and has a fully supported Java API. Play 2 Java is probably the best option for building scalable web applications with simplicity in mind without sacrificing scalability and other features.

While I contributed little to Play 2's features codewise, my main contribution to Play 2 adoption is this book. I hope it will become an invaluable aid to professional Play developers. In truth, my coauthor Sietse and I could have added even more information to this book, but we hope that we've struck a good balance between useful content and weight. We also hope that you will enjoy the book and that it will help you unleash the full potential of Play while keeping its simplicity in mind.

NICOLAS LEROUX

Soon after Nicolas introduced Play at Lunatech, it became clear that this was going to be the framework we'd be using for all new projects. Play "gets it." For "it," in this case, a lot of things can be substituted. Play "gets" HTTP and the web in general, how developing web application works, what makes a nice and clean API, and more. This was clear from the early Play 1 beta versions, and that's why we've used it on many projects since 1.0 came out. It didn't disappoint.

Now, with Play 2, Play continues to improve web development for the Java platform.

It's interesting that we have to say "Java platform," rather than just Java. The Java platform is no longer synonymous with the Java language—there are a lot of different languages targeting the JVM, all trying to improve the developer experience in their own way. Play 2 embraces Scala, partly for its benefits as a reactive[1] language, but also for all the benefits that a strictly type-safe language provides. By supplying a first-class Java API to the framework, Play 2 provides the best of both worlds.

We wrote this book in the hope that it will help you take advantage of all the benefits that web development using Play offers. But, perhaps more importantly, we also wanted to teach you all the core concepts behind Play. They're just good principles when developing for the web, and Play makes it easy to apply them. We hope we succeeded in these goals, and that you'll enjoy this book and developing Play applications.

SIETSE DE KAPER

---

[1] Read the Reactive Manifesto at http://www.reactivemanifesto.org/ if you want to know what that means, exactly.

acknowledgments

We first want to thank Karen Miller, our development editor at Manning, who put up with our many missed deadlines and gave us great feedback during the writing process. We'd also like to thank our awesome copyeditors, Benjamin Berg, Melinda Rankin, and Andy Carroll, for catching an amazing number of grammatical errors in the early revisions of the book. The greater Manning team deserves kudos as well; they've made for a very pleasant writing experience over the past year and a half.

We would like to think James Ward for writing such a great foreword to our book.

Thanks to Wayne Ellis for being our technical proofreader, catching those bugs we missed, and helping improve the source code for the book.

Big thanks to our team of reviewers, who provided invaluable feedback during various stages of the book's development: Dr. Lochana C. Menikarachchi, Franco Lombardo, Jeroen Nouws, John Tyler, Koray Güçlü, Laurent DeCorps, Michael Schleichardt, Patria H. Lukman, Ricky Yim, Rob Williams, Ryan Cox, Santosh Shanbhag, and William E. Wheeler.

Special thanks to the *Play for Scala* book team—our colleagues Peter Hilton, Erik Bakker, and Francisco Canedo—for cooperating with us on the book. We'd like to thank Lunatech for providing us with a great work environment that makes it possible to do cool stuff like work with and contribute to Play.

In addition, we'd like to give a big warm thank you to the Play community. Without the community, the Play project wouldn't be as successful as it is today. In addition to the Play community, we would like to especially thank all our readers who posted on the Manning Online Author forum after reviewing the Early Access (MEAP) chapters.

Special thanks to Steve Chaloner, "Infra," "Askar," and all others for providing such great feedback.

   Of course, our biggest supporters are our families, who supported us even though they don't have a clue what the book is about.

NICOLAS would like to thank his wife Sylke for her support during the book project, and his girls Emilie and Isabelle for distracting him when in need of a break.

SIETSE would like to thank his wife Joekie for her endless patience and loving support—not just during the writing of this book, but always.

about this book

This book will get you started developing web applications with Play 2, using the Java programming language. But, perhaps more importantly, it'll also teach you the concepts behind web development with Play.

There are many Java web frameworks, but most of them have a key flaw: they try to hide the web behind an abstraction layer, rather than embracing it. That is the most important difference between Play and most other Java web frameworks (Servlets, we're looking at you!).

Developing a web application with Play requires a certain mindset. Throughout the book, we try to teach you how to achieve that. If you're a Java EE veteran, we'll do our best to lessen the culture shock. But if you're new to web development with Java, or web development in general, we've got your back, too. We do our best to explain everything about web development that you need to know.

The only assumption we make is that you have *some* background in Java programming—you should be comfortable reading and writing Java code. We've used Java 7 syntax throughout this book, since that is the supported version of Java at the time of writing.

You've probably already heard that Play 2 is written in Scala. That is absolutely true, and we feel that the language and the tools available for the platform are an excellent choice to write a web *platform* in. We also feel that there is no reason you should have to build a web *application* in Scala. Play developers apparently agree, because Play has a first-class Java API, which means you can write a full application using Play 2 without writing a single line of Scala.

In this book, we avoid discussing Scala wherever possible. There is one subject where this wasn't avoidable: view templates in Play 2 are based on the Scala language. But in the rest of the book we treat it as just another template language, showing you the basic constructs you need to create your templates. We promise you don't need to learn any Scala to follow along with this book.

As we write this, the current version of Play is 2.2. That means that all the code we demonstrate assumes a Play version of 2.2.x, and we've tested every code sample under version 2.2.0.

Roadmap

This book is organized in three parts. The first part introduces you to all the basic concepts of Play. The second part dives deeper into the core elements of a Play application, while the third part demonstrates more advanced things that you can do with Play. Here's a quick overview of all the chapters.

Chapter 1 introduces Play, and highlights some of its important features. It then shows you how to install Play and create a simple "Hello World" application.

Chapter 2 takes a look at what makes up a Play application. It goes over all the directories and files, and explains what every component is for. We also show you how you can import a Play application into your IDE.

Chapter 3 shows a simple web application, without going into too much detail. In this chapter, we'll see every important part of Play in action: controllers, actions, templates, and forms. This is the start of an application that we'll develop in the book.

Chapter 4 takes a step back and looks at where Play fits in a more conventional enterprise architecture. It contrasts Play with conventional JEE development, and shows how Play can tackle major challenges in such an architecture.

Chapter 5 is all about controllers. It explains what controllers are and how action methods help you interface with the web. It also explains how routing works and introduces the different scopes.

Chapter 6 covers how to handle user input. We show you how to use Play's Form API, as well as how binding and validation work.

Chapter 7 introduces database persistence. We explain the concept of an ORM and show you how to use the Ebean ORM tool with Play. At the end of the chapter, we discuss how you can use JPA with Play instead of Ebean, should you choose to do so.

Chapter 8 explains how view templates work. It explains the template syntax, and shows how to use composition to structure your pages in a reusable manner. At the end of the chapter, we look at using Play's support for LESS and CoffeeScript, and introduce the internationalization API.

Chapter 9 covers one of the more powerful features of Play: asynchronous request handling. It explains why long-running tasks are better performed "in the background," and how to achieve that easily. It also shows how you can have a web application with streaming data, using WebSockets or Comet.

Chapter 10 explains how you can build a secure application in Play. It also explains how you can avoid common security problems, and how you can use filters to implement authentication.

Chapter 11 covers the build process of Play. It explains the configuration files, and shows you how to package your code in reusable modules. Finally, it shows you what's involved with taking your application to production.

Chapter 12 introduces the tools that Play has for testing your application. It explains the different kinds of automated tests there are, and how you can write them for your application.

Code conventions and downloads

All source code in listings or in text is in a `fixed-width font like this` to separate it from ordinary text. Code annotations accompany many of the listings, highlighting important concepts. The current version of Play is 2.2 at the time of writing. That means that all the code we demonstrate assumes a Play version of 2.2.x, and we've tested every code sample under version 2.2.0.

Source code for all working examples in this book is available for download from GitHub at https://github.com/playforjava, as well as from the publisher's website at www.manning.com/PlayforJava.

Author Online

The purchase of *Play for Java* includes free access to a private web forum run by Manning Publications where you can make comments about the book, ask technical questions, and receive help from the authors and other users. To access the forum and subscribe to it, visit www.manning.com/PlayforJava. This page provides information on how to get on the forum once you're registered, what kind of help is available, and the rules of conduct on the forum.

Manning's commitment to readers is to provide a venue for meaningful dialogue between individual readers and between readers and the authors. It is not a commitment to any specific amount of participation on the part of the authors, whose contribution to the forum remains voluntary (and unpaid). Let your voice be heard, and keep the authors on their toes!

The Author Online forum and the archives of previous discussions will be accessible from the publisher's website as long as the book is in print.

About the authors

NICOLAS LEROUX is a senior architect and Technical Director at Lunatech Research where he's worked since 2001 and where he is mainly involved in JEE projects for Lunatech's customers. Since 2009, Nicolas has developed a passion for the Play framework and is a core developer of its open source project. He was involved in the first version of the Play framework and is contributing to the second one. Nicolas also enjoys introducing Play to new audiences and is a frequent speaker at conferences.

SIETSE DE KAPER started his career as a software developer at Lunatech Research in 2007. He has worked on several commercial web applications using various web frameworks—mostly Java, but also PHP, Ruby, and Scala. Sietse started developing applications with the Play framework when version 1.0 came out in October 2009. After using Play on several projects, he now considers it the most effective framework in the Java ecosystem.

About the cover illustration

The figure on the cover of *Play for Java* is captioned a "Farmer from Dobrota, Montenegro." The illustration is taken from the reproduction, published in 2006, of a nineteenth-century collection of costumes and ethnographic descriptions entitled *Dalmatia* by Professor Frane Carrara (1812–1854), an archaeologist and historian, and the first director of the Museum of Antiquity in Split, Croatia. The illustrations were obtained from a helpful librarian at the Ethnographic Museum (formerly the Museum of Antiquity), itself situated in the Roman core of the medieval center of Split: the ruins of Emperor Diocletian's retirement palace from around AD 304. The book includes finely colored illustrations of figures from different regions of Dalmatia, accompanied by descriptions of the costumes and of everyday life.

Dobrota is a small town on the Adriatic coast, officially a part of the municipality of Kotor, an ancient Mediterranean port on Kotor Bay, surrounded by fortifications built in the Venetian period. Today it is increasingly a tourist destination, due to the dramatic limestone cliffs and beautiful coastal vistas. The man on the cover is wearing an embroidered vest over black woolen pantaloons and a wide colorful sash. He is carrying a long pipe, a musket, and has pistols inserted in his sash. The rich and colorful embroidery on his costume is typical for this region, and marks this as an outfit for special occasions and not for working the land.

Dress codes have changed since the nineteenth century, and the diversity by region, so rich at the time, has faded away. It is now hard to tell apart the inhabitants of different continents, let alone different towns or regions. Perhaps we have traded cultural diversity for a more varied personal life—certainly for a more varied and fast-paced technological life.

At a time when it is hard to tell one computer book from another, Manning celebrates the inventiveness and initiative of the computer business with book covers based on the rich diversity of regional life of two centuries ago, brought back to life by illustrations from collections such as this one.

Part 1

Introduction and first steps

In part 1, we introduce Play and show the basics of creating a Play application.

Chapter 1 introduces Play, its core concepts, and its key features. We install Play and create our first application.

Chapter 2 breaks down the structure of a Play application, explaining what each file and folder is for.

Chapter 3 shows how to create a more fleshed-out application, giving you a taste of the key MVC components in a Play application.

An introduction to Play

This chapter covers

- What the Play framework is
- What high-productivity web frameworks are about
- Why Play supports both Java and Scala
- Reactive programming
- Play 2 enterprise features
- What a minimal Play application looks like

Play isn't really a Java web framework. Java's involved, but that isn't the whole story.

The first version of Play may have been written in the Java language, but it also ignored the conventions of the Java platform, providing a fresh alternative to excessive enterprise architectures. Play was not based on Java Enterprise Edition APIs and made for Java developers; Play is for *web* developers.

Play wasn't written *for* web developers, it was written *by* web developers, and they brought high-productivity web development from modern frameworks like Ruby on Rails and Django to the JVM. Play is for productive web developers.

Play 2 is written in Scala, but that doesn't mean you have to write your web applications in Scala or even know anything about Scala. This is because Play 2 comes with a complete Java API, giving you the option to pick the language that suits you best. If you've used Play 1.x before, you'll notice that the API has become more type-safe.

Play isn't about Scala and type safety, either. An important aspect of Play is the usability and attention to detail that results in a better developer experience (DX). When you add this to higher developer productivity and more elegant APIs and architectures, you get a new emergent property: Play is fun.

1.1 What Play is

Play is fun. Play makes you more productive. Play is also a web framework whose HTTP interface is simple, convenient, flexible, and powerful. Most importantly, Play improves on the most popular non-Java web development languages and frameworks—PHP and Ruby on Rails—by introducing the advantages of the Java Virtual Machine (JVM).

1.1.1 Key features

A variety of features and qualities make Play productive and fun to use:

- Simplicity
- Declarative application URL scheme configuration
- Type-safe mapping from HTTP to an idiomatic Scala or Java API
- Type-safe template syntax
- Architecture that embraces HTML5 client technologies
- Live code changes when you reload the page in your web browser
- Full-stack web-framework features, including persistence, security, and internationalization
- Support for event-driven, resilient, and scalable applications

We'll get back to why Play makes you more productive, but first let's look a little more closely at what it means for Play to be a full-stack framework. A full-stack framework gives you everything you need to build a typical web application, as illustrated in figure 1.1.

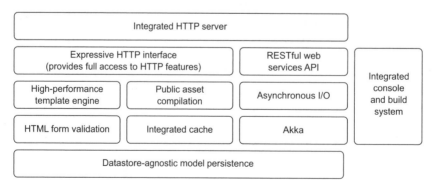

Figure 1.1 Play framework stack

Being "full stack" is not only a question of functionality, which may already exist as a collection of open source libraries. After all, what's the point of a framework if these libraries already exist and already provide everything you need to build an application? The difference is that a full-stack framework also provides a documented pattern for using separate libraries together in a certain way, and therefore provides confidence that a developer can make the separate components work together. Without this, you never know whether you're going to end up instead with two incompatible libraries or a badly designed architecture.

When it comes to building a web application, what this all means is that the common tasks are directly supported in a simple way, which saves you time.

1.1.2 Java and Scala

Play supports Java, and is in fact the best way to build a Java web application. Java's success as a programming language, particularly in enterprise software development, means that Play 1.x has been able to quickly build a large user community. If you're planning to use Play with Java, you particularly get to benefit from this community's size.

But recent years have seen the introduction of numerous JVM languages that provide a modern alternative to Java, usually aiming to be more type-safe, resulting in more concise code and support for functional programming idioms, with the ultimate goal of allowing developers to be more expressive and productive when writing code. Scala is currently the most evolved of the new statically typed JVM languages, and it's the second language that Play supports. Scala is meant (and proven) to be a *scalable* language, hence the name. Play 2 takes full advantage of the scalability that Scala offers, which means your Java applications will get these benefits, too.

Scalability is one of the major features of Play: it allows you to easily create highly scalable web applications. Scalability can mean a lot of different things, and throughout the book you'll see examples of how Play enables you to scale both horizontally and vertically. Most of this is thanks to Play's stateless nature, but also its foundation of Scala (and Akka), which enabled the developers of the framework to provide concurrent and nonblocking request processing. It also enabled developers to support applications in an event-driven way without sacrificing scalability. Nowadays, applications need to react to events and display live feeds rather than batch process during the night. Play was conceived with this perspective in mind. We'll talk more about this subject in the reactive programming section in this chapter.

> **Our sister book: *Play for Scala***
> If you're also interested in using Play to build web applications in Scala, then you should look at *Play for Scala*, which was written at the same time as this book. The differences between Scala and Java go beyond the syntax, and the Scala book is much more than a copy of this book with code samples in Scala. *Play for Scala* is focused on the idiomatic use of the Scala language with Play 2.

1.1.3   *Play is not Java EE*

Before Play, Java web frameworks were based on the Java Servlet API, the part of the
Java Enterprise Edition (Java EE) stack that provides the HTTP interface. Java EE and
its architectural patterns seemed like a really good idea, and brought some much-
needed structure to enterprise software development. But this turned out to be a
really bad idea, because structure came at the cost of additional complexity and low
developer satisfaction. Play is different, for several reasons, which we'll detail later in
this chapter. The biggest difference between Java EE and Play is simplicity. Play focuses
on providing simplicity to developers so that they can focus on their business problems and not on the framework itself. In contrast, Java EE used to be quite complex.

Java's design and evolution is focused on the Java platform, which also seemed like
a good idea to developers who were trying to consolidate various kinds of software
development. From a Java perspective, the web is only another external system. The
Servlet API, for example, is an abstraction layer over the web's own architecture that
provides a more Java-like API. Unfortunately, this turned out to be a bad idea as well,
because the web is more important than Java. When a web framework starts an architecture fight with the web, the framework loses. What we need instead is a web framework whose architecture embraces the web's, and whose API embraces HTTP.

1.2   *High-productivity web development*

Web frameworks for web developers are different. They embrace HTTP and provide
APIs that use HTTP's features instead of trying to hide HTTP, in the same way that web
developers build expertise in the standard web technologies—HTTP, HTML, CSS, and
JavaScript—instead of avoiding them.

1.2.1   *Working with HTTP*

Working with HTTP means letting the application developer make the web application
aware of the different HTTP methods, such as GET, POST, PUT, and DELETE, instead of
having an RPC-style layer on top of HTTP requests in order to tell the application
whether you want to create, update, or delete data. It also means accepting that application URLs are part of the application's public interface and should therefore be up
to the application developer to design instead of fixed by the framework.

This approach is for developers who not only work with the architecture of the
World Wide Web instead of against it, but who may have even read it. [1]

In the past, none of these web frameworks were written in Java, because the Java
platform's web technologies failed to emphasize simplicity, productivity, and usability.
This is the world that started with Perl (not Lisp as some might assume), was largely
taken over by PHP, and in more recent years has seen the rise of Ruby on Rails.

---

[1]   *Architecture of the World Wide Web, Volume One*, W3C, 2004 (http://www.w3.org/TR/webarch/).

1.2.2 *Simplicity, productivity, and usability*

In a web framework, simplicity comes from making it easy to do simple things in a few lines of code without extensive configuration. A "Hello World" in PHP is a single line of code; the other extreme is JavaServer Faces, which requires numerous files of various kinds before you can even serve a blank page.

Productivity starts with being able to make a code change, reload the web page in the browser, and see the result. This has always been the norm for many web developers, whereas Java web frameworks and application servers often have long build-redeploy cycles. Java hot-deployment solutions exist, but are not standard and come at the cost of additional configuration. Although there is more to productivity, this is what matters most.

Usability is related to developer productivity, but also to developer happiness. You're certainly more productive if it's easier to simply get things done, no matter how smart you are, but a usable framework can be more than that; it can be a joy to use. Fun, even.

1.3 *Reactive programming*

Play has unique features in the Java world. It allows applications to be nonblocking, asynchronous, and reactive. But what does this mean exactly? As we'll see in chapter 4, application requirements have changed dramatically in recent years. Today applications are deployed on everything from mobile devices to cloud-based clusters. User expectations are high: applications need to respond in milliseconds, and no downtime is allowed. Data needs are expanding into the petabytes.

Before Play and similar frameworks, scaling was achieved through buying larger servers, and concurrent processing via multithreading. Applications were running inside managed servers and containers. Applications were making little use of the multiple processors made available to them.

Reactive programming is about providing an architecture that allows developers to build systems that are event-driven, scalable, resilient, and responsive: delivering highly responsive user experiences with a real-time feel, backed by a scalable and resilient application stack, ready to be deployed on multicore and cloud computing architectures. The Play framework has these goals in mind and attempts to fulfill them.

Let's review each of the goals.

1.3.1 *Event-driven*

An application based on *asynchronous* communication implements a loosely coupled design. The sender and recipient can be implemented without regard to the details of how the events are propagated, allowing the interfaces to focus on the communication. Because the recipient of asynchronous communication can remain dormant until an event occurs or a message is received, an event-driven approach can make efficient use of existing resources, allowing large numbers of recipients to share a single hardware thread. A *nonblocking* application that is under heavy load can have lower latency and higher throughput than a traditional application based on blocking synchronization.

1.3.2   *Scalable*

A scalable application is one that can be expanded according to its demand. This can be achieved by adding elasticity to the application by adding or removing application nodes (servers or CPUs, for example). The architecture should handle elasticity without redesigning or rewriting the application. Cloud-computing environments tend to provide near to perfect elasticity to your application. An event-driven system provides the foundation for scalability because it provides loose coupling and location independence between components and subsystems.

1.3.3   *Resilient*

Application downtime nowadays is not allowed, and business users expect 24/7 uptime. If an application component crashes for one reason or another, the rest of the application should still work as expected. This means that each component needs to be isolated from other components' failure. The event-driven model has the necessary primitives to realize this model of failure management.

1.3.4   *Responsive*

Responsive applications are real-time and collaborative applications. Today, businesses try to engage their customers more and more. They are also trying to be really responsive to any customer feedback. Applications should therefore be real time and allow you to react to any customer feedback. Responsive applications are about real-time interaction between the different users. One example is Google Docs, which enables users to edit documents collaboratively in real time—allowing them to see each other's edits and comments live as they're made.

Now that we know all about Play's goals, let's see how Play fits at work. Not all enterprise applications have to be reactive.

1.4   *Play 2 enterprise features*

Play is also adapted to an enterprise environment. Mainly it satisfies the following enterprise requirements.

1.4.1   *Simplicity*

Play provides a clean component model that makes it easy to build scalable web applications that are testable. Simplicity has always been the Play framework's strong point and is important in an enterprise context. Developers need to concentrate on their business problems at hand and not on the framework. The framework should help them and not be in the way. The Play framework's first focus was always on simplicity. Simplicity doesn't mean a simple application: quite the opposite. Play provides simple but efficient building blocks, allowing development of complex applications. Simplicity is important in an enterprise context because it allows wide adoption of the framework within the company by lowering the barrier of entrance.

1.4.2 *Traditional data access*

Play provides all the necessary data access to enterprise data. This usually means accessing several databases from within one application. With Play, by default, you can access those data via JPA, the standard Java EE Java Persistence API, or via Ebean. JPA is currently widely adopted in the enterprise, so developers won't feel lost. Ebean is quite similar to JPA, but tries to be stateless with data access. You can also use Play's JDBC helpers if you want more low-level data access.

1.4.3 *Flexibility*

Play is flexible: almost everything is pluggable, configurable, and customizable. This means it's easy to change or extend any part of the framework. For example, you can rewrite the way Play handles request parsing. You can also plug your own logic inside the framework lifecycle, for example, before your application is started. Play is modular from the start. The Play framework is composed of several modules: `core`, `jdbc`, `jpa`, `json`, `cache`, and more.

1.4.4 *Integration*

Because Play is so flexible, it's easy to integrate a Play framework application with other (legacy) systems. For example, you can easily integrate with an LDAP server to authenticate using third-party libraries and make calls into it. Play provides hooks to plug in your custom code throughout the framework. Out of the box, you can integrate with any existing database through JPA, JDBC, or you can add your own persistence layer.

Through the use of modules, Play provides even more ways to integrate with other systems. As an enterprise, you can write your own reusable modules to integrate with legacy systems.

1.4.5 *Large-team applications*

Play is also made to work with large teams; it's possible to set up a project with multiple subprojects. The project can then be split among multiple teams with each team working on a subproject. Play provides support to manage those subprojects so they're automatically built and updated when releasing the application: applications can depend on other applications, and Play allows you to declare that and make it explicit.

1.4.6 *Security*

Play provides the backbone for handling authentication and authorization. As a developer, you need to hook into the Play security mechanism and provide the implementation that authenticates against your enterprise servers. Play goes even a step further, because it allows you to completely rewrite that part as well if the model doesn't fit your enterprise security model. Because Play stays simple, it's not difficult to plug in your own mechanism.

1.4.7   *Modularity*

Play is modular by design and allows developers to build simple, reusable pieces of software. Stacking up those reusable pieces makes it possible to build quite complex and robust systems. Each team can concentrate on a piece of the puzzle and each piece of the puzzle can be tested independently. Reusable modules can be shared among developers and enterprise departments. For example, an enterprise can build its authentication module once and make it available as a module to be reused by all applications.

After this Play framework overview, it's now time to experience simplicity!

1.5   *Hello Play!*

As you'd expect, it's easy to do something as simple as output "Hello world!" All you need to do is use the Play command that creates a new application and write a couple of lines of Java code. To begin to understand Play, you should run the command and type the code, because only then will you get your first experience of Play's simplicity, productivity, and usability. But to do that, you'll need to have Play installed. We'll get to that in a minute.

First, it's interesting to talk about why there even *is* an installation step with Play 2. Most web frameworks in the Java world are libraries that you add to your project and bootstrap with some configuration file (such as web.xml) or boilerplate code to run in a Servlet container or application server. With these frameworks, there *is* no install step. Play is more than a library; it provides a complete tool suite, including a web server and a build tool.

Installing Play is easy; here's how.

1.5.1   *Installing Play*

First, download Play 2.2 from the web site at http://playframework.org. Extract the .zip file to the location at which you want to install Play 2 (your home directory is fine). Next, you need to add this directory to your PATH system variable, which will make it possible for you to launch Play from anywhere.

Setting the PATH variable is OS-specific. Here are the instructions for OS X, Linux, and Windows:

- *Mac OS X*—Open the file /etc/paths in a text editor, and add the path where you installed Play to the file.
- *Linux*—Open your shell's startup file in a text editor. The name of the file depends on which shell you use; for example, .bashrc for bash or .zshrc for zsh. Add the following line to it: PATH="$PATH":/path/to/play (with the proper path substituted).
- *Windows 7*—Go to Control Panel > System and Security > System and click *Advanced System Settings* on the right side. Click the button *Environment Variables*. You'll see a window listing variables (as in figure 1.2), and there should be a user variable called PATH. Simply add the path to your Play installation to the end of its value.

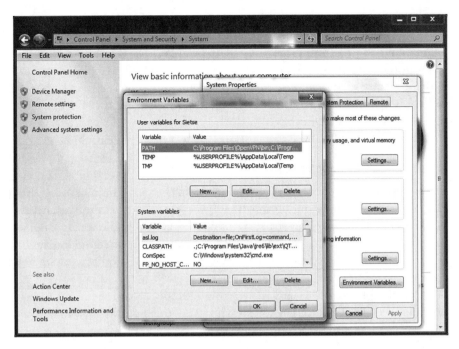

Figure 1.2 The Windows Environment Variables dialog

Mac users can use Homebrew

If you're using Mac OS X, you could also use Homebrew to install Play 2. Use the command `brew install play` to install, and Homebrew will download and extract the latest version and take care of adding it to your path, too.

Now Play should be available from any new shell you open. Go ahead and try it out; open a shell, and enter the `play` command. You should get output similar to this:

```
      _            _
 _ __ | | __ _ _  _| |
| '_ \| |/ _' | || |_|
|  __/|_|\___|\_  (_)
|_|             |__/

play! 2.1.1 (using Java 1.7.0_21 and Scala 2.10.0),
http://www.playframework.org

This is not a play application!

Use `play new` to create a new Play application in the current
directory, or go to an existing application and launch the development
console using `play`.

You can also browse the complete documentation at
http://www.playframework.org.
```

As you can see, this command didn't do much yet. But Play *does* try to be helpful; it tells you why it couldn't do anything ("This is not a play application!"), and it suggests a command you can use to get started (`play new`). This will be a recurring theme when using Play; whenever something goes wrong, Play will guess what you're trying to do, explain exactly where things went wrong, and suggest a next step to fix it. This isn't limited to the command-line output, though; we'll see useful error messages like this in our browsers later on, too.

For now, let's follow Play's suggestion: create a new application.

1.5.2 *Creating your first application*

A *Play application* is a directory on the filesystem that contains a certain structure that Play uses to find configuration information, code, and any other resources it needs. We don't need to create this structure ourselves; Play will do it for us when we use the `play new` command. This command will turn the current directory into a Play application, or you can add the desired name of your new application as a parameter, and it'll create that directory for you.

According to tradition, any first example in any sort of technical tutorial should be called "Hello World." Go ahead and type the following command: `play new HelloWorld`. Play will ask you to confirm the name, so hit Enter when the question comes up.

```
       _            _
 _ __ | | __ _ _  _|  |
| '_ \| |/ _' |  | ||  |_|
|  __/|_|\___|\__ (_)
|_|            |_/

play! 2.1.1 (using Java 1.7.0_21 and Scala 2.10.0)
http://www.playframework.org

The new application will be created in /Users/sietse/Hello World

What is the application name? [HelloWorld]
> HelloWorld

Which template do you want to use for this new application?

  1              - Create a simple Scala application
  2              - Create a simple Java application

>
```

Play is now asking us what kind of project we want. Pick option 2, Java.

```
> 2

OK, application HelloWorld is created.

Have fun!
```

Congratulations, you've created your first Play 2 application. Let's see what's inside.

1.5.3 Play application structure

The play new command always creates a default application with a basic structure, including a minimal HTTP routing configuration file, a controller class for handling HTTP requests, a view template, jQuery, and a default CSS stylesheet. Don't worry if you don't know what all these terms mean yet; we'll cover them in detail in chapter 2.

The full contents of a newly created application are shown next.

Listing 1.1 Files in a new Play application

```
├── README
├── app
│   ├── controllers
│   │   └── Application.java
│   └── views
│       ├── index.scala.html
│       └── main.scala.html
├── conf
│   ├── application.conf
│   └── routes
├── project
│   ├── build.properties
│   └── plugins.sbt
├── public
│   ├── images
│   │   └── favicon.png
│   ├── javascripts
│   │   └── jquery-1.9.0.min.js
│   └── stylesheets
│       └── main.css
├── build.sbt
└── test
    ├── ApplicationTest.java
    └── IntegrationTest.java
```

This directory structure is common to all Play applications.

Now that we've seen the files that make up our application, let's see what it looks like. Time to run the application.

1.5.4 Running the application

Play 2 always needs to be started from within an application directory, so cd into it: cd HelloWorld. Now start Play simply by typing play.

```
~$ cd HelloWorld
~/HelloWorld$ play
[info] Loading global plugins from /Users/sietse/.sbt/plugins
[info] Loading project definition from /Users/sietse/HelloWorld/project
[info] Set current project to HelloWorld

       _            _
 _ __ | | __ _ _  _| |
| '_ \| |/ _' || | |_|
|  __/|_|\____|\__ (_)
|_|            |__/
```

```
play! 2.2.0 (using Java 1.7.0_21 and Scala 2.10.0),
http://www.playframework.org

> Type "help play" or "license" for more information.
> Type "exit" or use Ctrl+D to leave this console.

[Hello World] $
```

You're now in Play's *console*. In the console, you can run several commands to interact with your application. We'll be introducing some of them in this chapter and others throughout the rest of the book, but you can always type play help to get a list of commands.

For now, we'll stick to running the application. Type run.

```
[Hello World] $ run

[info] Updating {file:/Users/sietse/Hello%20World/}Hello World...
[info] Done updating.
--- (Running the application from SBT, auto-reloading is enabled) ---

[info] play - Listening for HTTP on port 9000...

(Server started, use Ctrl+D to stop and go back to the console...)
```

Play has checked your application and its dependencies for updates, and started a web server that serves your application. Let's see what it's serving.

1.5.5   *Accessing the running application*

Now that the application is running, you can access a default welcome page at http://localhost:9000/. You should see the page shown in figure 1.3.

This is already a kind of "hello world"—an example of a running application that outputs something, so you can see how things fit together. This is more than a static HTML file that tells you that "the web server is running." Instead, this is the minimal amount of code that can show you the web framework in action. This makes it easier to create a "hello world" example than it would be if we had to start with a completely blank slate—an empty directory that forces you to turn to the documentation each time you create a new application, which is probably not something you'll do every day.

Now leaving our example application at this stage would be cheating, so we need to change the application to produce the proper output. Besides, it doesn't say "Hello world" yet. Let's change the welcome message.

1.5.6   *Changing the controller class*

The file in your application that controls what result is sent in response to the request for http://localhost/ is app/controllers/Application.java. It's a regular Java class, which currently contains one method, index. The method looks like this:

```java
public static Result index() {
  return ok(index.render("Your new application is ready."));
}
```

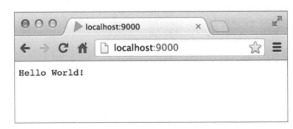

Figure 1.3   The default welcome page for a new Play application

The `index` method is called an *action* method. It contains the logic that determines the response to the current HTTP request. We'll get into more detail about what this specific code means later, but for now it's enough to understand that this is how Play renders the default welcome page.

Let's change the output to something else. Simply edit the file `app/controllers/Application.java` and replace the `Application` class's `index` method with the following.

```
public static Result index() {
  return ok("Hello World!");
}
```

This defines an action method that generates an HTTP "OK" response with text content. If you still have the application running, you can save the file and reload `http://localhost:9000/`; it will serve a plain text document containing the customary greeting, as seen in figure 1.4.

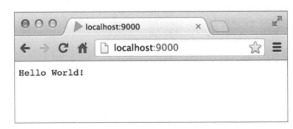

Figure 1.4   Simple text output

As you can see, the output is a little boring. In this case, it's more interesting if you make a mistake.

1.5.7   Add a compilation error

In the action method, remove the closing quote character from `"Hello world"`, save the file, and reload the page in your web browser. You'll get a helpful compilation error, as in figure 1.5.

Fix the error in the code, save the file, and reload the page again. It's fixed! Play dynamically reloads changes, so you don't have to manually build the application every time you make a change.

1.5.8   Use an HTTP request parameter

This is still not a proper web application example, though, because we didn't use HTTP or HTML yet. Let's make it a little more interactive and make it a proper HTML page. To start, add a new action method with a String parameter to the controller class:

```
public static Result hello(String name) {
  return ok("Hello " + name);
}
```

Now if you want to try to run this new method, you need to set up an HTTP path (say, `/hello`) that corresponds to this method. You'll also want to link an HTTP query parameter called `name` to our method's `name` parameter. This is called *binding* the parameter. To get this to work, we need to tell Play what we want to do.

The key to setting up this binding is in the file `conf/routes`. In fact, this file is the reason why the `index` method we saw before works in the first place. If you open up the file, you'll see the following line:

```
GET /         controllers.Application.index()
```

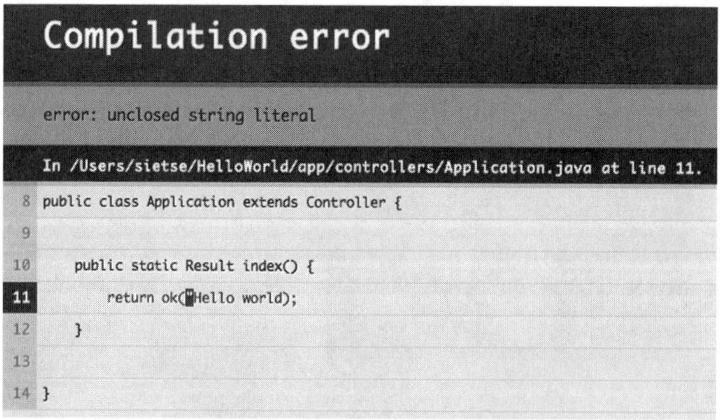

```
Compilation error

error: unclosed string literal

In /Users/sietse/HelloWorld/app/controllers/Application.java at line 11.
 8  public class Application extends Controller {

 9

10      public static Result index() {
11          return ok(▮Hello world);
12      }

13

14  }
```

Figure 1.5   Compilation errors are shown in the web browser, with the relevant source code highlighted.

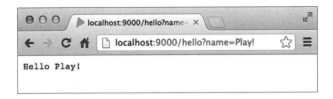

Figure 1.6 Output using an HTTP query parameter

That line is called a *route*, and it maps an HTTP path to an action method in our application. In this case, it maps the root URL (/) to `Application.index()`.

In order to give our new `hello()` method a URL to reach it by, we'll need to create a route for it. Add a new line to the `conf/routes` file to map the `/hello` to our new method, including the `String` parameter called name:

```
GET /hello    controllers.Application.hello(name:String)
```

Now open `http://localhost:9000/hello?name=Play!` and you can see how the URL's query string parameter is passed to the controller action. You should get output as in figure 1.6.

An example web application that outputs only text isn't very useful; we want HTML output. Let's create an HTML template to go with our action method.

1.5.9 Add an HTML page template

Under the `app/views` directory, add a file named `hello.scala.html` with the following content:

```
@(name:String)
<!doctype html>
<html>
  <head>
    <meta charset="UTF-8">
    <title>Hello</title>
  </head>
  <body>
    <h1>Hello <em>@name</em></h1>
  </body>
</html>
```

This is a *Scala template*, a template with syntax based on the Scala programming language. Don't worry, you don't have to learn Scala! Think of it as any other new template language.

The first line of our template defines the parameter list—a `name` parameter in this case. The rest of the file is an HTML document layout of a simple page. If you take a closer look at the HTML body, you'll see that it includes an HTML `em` tag whose content is an expression, `@name`. That will output the value of the `name` parameter.

In order to use this template, we have to edit the `hello` action method to return a result that wraps a call to the template instead of a `String` literal:

```
public static Result hello(String name) {
  return ok(views.html.hello.render(name));
}
```

Figure 1.7   Output using our HTML template

Reload the web page—http://localhost:9000/hello?name=Play!—and you will see the formatted HTML output, like in figure 1.7.

Congratulations, you've created your first Play application! You've seen all the major parts that make up a Play application. There's one more thing to look at that's not really part of a Play application, but still important while developing one; the Play console. Let's see what exactly the console is for.

1.6   *The console*

Web developers are used to interacting with their applications through the browser. With Play, you can also use the console to interact with your web application's development environment and build system. This is important for both quick experiments and automating things.

To start the console, run the play command in the application directory without an additional command:

```
play
```

If you're already running a Play application, you can type Control+D to stop the application and return to the console.

The Play console gives you a variety of commands, including the run command that you saw earlier. For example, you can compile the application to discover the same compilation errors that are normally shown in the browser, such as the missing closing quotation mark that you saw earlier:

```
[hello] $ compile
[info] Compiling 1 Java source to hello/target/scala-2.9.1/classes...
[error] hello/app/controllers/Application.java:11:
        unclosed string literal
[error]     return ok(index.render("Hello world));
[error]                            ^
[error] hello/app/controllers/Application.java:11:
        ')' expected
[error]     return ok(index.render("Hello world));
[error]                                          ^
[error] hello/app/controllers/Application.java:12:
        ';' expected
[error]   }
[error]    ^
[error] hello/app/controllers/Application.java:14:
        reached end of file while parsing
[error] }
[error]  ^
```

```
[error] 4 errors
[error] {file:hello/}hello/compile:compile:
        javac returned nonzero exit code
[error] Total time: 0 s, completed Mar 19, 2012 11:29:53 AM
[hello] $
```

You can also start a Scala console, which gives you direct access to your compiled Play application:

```
[hello] $ console
[info] Starting scala interpreter...
[info]
Welcome to Scala version 2.9.1.final
CO (Java HotSpot(TM) 64-Bit Server VM, Java 1.6.0_29).
Type in expressions to have them evaluated.
Type :help for more information.

scala>
```

As the name suggests, the Scala console uses Scala. This is because the build tool (sbt—Scala Build Tool) and the core framework are Scala-based. Like we said before, you don't have to learn Scala to be able to use Play, but we did want to show you this useful feature of Play's console. Certain things are easy enough to do, and are not particularly different from how you would do things in Java. One example of this is rendering a template, which is a Scala function that you can call like this:

```
scala> views.html.hello.render("Play!")
res1: play.api.templates.Html =

<!doctype html>
<html>
  <head>
    <meta charset="UTF-8">
    <title>Hello</title>
  </head>
  <body>
    <h1>Hello <em>Play!</em></h1>
  </body>
</html>
```

We rendered a dynamic template in a web application that is not running. This has major implications for being able to test your web application without running a server.

1.7   Summary

Play was built "by web developers, for web developers"—taking good ideas from existing high-productivity frameworks and adding the JVM's power and rich ecosystem without sacrificing enterprise features. Play 2 also introduces new goals expressed through the reactive-programming model. The result is a web framework that offers simplicity, productivity, and usability as well as structure and scalability. After starting with a first version implemented in Java, Play 2 introduces more type safety throughout the framework.

As soon as you start writing code, you go beyond Play's background and its feature list to what really matters—the user experience that determines how much you'll enjoy using Play. The good news is that Play achieves a level of simplicity, productivity, and usability that means that you can look forward to enjoying Play and, we hope, the rest of this book.

The parts of
an application

Now that you know what Play is all about, it's time to start building a serious application. In this chapter, we'll dive deeper into what makes up a Play application, and give you an introduction to all the important concepts you'll need to know about when building a Play application. The following chapters will then explore each concept in more detail.

In this chapter, we'll also introduce the example application that we'll evolve into an enterprise-like application as we progress through the chapters of this book. The application we chose will be an example of a real-world application; not the next Twitter or Facebook, which have specific and uncommon requirements and challenges,[1] but something your customer might ask you to build. We start by creating a

---

[1] Although you could certainly use Play for them!

21

new application and identifying all the files that make up the new application. After that, we'll set up an IDE so that we're ready to start the coding in the next chapter.

Let's see what we're going to build.

2.1   *Introducing our application*

Throughout the rest of this book, we'll build an enterprise web application from the ground up. The Acme Paperclip Company has asked us to build them a web-based warehouse management application. They have all sorts of plans for automation of their warehouse processes, but they first want us to show them that we're up to the job by building a simple product catalog for their product range.

The application we'll build for them in this chapter is a simple CRUD[2] application for maintaining a product catalog. Users will be able to browse a list of products, as well as add new ones. Because this is only a proof of concept, we'll simulate storing these products; the data storage will be mocked, rather than use a database. We'll add persistence in chapter 7.

But first, let's create a new Play application that will become our warehouse application. As we did in chapter 1, when we created the "Hello World" example, we'll use the play new command. Go ahead and run play new warehouse, and you'll have a new directory, warehouse, that will contain a default Play application. Let's see what's inside.

2.2   *A rundown of a Play application*

If you take a look at your application's directory, you'll see it contains the following files and directories:

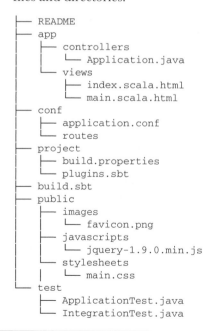

```
├── README
├── app
│   ├── controllers
│   │   └── Application.java
│   └── views
│       ├── index.scala.html
│       └── main.scala.html
├── conf
│   ├── application.conf
│   └── routes
├── project
│   ├── build.properties
│   └── plugins.sbt
├── build.sbt
├── public
│   ├── images
│   │   └── favicon.png
│   ├── javascripts
│   │   └── jquery-1.9.0.min.js
│   └── stylesheets
│   │   └── main.css
└── test
    ├── ApplicationTest.java
    └── IntegrationTest.java
```

---

[2] Create, Retrieve, Update, Delete

We'll take a closer look at each of the top-level directories. The app directory is the most important one, but we'll cover that last, and talk about the others first.

To start, we'll discuss a directory that doesn't show up in a newly created application, but which will be there after you run it once: the target directory. There's only one thing you have to know about the target directory: you should ignore it. The target directory is the build process's working directory. This is where your compiled classes are stored, among other things. Be sure to never commit it in your versioning system. If you're using Git as your versioning system, you probably won't; Play also generated a .gitignore file for you, making sure you never commit files that are generated at runtime.

Now that we know what to ignore, let's start discussing the first directory of interest, the conf directory.

2.3   *Play's configuration files*

The conf directory is where you *configure* the application. Its contents look like this:

```
.
├── application.conf
└── routes
```

As you can see, this directory contains two files: application.conf and routes. The application.conf file contains configuration information about your Play application. This is where you'll configure things like logging, database connections, which port the server runs on, and more.

The application configuration file is loaded at startup time and is globally readable. This means that any code that needs to can access it. If you need some configuration options for your application, you can add some custom options to the file, and use them in your own code. Play generated an example configuration when you ran play new, so open it up and poke around if you're curious. We'll cover some of the options in here when we run into them, both later in this chapter and through the rest of the book.

The other file in the conf directory is the routes file. Here you can define your application's *routes*, mappings from HTTP URLs to application code. It already contains two example routes:

```
# Home page
GET     /   controllers.Application.index()

# Map static resources from the /public folder to the /assets URL path
GET     /assets/*file    controllers.Assets.at(path="/public", file)
```

Every line of the routes file defines a single route. Let's focus on the first route; we'll explain what the second route does in section 2.5.

Any route consists of three parts: the HTTP *method*, the *path*, and the *action method*, as illustrated in figure 2.1.

Our example route maps any HTTP GET request for '/' to controllers.Application .index(). This means that any GET request for the / (root) URL is *handled* by the index

Figure 2.1   Components of a route

About HTTP methods

If you're unfamiliar with the HTTP protocol, the concept of an HTTP "method" may be new to you. An HTTP method has nothing to do with the kinds of methods you find in Java. There's a lot of documentation to be found about the HTTP protocol and its methods and what they imply; search the web if you're curious, but here's a summary that will get you through the chapter.

The method of an HTTP request signifies the purpose of your request: whether you want to retrieve a resource from the server or post information to it, for example. A number of different methods are defined in the HTTP specification, and some extensions to the protocol add even more, but the two most-used methods in the HTTP standard are GET and POST.

GET is a retrieval request for a resource, and it contains no body, although the URL used may contain parameters (everything that comes after the ?). It's important that a GET request may *never* have any lasting effects on the server; every time you GET a URL it should have the same effect. The fancy word for this is *idempotence*. The most important thing to remember is that you should only use it for information *retrieval*, not for submission of data.

The POST method, on the other hand, is a request for data *submission*, and may contain a body. It is still directed at a URL, but a POST request has effects server-side. A POST request is often used for forms that create or modify information. This is why your browser will likely warn you when you reload a URL that you POSTed to before.

There are more methods in the HTTP standard, such as PUT and DELETE, but we'll talk about those when we discuss HTTP APIs.

---

method on the Application class in the controllers package. We call methods that handle requests *action methods*.

The routes file is important to any Play application. It allows you to "design" your URLs. This is a big deal. Some (if not most) other Java web frameworks dictate what your URLs should be, or the framework can't do its job. Because Play gives you full control over your URL schema, you can design clean, human-readable, bookmarkable URLs.

The next directory in our list is the project directory, and it contains files that configure the build process.

2.4 Build configuration files

The `project` directory looks like this:

```
├── README
├── app
├── conf
├── project
│   ├── build.properties
│   └── plugins.sbt
├── build.sbt
└── public
```

Of these files, you'll only deal with `build.sbt` at the top root directory. Both `build.properties` and `plugins.sbt` are SBT configuration files, which describe the Play version to use and the SBT version to use. SBT (Scala Build Tool) is the build tool that Play's console and build process is based upon. We'll tell you more about what this file does whenever we need to change it, but don't worry about it for now.

The file `build.sbt` is a file you *will* have to edit occasionally. The file looks like this when newly generated:

```
name := "warehouse"

version := "1.0-SNAPSHOT"

libraryDependencies ++= Seq(
  javaJdbc,
  javaEbean,
  cache
)

play.Project.playJavaSettings
```

In this file you define your application's version number as well as any *managed dependencies* it might need. Managed dependencies are libraries and modules you use in your application that Play[3] can look up and download automatically. This is called *resolving* dependencies. You might be familiar with this process if you've used Maven or Ivy before.

As you can see, Play has already added some default modules for you. Every Java Play project uses by default the `javaJdbc` component to interact with databases, the `javaEbean` component to add object-relational mapping, and the `cache` module to provide caching capabilities. You can read more about the database modules in chapter 7.

If you want to add a dependency on a library, you need to add a line describing it to the list of dependencies. As an example, suppose you want to use Google's Guava library[4] to get some useful extra functionality on top of what the JDK standard library provides. You'd add a dependency on version 14.0 like this:

```
name := "warehouse"

version := "1.0-SNAPSHOT"
```

---

[3] Play delegates this to SBT.

[4] Visit http://code.google.com/p/guava-libraries/ for more information on Guava.

```
libraryDependencies ++= Seq(
  javaJdbc,
  javaEbean,
  cache,
  "com.google.guava" % "guava" % "14.0"
)

play.Project.playJavaSettings
```

The next time the application is started, Play will resolve the dependency, automatically download the correct JAR, and add it to the classpath.

The way dependency resolving works is that several preconfigured *dependency repositories* are queried for the correct versions of the files you need. There are various dependency repositories on the internet that serve the majority of the libraries available in the Java ecosystem. The best-known repository is the Maven central repository at http://search.maven.org/.

The dependency management system is smart enough to also download your dependencies' dependencies, also called *transitive dependencies*. If you're using transitive dependencies, and you want to include a library that has lots of dependencies itself, you no longer have to keep track of what version of what JAR to put where. The dependency management system does all of this for you.

Another great benefit of using managed dependencies is that you don't need to keep any library files with your source files, keeping your codebase nice and small, while ensuring that it will always build (as long as any repository server containing the files is still available). Another bonus you get is that it's easy to upgrade a library to a different version: change the version in your dependency declaration, and you're done.

Play 2 will automatically resolve any dependencies as soon as it finds any change in this file when your application starts, so you don't need to worry about having to trigger a dependency update.

If you want to use a library that's not in any repository (yet)—for example, when it's a new library, or one you developed in-house—you don't *have* to use dependency management to use that library. You can create a new directory called lib in your application's root directory, and any JAR Play finds there will automatically be added to the classpath for your application.

We'll talk more about dependencies and dependency management in chapter 11. Let's move on to the next directory, public.

2.5   *Public assets*

The public directory contains a few files already:

```
├── README
├── app
├── conf
├── project
├── public
│   ├── images
```

```
|   |       └─ favicon.png
|   ├─ javascripts
|   |       └─ jquery-1.7.1.min.js
|   └─ stylesheets
|           └─ main.css
└─ target
```

As you can maybe guess from its contents and its name, the `public` directory contains resources that are served directly, without any processing. This is what the second route we saw in section 2.3 does: it makes the contents of this directory available as *public assets*, files that are available to the client directly.

```
# Map static resources from the /public folder to the /assets URL path
GET  /assets/*file   controllers.Assets.at(path="/public", file)
```

Public assets are usually support files that are not your application. Things like images, stylesheets, JavaScript files, and static HTML pages are all public assets. Public assets are not generated by your application; they're served straight to the client.

Play adds some additional features to requests serving public assets. It adds support for *caching* by providing ETag headers and for *compression* using gzip.

If you're interested in *preprocessing* certain files, such as LESS stylesheets, Coffee-Script files, or JavaScript files, be sure to read section 2.6.1 about *compiled assets*. But first, let's move on to the app directory.

2.6 *Application code*

The `app` directory is the most important directory of your application. It contains your application code—any part of your application that will need to be compiled, such as your Java source files and view templates, which we'll discuss in a bit. When newly generated, the `app` directory contains the following files:

```
├─ app
|   ├─ controllers
|   |       └─ Application.java
|   └─ views
|           ├─ index.scala.html
|           └─ main.scala.html
├─ conf
├─ project
├─ public
└─ target
```

The files that are there are responsible for generating the welcome page we saw when we navigated to http://localhost:9000/ in section 1.5.5 in chapter 1.

There is one file, `Application.java`, that contains Java code implementing the *business logic* for generating the web page. Classes that take an HTTP request, run some logic on it, and return an HTTP result are called *controller* classes, which explains why they're in the `controllers` folder.

There are two *template* files, `index.scala.html` and `main.scala.html`, which are responsible for defining the HTML page. Any content that's generated on the server and sent to the client in an HTTP body, such as an HTML page, is called a *view*, therefore, the files are in the `views` folder.

The template files contain a template in Play's Scala template syntax. An important aspect of Scala templates is that they're compiled to regular classes. This has all sorts of advantages, the most important of which are compile-time syntax and type checking.

You *don't* have to learn Scala

Although Play's Scala templates in fact contain Scala code, this does *not* mean you have to learn or understand Scala. Any template language has structures you need to know to build your templates, and Scala templates are no different. Once you know what you have to do to, for example, iterate over a collection or insert a variable value somewhere, you know all you have to know to use that feature. You don't have to think of it as Scala if you don't want to. Think of it as another template language.

Now if you *happen* to know Scala, you will recognize the structures used in the tags and understand why they work the way they work. But the point is that you don't *have* to in order to use the template syntax and enjoy all the benefits it brings.

Another thing that's important to note about the `app` directory is that it's the root for all your source code, meaning that any subfolder will automatically have to be a package, as with any regular Java project.

You might be used to having your packages look more like a domain space, such as `org.mycompany.myproject.mypackage`, but there's nothing in the Java language that forces you to do that. It happens to be convention, and that convention mainly exists for namespacing purposes, to prevent classes with the same name stepping on each other's turf. Because you won't be running two Play apps in the same JVM at the same time, you don't have to worry about that in your Play apps, so Play doesn't follow that convention. That's why your controllers are in the `controller` package, your views in the `views` package, and so on. Nice, concise, and easy to follow.

Now let's look at another cool feature in Play that also uses the `app` directory: compiled assets.

2.6.1 Compiled assets

We've seen what assets are in section 2.5, where we introduced assets as files served to the client, but assets *can* also be the result of compilation. A CSS or JavaScript file doesn't have to be compiled, but there are certain tools that generate them. Play has the option to preprocess assets before they're served to the client, giving you more convenience and flexibility over these files. Out of the box, Play 2 comes with support for LESS, CoffeeScript, and Google's Closure compiler. Using them is completely optional, but Play makes it easier for you to use these technologies if you want to.

The source files for compiled assets should be kept in your application's `app/assets` directory. That directory is not auto-generated by Play, so create it if you want to use this feature.

LESS

LESS (http://lesscss.org) is a dynamic stylesheet language that is compiled to CSS, offering a more powerful and flexible stylesheet language that is still compatible with any browser. Any `.less` file saved in the `app/assets` directory will be compiled into the application's `public` folder, which means the result will be available as a regular public asset.

COFFEESCRIPT

CoffeeScript (http://coffeescript.org) is a programming language that compiles to JavaScript. It's generally considered a cleaner and more readable language than JavaScript, and is gaining popularity. Any `.coffee` file placed in `app/assets` will be compiled to the application's `public` folder, like LESS files.

JAVASCRIPT

If you're not using CofeeScript, but JavaScript, you might want to use Google's Closure compiler (https://developers.google.com/closure/compiler/; not to be confused with the programming language "Clojure"). The Closure compiler analyzes your JavaScript code, tries to make it run faster, and warns you about potential problems. It also makes your code smaller (this is called *minifying*), which will make it download and run faster. Like LESS and CoffeeScript, place any `.js` files you want to compile in the `app/assets` directory, and they will be compiled to `/public/`.

2.7 Setting up an IDE

Now that we know what all the directories and files are for, we're going to edit some of them in a moment, and then start implementing our proof-of-concept application. You could edit the files with a plain text editor. But if you use a Java IDE such as Eclipse or IntelliJ, you'll find that editing your source code becomes a lot easier, and you'll be more productive. One of the advantages of using a type-safe language like Java is that tools like IDEs can do a lot to make coding faster and easier (and therefore more fun). Most IDEs offer features such as autocompletion, automated refactoring, and static code analysis. In short, an IDE makes your life easier.

Play makes it easy to import your applications into most well-known IDEs by including commands that will set up a project for you. Play comes with support for Eclipse and IntelliJ IDEA. This does *not* mean that you can't use any IDE you want; it means that you have to set up the project in your IDE yourself if you use an IDE other than Eclipse or IntelliJ IDEA.

2.7.1 Eclipse

Eclipse is one of the most well-known and widely used Java IDEs. It's open source and free to use. Figure 2.2 shows how you set up your application for Eclipse.

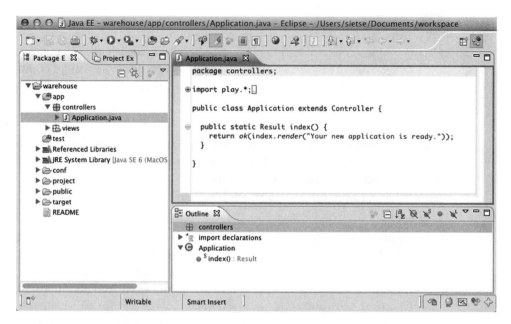

Figure 2.2   A new Play application in Eclipse

First of all, you need to generate the Eclipse-specific files that instruct Eclipse how to load your application and its dependencies and how to build it. Play generates the necessary files for you when you run the `eclipse` command from the Play console.

Once these files have been generated, Eclipse will be able to recognize your application's directory as an Eclipse project, and you can import it directly. To do so, use the *Import* command under the *File* menu in Eclipse's menu bar. When Eclipse asks you what you want to import, choose *General > Existing Projects into Workspace*. On the next screen, click *Browse* to select your application's root directory, and Eclipse will recognize the project as figure 2.3 shows. Click the *Finish* button, and you're all done setting up your Eclipse project.

2.7.2   *NetBeans*

NetBeans is another well-known and widely used Java IDE. It's open source and free to use. NetBeans 7.3 supports Play natively. All you need to do is to install the NBPlay plugin in your NetBeans IDE. To do so, go to http://plugins.netbeans.org/plugin/47637/.

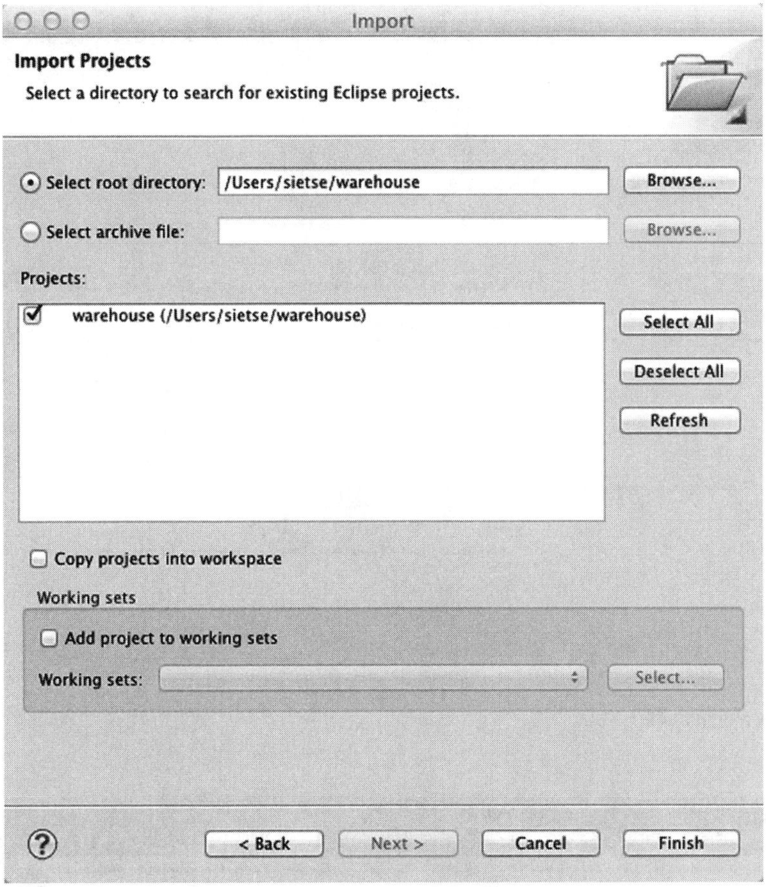

Figure 2.3 Importing a project in Eclipse

You should see a screen similar to figure 2.4.

Download the plugin by clicking the *Download* button and save the plugin in a known location. Once you have it downloaded, in NetBeans IDE, select the menu *Tools* and *Plugins*. Select the *Downloaded* tab and then click the *Add Plugins* button. Select the previously saved NBPlay plugin as shown in figure 2.5.

You are now installing the plugin.

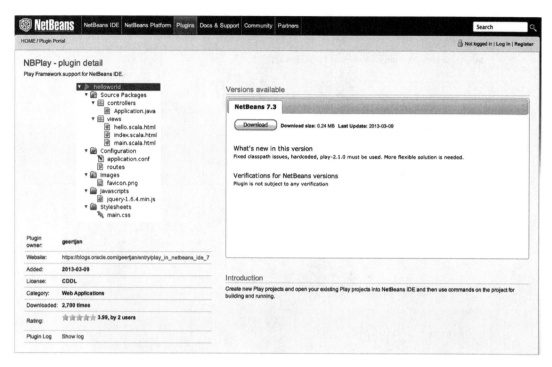

Figure 2.4   NetBeans plugin center

Figure 2.5   Install the NetBeans plugin

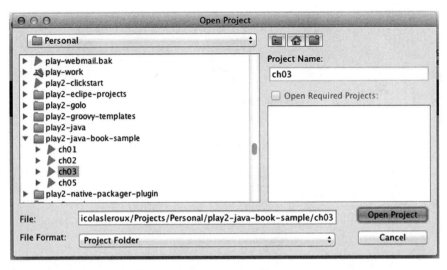

Figure 2.6   Open a new Play project in NetBeans IDE

Now, open your previously created project. NetBeans now recognises that it is a Play 2 project, as shown in figure 2.6.

The Play NetBeans plugin provides syntax highlighting, syntax checking, and auto-complete in Play 2 templates and routes files as figure 2.7 shows.

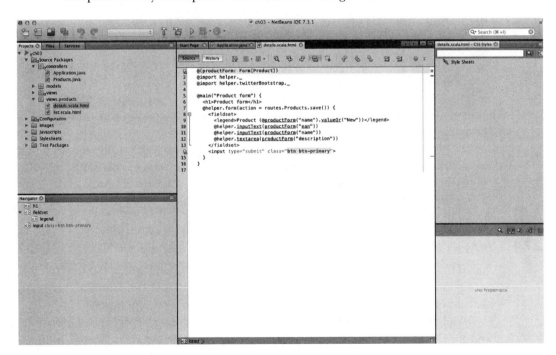

Figure 2.7   A new Play application in NetBeans IDE

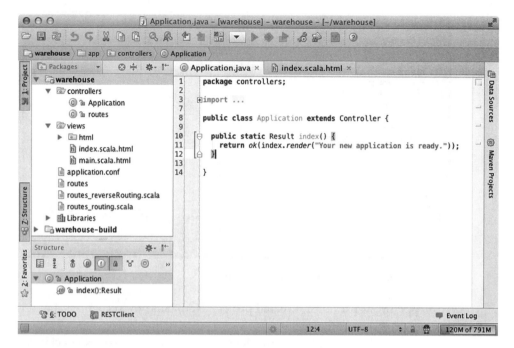

Figure 2.8 A new Play application in IntelliJ IDEA

2.7.3 *IntelliJ IDEA*

IntelliJ IDEA is a commercial IDE from JetBrains. It is open source, and the community edition is free to use, with more powerful features available in the paid "ultimate" edition.

Since version 12, IntelliJ has support for Play 2. This means you get syntax highlighting, syntax checking, and autocomplete in Play 2 templates and routes files as shown in figure 2.8.

Play 2 can make an IntelliJ "project" out of your application, but the model that is part of this project can also be imported into any existing project you might have. To create the IntelliJ project, run the `idea` command from the Play 2 console.

To open the project in IntelliJ, select *File > Open project...* from the menu bar, and choose the directory for your application.

2.7.4 *Using a debugger*

One of the most useful features in Java IDEs is their debuggers, which tap into the JVM that's running your application and allow you to pause code execution at any point (such a point is called a *break point*) to inspect the state of your application.

To debug a Play application, you need to start it in debug mode, and then configure your debugger to use *remote debugging*, which means that your debugger will connect to a JVM that's already running, rather than the IDE launching one and connecting to that.

To start Play in debug mode, start it with the `debug` parameter. Play will tell you which port to connect your debugger to, which is port 9999 by default:

```
~/warehouse  > play debug
Listening for transport dt_socket at address: 9999
[info] Loading project definition from /Users/sietse/hello/project
[info] Set current project to hello (in build file:/Users/sietse/hello/)
```

If you want to use Eclipse's debugger with your Play application, you need to set up a new *debug configuration* under the *Run* menu. Select *Remote Java Application* and click the *New* button to create a new remote debug configuration. Set it to connect to your Play application on `localhost`, by default on port 9999. To start debugging, select *Run > Debug* in the menu bar as shown in figure 2.9.

To use IntelliJ's debugger with a Play application, select *Run > Edit Configurations* from the menu bar, and then click the plus button in the upper-left corner. From the

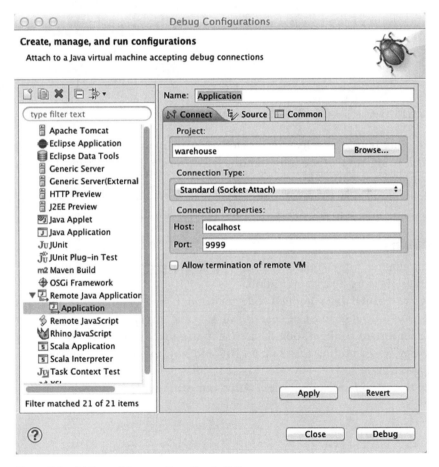

Figure 2.9   Adding a debug configuration in Eclipse

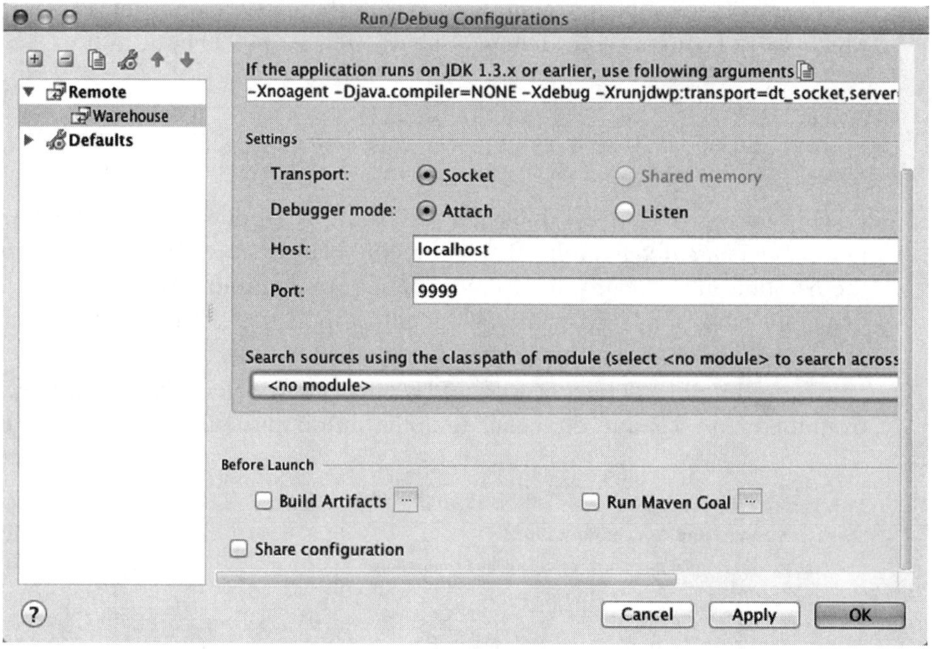

Figure 2.10 Adding a debug configuration in IntelliJ

menu that pops up, select *Remote* to create a new remote debug configuration. To start using your new configuration, select *Run > Debug...* from the menu bar as shown in figure 2.10.

Explaining how to use the debugger is beyond the scope of this book, but this should be enough to get you started debugging with Eclipse or IntelliJ.

2.8 Summary

In this chapter, we've created a new Play 2 Java project and identified what directories and files make up a Play application.

We've learned that compiled code goes under /app/, and that includes any *compiled assets*, such as LESS and CoffeeScript files. Static assets go in /public/, and /conf/ holds important configuration data, such as the routes file and application.conf.

We've also seen how to set up an IDE and how to attach a debugger to a running Play application.

In the next chapter, we'll start coding our example application.

A basic CRUD application 3

This chapter covers

- An introduction to all major Play concepts
- Creating a small application

In the previous chapter, we introduced our example application: the paper clip warehouse management system. Now that we know what we're going to build, and have our IDE all set up, it's time to start coding.

In this chapter, we'll start implementing our proof-of-concept (POC) application. It will be a simple CRUD[1] application, with data stored in-memory rather than in a database. We'll evolve our POC application in later chapters, but this simple application will be our starting point.

We'll start by setting up a controller with some methods and linking some URLs to them.

---

[1] Create, Retrieve, Update, Delete

3.1   *Adding a controller and actions*

In chapter 1 we edited the `Application` class, changing the default output and adding custom operations. The `Application` class is an example of a *controller* class. Controller classes are used as a home for action methods, which are the entry points of your web application. Whenever an HTTP request reaches the Play server, it is evaluated against a collection of rules in order to determine what action method will handle this request. This is called *routing* the request, which is handled by something aptly named the *router*, which, in turn, is configured using the `conf/routes` file, as described in section 2.3. After the correct action method is selected, that method executes the logic necessary to come up with a *result* to return to the client in response to the request. This process is illustrated in figure 3.1.

Let's create a controller for the new warehouse application that we created in the previous chapter. The only requirement of a controller class is that it extends `play.mvc.Controller`. It does *not* have to be part of a specific package, although it is convention to put controllers in the `controllers` package. Let's create one for our product catalog. Because we're dealing with products, we'll call it `Products`. Create the `Products` class under the `controllers` package (that means the file is named `/app/controllers/Products.java`). Have this class extend `Controller`, like so:

```
package controllers;

import play.mvc.Controller;

public class Products extends Controller {

}
```

An empty controller doesn't do anything. The whole purpose of controllers is to provide action methods. An action method has to conform to the following requirements:

- It has to be *public.*
- It has to be *static.*
- It has to have *a return type (a subclass) of* `Result`.

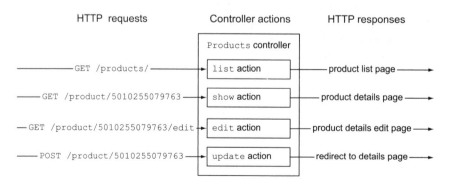

Figure 3.1   Requests routed to actions

Let's add some action methods to our controller. For our proof-of-concept application, we'll want to *list* products in our catalog, show *details* for an individual product, and *save* new and updated products. We'll add actions for these operations later, but for now we'll make them return a special type of result: TODO. A TODO result signifies that the method is yet to be implemented. Add the corresponding actions, as shown in the following listing.

Listing 3.1   Adding action methods

```
package controllers;

import play.mvc.Controller;
import play.mvc.Result;

public class Products extends Controller {

  public static Result list() {              ◁─── List all products
    return TODO;
  }

  public static Result newProduct() {        ◁─── Show a blank product form
    return  TODO;
  }

  public static Result details(String ean) {  ◁─── Show a product edit form
    return TODO;
  }

  public static Result save() {              ◁─── Save a product
    return TODO;
  }

}
```

Now that we have some action methods, let's give them URLs so that we can reach them.

3.2   *Mapping URLs to action methods using routes*

In order to determine which action method will handle a given HTTP request, Play takes the properties of that request, such as its method, URL, and parameters, and does a lookup on a set of mappings called *routes*. Like we saw before, in section 2.3, routes are configured in the routes file in your application's conf directory. Add routes for our new operation, as shown in the following listing.

Listing 3.2   Adding routes for our product catalog

```
GET  /products/          controllers.Products.list()
GET  /products/new       controllers.Products.newProduct()
GET  /products/:ean      controllers.Products.details(ean: String)
POST /products/          controllers.Products.save()
```

Now that we have some routes, let's try them out. Start your application if it's not already running, and point your browser at http://localhost:9000/products/. You should see the page shown in figure 3.2.

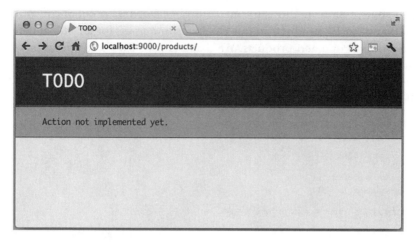

Figure 3.2   Play's TODO placeholder at /products

If you see the TODO placeholder page, that means the controller, action method, and route are all correctly set up. Time to add some functionality. The first step is adding a class that will model our products.

3.3   *Adding a model and implementing functionality*

In order to create a product catalog, we need a class to represent "a product" in our application. Such classes are called *model* classes, because they model real-world concepts.

3.3.1   *Creating a model class*

We'll keep our product model simple for now: an article number, name, and description will do. For the article number, we'll use an EAN code, which is a 13-digit internationally standardized code. Although the code consists of digits, we're not going to perform math on it, so we'll use `String` to represent the EAN code.

Create a class called `Product` under a new package called `models`. Again, there's nothing about Play that requires you to put model classes in the `models` package, but it's convention to do it that way. Add the properties we mentioned previously to your new class, and add a constructor that sets them on instantiation for convenience. In addition, add a default no-argument constructor, because we'll need that when we add database persistence later. The last thing we'll add is a `toString()` method, because that will make it easier for us to see what product object we have.

We end up with a class as shown in the following listing.

Listing 3.3   /app/models/Product.java

```
package models;

public class Product {

    public String ean;
    public String name;
```

```
public String description;

public Product() {}

public Product(String ean, String name, String description) {
  this.ean = ean;
  this.name = name;
  this.description = description;
}

public String toString() {
  return String.format("%s - %s", ean, name);
}
}
```

DON'T BE ALARMED BY PUBLIC PROPERTIES If you've been a Java developer for some time, you're probably surprised that we chose to use public properties. You're probably more used to making properties private and exposing them using getter and setter methods instead, creating a "Java Bean." Don't worry, we know what we're doing. For now, bear with us. Everything will be explained in detail in chapter 7.

We've created our first model class. In most cases, instances of these model classes are also stored in a database. To keep things simple, we'll fake this functionality for now by maintaining a static list of products. Now let's create some data.

3.4 Mocking some data

We'll mock data storage by using a static `Set` of `Products` on the `Product` model class, and we'll put some data in the class's static initializer, as shown in the following listing.

> **Listing 3.4 Adding some test data to `/app/models/Product.java`**

```
import java.util.ArrayList;
import java.util.List;

public class Product {

  private static List<Product> products;

  static {
    products = new ArrayList<Product>();
    products.add(new Product("1111111111111", "Paperclips 1",
        "Paperclips description 1"));
    products.add(new Product("2222222222222", "Paperclips 2",
        "Paperclips description "));
    products.add(new Product("3333333333333", "Paperclips 3",
        "Paperclips description 3"));
    products.add(new Product("4444444444444", "Paperclips 4",
        "Paperclips description 4"));
    products.add(new Product("5555555555555", "Paperclips 5",
        "Paperclips description 5"));
  }
...
}
```

NEVER DO THIS IN A REAL APPLICATION   Although having a static property serve as a cache for data is convenient for this example, never do it in a real-world app. Because we'll only be using this List in dev-mode, which has only one thread running by default, we won't run into any serious trouble. But when you try this in any environment with multiple threads, or even multiple application instances, you'll run into all sorts of synchronization issues. Depending on the situation, either use Play's caching features, or use a database (see chapter 7).

Now that we have some data, let's also add some methods to manipulate the collection of Products. We'll need methods to retrieve the whole list, to find all products by EAN and (part of the) name, and to add and remove products. Add the methods shown in listing 3.5. We'll let their implementations speak for themselves.

Listing 3.5   Data access methods on the Products class

```java
public class Product {

...
  public static List<Product> findAll() {
    return new ArrayList<Product>(products);
  }

  public static Product findByEan(String ean) {
    for (Product candidate : products) {
      if (candidate.ean.equals(ean)) {
        return candidate;
      }
    }
    return null;
  }

  public static List<Product> findByName(String term) {
    final List<Product> results = new ArrayList<Product>();
    for (Product candidate : products) {
      if (candidate.name.toLowerCase().contains(term.toLowerCase())) {
        results.add(candidate);
      }
    }

    return results;
  }

  public static boolean remove(Product product) {
    return products.remove(product);
  }

  public void save() {
    products.remove(findByEan(this.ean));
    products.add(this);
  }

}
```

Now that we have the plumbing for our products catalog, we can start implementing our action methods.

3.5 *Implementing the list method*

We'll start with the implementation for the list method. As we said before, an action method always returns a *result*. What that means is that it should return an object with a type that is a subclass of play.mvc.Result. Objects of that type can tell Play all that it needs to construct an HTTP response.

An HTTP response consists of a status code, a set of headers, and a body. The status codes indicate whether a result was successful and what the problem is if it wasn't. Play's Controller class has a lot of methods to generate these result objects. Let's go ahead and replace our TODO result with a code 200 result, which means "OK." To do this, use the ok() method to obtain a new OK result, like this:

```
public static Result list() {
  return ok();
}
```

If you were to try this out in a browser, you'd get an empty page. If you were to check the HTTP response,[2] you'd see that the response status code has changed from 501 - Not Implemented to 200 - OK. The reason why our browser shows an empty page is because our response has no *body* yet. That makes sense, because we didn't put one in yet. To generate our response body, we want to generate an HTML page. For this, we'll want to write a template file.

3.5.1 *The list template*

As we saw in the previous chapters, a Play template is a file containing some HTML and Scala code that Play will compile into a class that we can use to render an HTML page. Templates go in your application's views directory and, to keep things clean and separated by functionality, we'll create a products directory there. Next, create a file called list.scala.html, and add to it the contents shown in the following listing.

> **Listing 3.6   /app/views/products/list.scala.html**

```
@(products: List[Product])

@main("Products catalogue") {

  <h2>All products</h2>

   <table class="table table-striped">
    <thead>
      <tr>
        <th>EAN</th>
        <th>Name</th>
        <th>Description</th>
      </tr>
    </thead>
    <tbody>
    @for(product <- products) {
```

---

2 Your browser probably has tools to do that.

```
    <tr>
      <td><a href="@routes.Products.details(product.ean)">
        @product.ean
      </a></td>
      <td><a href="@routes.Products.details(product.ean)">
@product.name</a></td>
      <td><a href="@routes.Products.details(product.ean)">
@product.name</a></td>
    </tr>
    }

  </tbody>
  </table>
}
```

When rendered (we'll get to how to do that in a moment), this template will produce a page as seen in figure 3.3.

Don't worry, we'll make it look better in a bit. But first, without going into too much detail (see chapter 8 for more detail on templates), let's see what happens in the template.

All products

EAN	Name	Description
3333333333333	Paperclips 3	Paperclips 3
4444444444444	Paperclips 4	Paperclips 4
1111111111111	Paperclips 1	Paperclips 1
5555555555555	Paperclips 5	Paperclips 5
2222222222222	Paperclips 2	Paperclips 2

Figure 3.3   Our products listing

HOW THE TEMPLATE WORKS

The first line of the list template is the *parameter list*:

```
@(products: List[Product])
```

With the parameter list, we define which parameters this template accepts. Every entry in the parameter list consists of a name, followed by a colon and the type of the parameter. In our example, we have one parameter called name, of type List <Product>,[3] to represent the list of products we want to render. This parameter list will be part of the method definition for this template's render method, which is how Play achieves type safety for its templates.

Let's take a look at the next line of code, which starts a block of code:

```
@main("Products catalogue") {
  ...
}
```

With this code we call another template, the one called main. This is the template at /app/views/main.scala.html, which Play created for us when we created the application. It contains some boilerplate HTML that we'll wrap around all of our pages, so we don't have to worry about that any more. The code we write in the block will end up in the <body> tag of our rendered HTML page. This is how you can compose templates in Play, and we'll see more of this in later chapters.

---

[3]   In Scala syntax, generic type arguments are indicated using square brackets instead of angle brackets as in Java.

The body of our code block is mainly HTML, which will be included in the rendered page verbatim. There's one bit of template code left—the bit that iterates over our products list:

```
@for(product <- products) {
    ...
}
```

This bit of code is comparable to a regular Java for-each loop: it iterates over a collection and repeats the code it wraps for every element in it, assigning the current element to a variable. In our example, it generates a pair of `<td>` elements for every `Product` in our products list. Listing 3.7 shows the full loop as a reminder.

Listing 3.7 `for` loop generating the product descriptions

```
@(products: List[Product])
    <table class="table table-striped">
     <thead>
      <tr>
        <th>EAN</th>
        <th>Name</th>
        <th>Description</th>
      </tr>
     </thead>
     <tbody>
     @for(product <- products) {
       <tr>
         <td><a href="@routes.Products.details(product.ean)">
           @product.ean
         </a></td>
         <td><a href="@routes.Products.details(product.ean)">
@product.name</a></td>
         <td><a href="@routes.Products.details(product.ean)">
@product.name</a></td>
       </tr>
       }

     </tbody>
    </table>
```

The pieces of code in the loop's body that start with an @ are Scala *expressions*; the code that follows the @ is evaluated, and the result is included in the output. In this case, we use it to print out properties of `product` and generate links to our action methods based on our routing configuration. For everything about routing, see chapter 5. We'll render our template soon, but first let's add some style.

ADDING BOOTSTRAP

During our examples, we focus more on functionality than styling; this is a book about Play, after all, and not about web design. But there is a way to make things look nicer with little effort: *Bootstrap*, by Twitter.

Bootstrap provides some CSS and image files that make HTML look good and maybe adding an HTML class here and there. It's easy to use Bootstrap in your Play applications. Here's how.

First, download the latest version of Bootstrap from the website at http://getbootstrap .com. Extract the contents of the zip file to a `bootstrap` directory under your application's `public` directory. This will make the files available from your application.

Next, we need to include the Bootstrap CSS in our templates. Because we're going to need it on all of our pages, the `main` template is the best place to do that. Open the file `/app/views/main.scala.html`, and add the following line below the existing `<title>` element, inside the `<head>` element:

```
<link href="@routes.Assets.at("bootstrap/css/bootstrap.min.css")"
    rel="stylesheet" media="screen">
```

This will allow your pages to be styled by Bootstrap, and, from now on, we'll use Bootstrap to make all of our examples look nicer. If you want to learn more about Bootstrap, check out the website at http://getbootstrap.com.

Now that we have our templates ready, let's see how to render them.

RENDERING THE TEMPLATE

Now that we have a template, all that's left for us to do is to gather a list of products and render the template in our `list` action method. The following listing shows how.

Listing 3.8   Rendering the `list` template

```
...
import views.html.products.list;

public class Products extends Controller {

  public static Result list() {
    List<Product> products = Product.findAll();
    return ok(list.render(products));
  }

  ...

}
```

As you can tell from the import in this example, the template `/views/products/ list.scala.html` results in a class called `views.html.products.list`. This `list` class has a static method called `render`, which, as your IDE can tell you, takes one parameter of type `List<Product>` and returns an object of type `Html`. The parameter is the one we defined at the top of our template, whereas the return type is determined by the `.html` extension of the template filename.

The `render` method on the template results in an HTML page, which we want to return to the client in the body HTTP response. To do this, we wrap it in a `Result` object by passing it to the `ok` method.

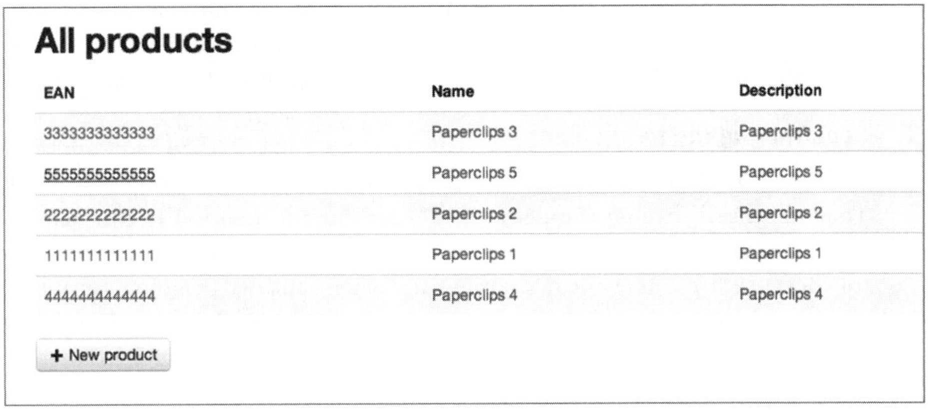

All products

EAN	Name	Description
3333333333333	Paperclips 3	Paperclips 3
5555555555555	Paperclips 5	Paperclips 5
2222222222222	Paperclips 2	Paperclips 2
1111111111111	Paperclips 1	Paperclips 1
4444444444444	Paperclips 4	Paperclips 4

+ New product

Figure 3.4 Our products listing

Time to try out our code. Navigate to http://localhost:9000/products/, and you should see a list as in figure 3.4.

Now that we can see our list of products, let's continue implementing features.

3.6   *Adding the product form*

A static product catalog isn't useful. We want to be able to add products to the list. We'll need a form for that, so create a new template called `details.scala.html` at `/app/views/products`. We'll create a form that will work both for creating new products and editing existing ones. The template is shown in the following listing.

Listing 3.9   Product form `/app/views/products/details.scala.html`

```
@(productForm: Form[Product])
@import helper._
@import helper.twitterBootstrap._

@main("Product form") {
  <h1>Product form</h1>
  @helper.form(action = routes.Products.save()) {
    <fieldset>
    <legend>Product (@productForm("name").valueOr("New"))</legend>
    @helper.inputText(productForm("ean"), '_label -> "EAN")
    @helper.inputText(productForm("name"),'_label -> "Name")
    @helper.textarea(productForm("description"), '_label -> "Description")
    </fieldset>
      <input type="submit" class="btn btn-primary" value="Save">
    <a class="btn" href="@routes.Products.index()">Cancel</a>
  }
}
```

As you can see in the first line of the template, this template takes a `Form<Product>` parameter, like our `list` template took a `List<Product>` parameter. But what's this `Form` class? `Form` is what Play uses to represent HTML forms. It represents name/value pairs that can be used to build an HTML form, but it also has features for input valida-tion, error reporting, and data binding. Data binding is what makes it possible to con-vert between HTTP (form) parameters and Java objects and vice versa.

3.6.1 Constructing the form object

Let's see how these forms work. First, we need to create one to pass to the template. That's as easy as calling the `play.data.Form.form()` method in our action method. The `form` method takes a class as a parameter, to tell it what kind of object the form is for. Because a product form is always the same, and we're going to use it in a few places in the `Products` controller, we might as well create a constant for it in the class, like so:

```
private static final Form<Product> productForm = Form
    .form(Product.class);
```

Now that we have an empty form, it's easy to pass it to the template. Implement the newProduct action method as shown here:

```
public static Result newProduct(){
  return ok(details.render(productForm));
}
```

With this action method implemented, you can see the form at `http://localhost:9000/products/new`. It should look like figure 3.5.

Let's see how to create the form.

3.6.2 Rendering the HTML form

Let's see how we make an HTML form from our `Form` object. At the top of the tem-plate, you can see how we import two helpers:

```
@import helper._
@import helper.twitterBootstrap._
```

Figure 3.5   The product form

These helpers are there to help us generate HTML. The first one imports generic HTML helpers, and the second one makes the generated HTML fit the Twitter Bootstrap layout. We first use one of these helpers when we start the form:

```
@helper.form(action = routes.Products.save()) {
    ...
}
```

The `form` helper generates an HTML `<form>` element. The `action` parameter tells it where the form should be submitted to. In our case, that's the `save` method on our `Products` controller. Play will turn this into an `action` attribute with the correct URL value for us.

A form is not much use without any fields. Let's see how those are constructed.

3.6.3 Rendering input fields

Our form contains a single fieldset, which is created using regular HTML. The value for the fieldset's `legend` element is interesting enough to take a closer look at. It starts off with regular text, "Product," but then we use the form object to construct the rest of the value:

```
@productForm("name").valueOr("New")
```

Here, we request the form field `name` by calling `productForm("name")`.[4] This object is of type `Form.Field`, and it represents the form field for the `name` property of the form. To get the value, we could call the `value` method on the field. But because we don't know *if* there is a value for this field, we use the `valueOr` method, which allows us to specify a default value to use in case the field has no value. This means we don't need to check for a value manually, saving us from a lot of messy, verbose code in our template.

The next few lines in our template render input elements—one for each property of our `Product` class:

```
@helper.inputText(productForm("ean"))
    @helper.inputText(productForm("name"))
    @helper.textarea(productForm("description"))
```

When our template is rendered, these lines are rendered as shown in the following listing.

Listing 3.10 Rendered input elements

```
<div class="clearfix  " id="ean_field">
    <label for="ean">ean</label>
    <div class="input">

    <input type="text" id="ean" name="ean" value="" >

        <span class="help-inline"></span>
        <span class="help-block"></span>
    </div>
</div>
```

---

[4] `productForm("name")` is short for `productForm.field("name")`.

```
<div class="clearfix  " id="name_field">
    <label for="name">name</label>
    <div class="input">

    <input type="text" id="name" name="name" value="" >

        <span class="help-inline"></span>
        <span class="help-block"></span>
    </div>
</div>
<div class="clearfix  " id="description_field">
    <label for="description">description</label>
    <div class="input">

    <textarea id="description" name="description" ></textarea>

        <span class="help-inline"></span>
        <span class="help-block"></span>
    </div>
</div>
```

With three simple lines of code, we've generated all that HTML! And because of the Bootstrap helper, it doesn't look bad, either.

The final line of our template's form adds a regular HTML Submit button, and with that, our form is ready. When you try it out, the form will submit to our unimplemented save method, so it doesn't do much yet. Let's take care of that now.

3.7 *Handling the form submission*

When you submit the product form in the browser, the form gets submitted to the URL specified in the action attribute of the HTML <form> element, which, in our case, ends up at our application's Products.save action method. It's now up to us to transform those HTML form parameters into a Product instance, and add it to the product catalog. Luckily, Play has some tools to make this job easy.

When we created the Form object in the previous section, we used it to create an HTML form based on the Product class. But Play's Forms work the other way around, too. This reverse process is called *binding*.

Play can bind a set of name/value combinations, such as a Map, to a class that has properties with the same names. In this case, we don't want to bind a map, but we do want to bind values from the request. Although we could obtain a Map of the name/value pairs from the HTTP request, this situation is so common that the Form class has a method to do this: bindFromRequest. This will return a new Form object, with the values populated from the request parameters. To obtain a Product from our form submission and add it to the catalog, we can write the following code:

Listing 3.11   Product binding

```
public class Products extends Controller {
...
  public static Result save() {
    Form<Product> boundForm = productForm.bindFromRequest();
    Product product = boundForm.get();
```

```
        product.save();
        return ok(String.format("Saved product %s", product));
    }
}
```

When you try out the form now, you'll get a simple text message informing you of the successful addition of the product. If you then check the catalog listing we made in section 3.5, you can verify that it worked.

But our current implementation isn't particularly nice. The user is free to omit the EAN code and product name, for example; at the moment this will work, but it's not something that we want. Also, the text message reporting the result isn't great. It would be a lot nicer to rerender the form with an error message on failure, and show the product listing with a success message if everything was correct.

First, let's tell Play that the ean and name fields are required. We'll leave the description optional.

We can make those fields required by using an annotation, play.data.validation .Constraints.Required. Play will check for those annotations and report errors accordingly. The following listing shows the constraint added.

Listing 3.12 Adding a pattern constraint

```
...
import play.data.validation.Constraints;

public class Product {
...

  @Constraints.Required
  public String ean;
  @Constraints.Required
  public String name;
  public String description;
...
}
```

What we need to do now is perform the validation in our controller and show an error or success message accordingly. The following listing shows a different version of save() that has that functionality.

Listing 3.13 A better save implementation

```
public static Result save() {
  Form<Product> boundForm = productForm.bindFromRequest();
  if(boundForm.hasErrors()) {
    flash("error", "Please correct the form below.");
    return badRequest(details.render(boundForm));
  }

  Product product = boundForm.get();
  product.save();
  flash("success",
      String.format("Successfully added product %s", product));

  return redirect(routes.Products.list());
}
```

In this version of our implementation, we use the *validation* functionality of Play's forms. On the second line of our method, we ask the Form if there are any errors, and, if there are, we add an error message and rerender the page. If there are no errors, we add a success message and redirect to the products list.

The error and success messages aren't visible yet. We've added them to something called the *flash scope*. Flash scope is a place where we can store variables between requests. Everything in flash scope is there until the following request, at which point it's deleted. It's ideal for success and error messages like this, but we still need to render these messages.

Because messages like these are useful throughout the application, let's add them to the main template, because that's what every page extends. That way, every page will automatically display any messages we put in flash scope. Add the lines shown in listing 3.14 to the start of the `<body>` element in `app/views/main.scala.html`.

Listing 3.14   Displaying flash success and error messages

```
@if(flash.containsKey("success")){
  <div class="alert alert-success">
    @flash.get("success")
  </div>
}

@if(flash.containsKey("error")){
  <div class="alert alert-error">
    @flash.get("error")
  </div>
}
```

Now try out the form. Load the form at `http://localhost:9000/products/new`, and try to submit the form while leaving the EAN field blank. You should see a page as in figure 3.6.

A lot more is possible using form validation, but for now this is enough. You can learn all about forms and validation in chapter 6.

Now that we have our form working, we can use it to edit existing products. To do this, we need to implement the `details` method as in the following listing.

Listing 3.15   Implementing the `details` method

```
public class Products extends Controller {
...
  public static Result details(String ean) {
    final Product product = Product.findByEan(ean);
    if (product == null) {
      return notFound(String.format("Product %s does not exist.", ean));
    }

    Form<Product> filledForm = productForm.fill(product);
    return ok(details.render(filledForm));
  }

...
}
```

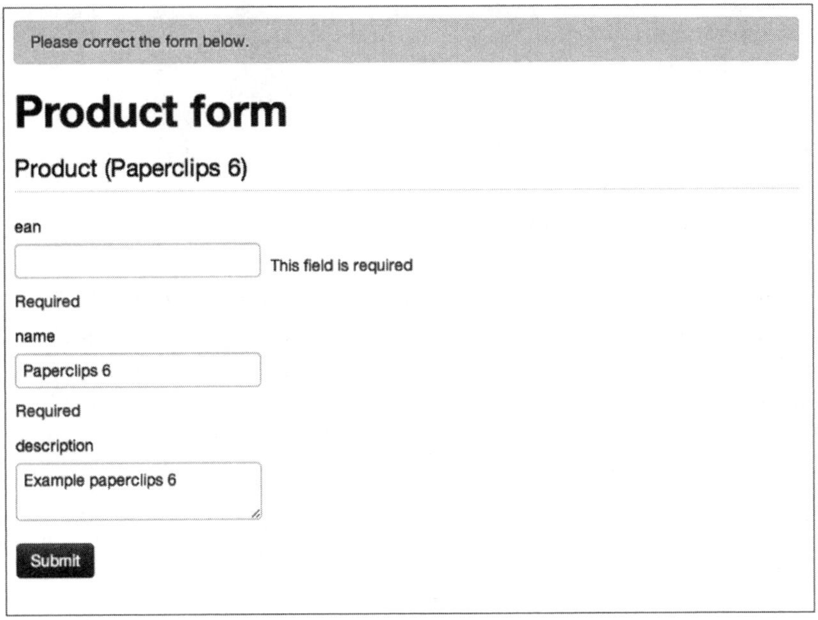

Please correct the form below.

Product form

Product (Paperclips 6)

ean

This field is required

Required

name

Paperclips 6

Required

description

Example paperclips 6

Submit

Figure 3.6 Validation errors in our form

As you can see, it doesn't take a whole lot of code to turn a "new product" form into a "product edit" form. This method takes an EAN code as a parameter from the URL, as we defined in the `routes` file in section 3.2. We then look up the product based on the EAN. If there's no product with that EAN, we return a `404 - Not Found` error.

If we *do* find a product, we create a new `Form` object, prefilled with the data from the product we found. We use the `fill` method on our existing empty form object for that. It's important to note that this does *not* fill in the existing form, but it creates a new form object *based on* the existing form.

Once we have the form, all that remains is to render the template and return the "ok" result, as in `newProduct`.

This action method is complete, and now the links in the product listing all work correctly. There's one more step left to complete our CRUD functionality: we need to implement delete functionality.

3.8   Adding a delete button

Let's start by adding a `delete()` method to our `Products` controller. The functionality is largely similar to the `details()` method; we take an EAN parameter, search for a corresponding `Product`, and return a 404 error if we can't find one. Once we have the `Product`, we delete it and redirect back to the `list()` method. Listing 3.16 shows the method.

Listing 3.16 The `delete()` action method

```
public static Result delete(String ean) {
  final Product product = Product.findByEan(ean);
  if(product == null) {
    return notFound(String.format("Product %s does not exists.", ean));
  }
  Product.remove(product);
  return redirect(routes.Products.list());
}
```

Now we need to add a route for this method in order to make it callable from the web. Because this is a method that changes something, we can't make this a GET operation. With a RESTful interface, we have to make this a DELETE operation. To do so, we'll use a bit of JavaScript to send a DELETE request, because we can't use a simple link (that would issue a GET operation). This is simple; the following code instructs your browser to issue a DELETE request to the server:

```
<script>
   function del(urlToDelete) {
      $.ajax({
        url: urlToDelete,
        type: 'DELETE',
        success: function(results) {
          // Refresh the page
          location.reload();
        }
      });
   }
</script>
```

Now, let's change our route to add a DELETE route, as shown here:

```
DELETE  /products/:ean  controllers.Products.delete(ean: String)
```

It's now time to add the user interface for our delete operation: the *Delete* button. Because the delete operation requires an HTTP DELETE call, we add a simple link that calls our JavaScript `del` method, which in turn calls the server and refreshes the page. We add a simple link with an `onclick` action handler that calls our JavaScript, and we're done. The following listing shows the updated `list` template.

Listing 3.17 Updated template—`app/views/products/list.scala.html`

```
@(products: List[Product])
@main("Products catalogue") {

  <h2>All products</h2>

    <script>
     function del(urlToDelete) {
        $.ajax({
          url: urlToDelete,
          type: 'DELETE',
          success: function(results) {
```

```
              // Refresh the page
              location.reload();
          }
        });
    }
  </script>

  <table class="table table-striped">
   <thead>
     <tr>
       <th>EAN</th>
       <th>Name</th>
       <th>Description</th>
       <th></th>
     </tr>
   </thead>
   <tbody>
   @for(product <- products) {

     <tr>
       <td><a href="@routes.Products.details(product.ean)">
         @product.ean
       </a></td>
       <td><a href="@routes.Products.details(product.ean)">
@product.name</a></td>
       <td><a href="@routes.Products.details(product.ean)">
@product.name</a></td>
       <td>
          <a href="@routes.Products.details(product.ean)">
<i class="icon icon-pencil"></i></a>
          <a onclick="del('@routes.Products.delete(product.ean)')">
<i class="icon icon-trash"></i></a>
       </td>
     </tr>
     }

   </tbody>
  </table>

 <a href="@routes.Products.newProduct()" class="btn">
   <i class="icon-plus"></i> New product</a>
}
```

The link calls our JavaScript del method, which in turn issues a request to the server

Go ahead and test it out. You should be able to delete products from the list page now.

With the delete functionality added, the functionality for our proof-of-concept application is now complete.

3.9   *Summary*

In this chapter, we implemented a simple proof-of-concept application. We added all the CRUD functionality, with a datastore in memory. We started with a *controller* with some basic *action methods* and linked them to URLs by setting up Play's *routing* system. We then introduced some *view templates* and added some *forms* with *validation*. Finally, we added the delete functionality by adding a DELETE action and a corresponding form.

This chapter was a quick introduction to all the core concepts of Play. All the topics in this chapter will be explained in detail in later chapters, but now you have the general idea of the most important concepts. You've also had a taste of what it means that Play is type-safe. If you followed along with the exercises, and you made an occasional mistake, you've probably also seen how soon mistakes are spotted because of the type safety, and how useful Play's error messages are when a problem is found.

In the next chapter, we're going to see how Play 2 fits in an enterprise environment and the enterprise challenges Play 2 is trying to solve.

Part 2

Core functionality

Part 2 takes a look at Play's place in a greater system architecture, and dives deeper into the concepts introduced in part 1.

Chapter 4 takes a step back and takes a look at where Play fits in a more conventional enterprise architecture. It contrasts Play with conventional JEE development, and shows how Play can tackle some major challenges in such an architecture.

Chapter 5 is all about controllers. It explains what controllers are and how action methods help you interface with the web. It also explains how routing works and introduces the different scopes.

Chapter 6 covers how to handle user input. We show you how to use Play's Form API, as well as how binding and validation work.

Chapter 7 introduces database persistence. We explain the concept of an ORM and show you how to use the Ebean ORM tool with Play. At the end of the chapter, we show how you could choose to use JPA instead of Ebean.

Chapter 8 explains how view templates work. It explains the template syntax, and shows how to use composition to structure your pages in a reusable manner. At the end of the chapter, we look at using Play's support for LESS and Coffee-Script, and introduce the internationalization API.

An enterprise app, Play-style 4

This chapter covers

- Recalling what an enterprise application is
- Determining today's enterprise application challenges
- Understanding Play applications in an enterprise context
- Defining our warehouse enterprise application

In this chapter, we'll review what an enterprise application is. We'll then explain what challenges enterprise applications face today. We'll also see how the Play framework can be used to create enterprise applications. From there, we'll architect the warehouse application we're going to implement throughout the book and put the application in an enterprise context.

4.1 Recalling what an enterprise application is

An enterprise application is usually a business application. Its purpose is to meet specific business requirements. It encodes business policies, processes, rules, and entities; is developed in a business organization; and is deployed in a manner responsive to business needs.

In today's corporate environment, enterprise applications are complex, scalable, distributed, component-based, and often mission critical. They are data-centric and must meet stringent requirements for security, administration, and maintenance. Most of the time, business applications are isolated. One enterprise application addresses business requirements for one specific business unit. But because of isolation and business constraints, most enterprise applications are unable to talk to each other. It's usual to see multiple business applications performing similar tasks because of that.

Enterprise applications usually live inside the IT department and are usually hosted within the organization.

Current enterprise applications are applications that are created to fulfill a business need such as IT service management, customer-relationship management, enterprise-resource planning, business intelligence, project management, collaboration, human-resource management, manufacturing, enterprise-application integration, and so on.

Figure 4.1 illustrates a typical enterprise application ecosystem.

As we can see, because an enterprise application is secured and usually satisfies one business need, it's isolated and confined within its business context. It's also not exposed to the outside world, and the information it holds is not accessible by other systems. Because of that, often new business applications are built to gather

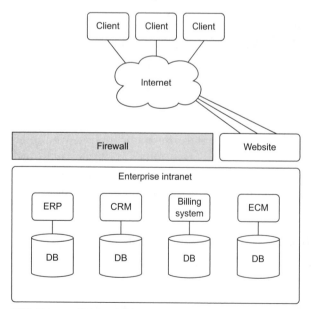

CRM: Customer Relationship Management
ERP: Enterprise Resource Planning
ECM: Enterprise Content Management

**Figure 4.1 Enterprise
application ecosystem**

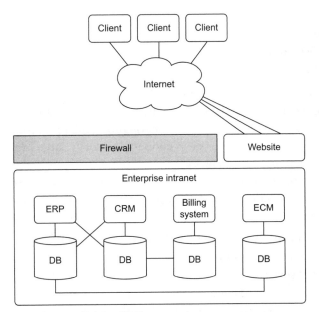

CRM: Customer Relationship Management
ERP: Enterprise Resource Planning
ECM: Enterprise Content Management

Figure 4.2   Enterprise application ecosystem after integration

information from the different systems and to distribute that information to other business applications.

Usually, these types of applications operate by batch during the night. For example, a batch is run every night to gather new customers from the CRM system and to feed the billing system. It allows the applications to stay isolated (as are their respective business units). Often, user interfaces are as complex as the applications, because little time was left to think about the users.

Integration with the existing systems is key. Most often, this isn't really part of the application requirements; it tends to be added along the way, leading to very complex and difficult-to-maintain architectures. Scalability also becomes a problem. Figure 4.2 illustrates a typical enterprise application system once integration has been performed.

As we can see, there is no real interaction between the systems per se. Most of the time, one application goes straight to another application's datasource. This leads to the following problems:

- Strong coupling, making it hard to update or upgrade applications
- No separation of concerns—the CRM application can now decide to act as an ERP
- Data-integrity problems

Nowadays, enterprise applications tend to be developed and architected with a new concept in mind: *service-oriented architecture*. The idea is that each application should be designed as a service. This allows for:

- Loose coupling
- Service reusability
- Standardized service contracts
- Service discoverability

Service-oriented architecture (SOA) is a software design and software architecture design pattern based on structured collections of discrete software modules, known as *services*, that collectively provide the complete functionality of a large software application. The purpose of SOA is to allow easy cooperation of a large number of applications that are connected over a network.

The most common implementations are done though the so-called ESB (enterprise service bus). Each service communicates through messages. An ESB usually performs the following tasks:

- Monitor and control routing of message exchange between services
- Control deployment and versioning of services
- Ensure reusability of services
- Provide commodity services like event handling, data transformation, message and event queuing, and security or exception handling

Figure 4.3 illustrates a typical SOA implementation of the applications from the previous figure.

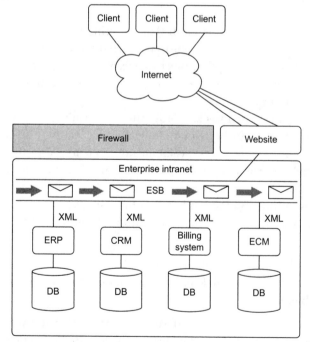

CRM: Customer Relationship Management
ERP: Enterprise Resource Planning
ECM: Enterprise Content Management

Figure 4.3   Enterprise applications with SOA

SOA is relatively new in enterprises. The main drawback is complexity due to the abundance of configurations and implementation details. The fact is that extra effort to maintain all the services is required. Most of the time communication between the different services happens through message exchange. Extra care is required to design the message exchange flow and message composition. SOA is also most often not web compliant, meaning that exposing services over the web still requires extra effort.

Obviously, something new is starting to change this status quo: the web. This is a game changer for enterprise applications, and it brings new challenges.

4.2   *Determining today's enterprise application challenges*

It seems natural today to request information and get it immediately. The internet has changed our everyday life. If we want to know what time a flight from Singapore arrives, we can connect to the airport website and get immediate results. We don't need to wait one or two hours to have the information. Even better, information is pushed to us; our phones can alert us when important (or not so important) events occur. For example, our phones can tell us as soon as the Celtics win the NBA tournament. *Applications are reactive.*

As users, we're now used to coping with multiple flows of information. *We are no longer pulling information; now information is pushed at us.*

A user's interaction with an IT system has also changed dramatically. We don't need to read a user manual before using a hotel reservation system, nor do we need a training session. *Software is now accessible and usable by everyone.*

Because the software is easily reachable and accessible, users can add more and more information to the different systems, creating more and more data. Today, we're dealing with a *large quantity of information.*

With such a large amount of information, most internet web applications provide a way to query that information through a public API, allowing third parties to combine that information and redistribute it *in real time. Web applications talk to each other in real time.*

Simplicity is also key. Most of the popular web applications focus on one problem and provide a simple solution. Enterprise applications should learn from them. Concentrate on your business problem and stay simple. This doesn't mean that the application is simple in itself; it means that the application can be easy to use and to extend.

Scalability is usually a strong requirement for an enterprise. But talking about enterprise scalability is not the same as talking about web-application scalability. In the latter case, we usually mean that the application can handle millions of users. Enterprise scalability means that the applications should be able to grow with enterprise needs. This can be in terms of users, but it also means that the applications should be able to scale to new business requirements. For example, if company X acquires company Z, the address book application from company X should be able to absorb company Z's address book. Scalability is a matter of supporting more users and more data but also integrating more systems. Cloud computing helps with the first part, and simple architecture and good APIs help in the second case. Again, modern web applications provide for these two requirements naturally.

You probably agree that all of this is now a given when we talk about web applications. But enterprise applications rarely meet these requirements. And as you guessed, enterprise has to address these challenges to stay on the competitive edge:

- Push real-time data to their customers/employees
- Deal with a large flow of data
- Improve scalability and integration
- Provide easy integration with the latest clients
- Ensure interoperability between applications and existing systems

The internet, HTML5, XML, JSON, and the HTTP protocol (and good developers) provide most of the low-level requirements to address these challenges, as we'll see in the next chapters. There's also a paradigm shift in which client-side programs are becoming more and more elaborate due to the hardware evolution; for example, your phone is more powerful than your two-year-old desktop computer. Enterprise will adapt to this new paradigm as well.

In enterprise, the main challenge is to aggregate and redistribute selected data to other systems or users. Usually the needed information is dispatched over multiple systems, and one needs to aggregate them. Because we're dealing always with more and more information, processing large amounts of data in real time will be the next big requirement. Another implicit requirement is overall simplicity and the tool's simplicity. The systems we're building should be comprehensive, and the tooling should make it easier for us to build a great system, removing complexity from our way. The Play framework certainly meets that requirement. Building simple software blocks allows us to create reliable and complex systems that match business needs. A modern framework should be able to help address the mentioned challenges. Obviously, we'll discover through the book that Play addresses exactly those challenges; but first, let's see how Play's application architecture should work in an enterprise context.

4.3 Understanding Play's application in an enterprise context

As we already explained in chapter 1, Play is a web framework that focuses on the following aspects:

- Simplicity
- High productivity
- Modern web application development

Simplicity doesn't mean that you can only build simple applications. On the contrary, it means that it should be easier to integrate your application components. The idea is to decompose your complex application with simple building blocks. Each building block should be simple enough that it's comprehensible by everyone without much thinking. It also allows new developers to join a project and be productive from the start without losing time setting up the environment or understanding the details of the other blocks.

High productivity means that any developers can produce working software within a matter of hours and can be able to demo it without external help.

Modern web framework means that the framework concentrates on the server side and delegates as much as possible to the (rich) clients. Play makes sure to delegate as much as possible to the web browser and allows easy integration with the latest browser specifications. Today, a lot of innovation happens at the client level. Our smartphones are now more powerful than the desktop computers of two years ago. Therefore, the server should delegate as much as possible to the clients. The less the server does for the client (for example, rendering or user-interface interaction), the more scalable the application is.

Play is also designed to easily integrate with other web applications through HTTP. Play forces you to think about the way your clients will interact with your applications. It also provides functionality to easily talk to other web applications.

How do such concepts fit the enterprise context? If you see the web as a giant company and the different web applications as business units, everything is explained. A lot of web applications are able to get data from other web applications. For example, most new web applications allow you to log in using your existing Facebook credentials; you don't need to reimplement user authentication. Let's see in more detail what we mean and how Play helps.

Play achieves reusability and interoperability between applications by promoting RESTful architecture web applications. This means that web applications should expose their methods and data using REST, and most of the time they should expose themselves as web services as well.

A RESTful web application is a web application implemented using HTTP and REST principles. It's a collection of resources, with four defined aspects:

- The base URI for the web application, such as http://example.com/ warehouses/
- The internet media type of the data supported by the web API
- The set of operations supported by the web API using HTTP methods (for example, GET, PUT, POST, or DELETE)
- A hypertext-driven API (that is, URLs define the API)

In order to facilitate communication within a web application, web APIs are usually part of the web application. REST promotes reusing the existing information systems. This means that web REST APIs tend to reuse the same architecture, making it easier for developers.

RESTful architecture goals are:

- Scalability of component interactions
- Generality of interfaces

- Independent deployment of components
- Intermediary components to reduce latency, enforce security, and encapsulate legacy systems

If we translate this into enterprise terms, it means greater interoperability between applications, standard ways to produce interfaces using predefined operations (for example, GET, PUT, POST, or DELETE), and loose coupling between components. This is exactly what enterprise applications are looking for.

The REST architectural style describes six architectural constraints:

- *Client–server*—A uniform interface separates clients from servers. This separation of concerns means that, for example, clients are not concerned with data storage, which remains internal to each server, so that the portability of client code is improved. Servers aren't concerned with the user interface or user state, so servers can be simpler and more scalable. Servers and clients may also be replaced and developed independently, as long as the interface between them isn't altered.
- *Stateless*—The client–server communication is further constrained by no client context being stored on the server between requests. Each request from any client contains all of the information necessary to service the request, and any session state is held in the client.
- *Cacheable*—As on the World Wide Web, clients can cache responses. Responses must therefore, implicitly or explicitly, define themselves as cacheable or not to prevent clients reusing stale or inappropriate data in response to further requests. Well-managed caching partially or completely eliminates some client–server interactions, further improving scalability and performance.
- *Layered system*—A client can't ordinarily tell whether it's connected directly to the end server or to an intermediary along the way. Intermediary servers may improve system scalability by enabling load-balancing and by providing shared caches.
- *Code on demand (optional)*—Servers can temporarily extend or customize the functionality of a client by sending executable code. Examples of this include client-side scripts such as JavaScript.
- *Uniform interface*—The uniform interface between clients and servers, discussed ahead, simplifies and decouples the architecture, which enables each part to evolve independently.

Complying with these constraints and conforming to the REST architectural style enables any kind of distributed hypermedia system to have desirable emergent properties, such as performance, scalability, simplicity, modifiability, visibility, portability, and reliability. The nature of Play enforces these principles, which means it has never been easier to implement a RESTful web application than with Play.

Going back to an enterprise context, when creating a new application, on a high level, we want to:

- Reuse existing software blocks
- Retrieve data from other systems
- Expose data to other systems

We saw that Play promotes the REST architectural style, which provides exactly the elements discussed and at the same time focuses on simplicity and reusing the existing information systems. Figure 4.4 shows how our enterprise applications would look using the REST-style architecture.

With Play, each enterprise application is a web application, and each enterprise application provides a REST web API. Enterprise applications communicate with each other using a RESTful web API through HTTP. The REST web API comes naturally when designing the web application. The web application architectural design is therefore key. We'll see in the next section how that all works when we architect our warehouse application. Typically, communication between the different applications occurs via HTTP, exchanging JSON, XML, or whatever format the developers agreed upon.

On a more practical level, enterprise tends to have large development teams. Distributing the work between the different teams is therefore key. Play provides two ways to achieve that goal:

- Create a Play module or Play sub-application for each team
- Create a web application (a.k.a., a web service)

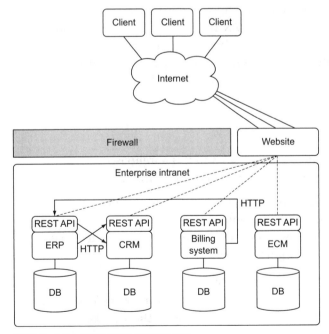

CRM: Customer Relationship Management
ERP: Enterprise Resource Planning
ECM: Enterprise Content Management

Figure 4.4 Enterprise applications with Play

A *Play module* or *Play sub-application* is a web application within your Play web application. For our discussion, it's important to know that modules allow you to build a subset of an application, and chapter 11 explains in more detail how to create modules and sub-applications. Again, the REST-style architecture allows the teams to agree on communication between the different application modules. Obviously, defining the interface to communicate between the applications is the most important part; that's why you usually need a web service API that follows the REST architecture, and Play makes it easy to include.

Using Play, it's also easier to build real-time web applications, query multiple systems, and deal with large amounts of data, thanks to its asynchronous nature. We'll detail this in chapter 9.

As we've already seen in chapter 1, Play focuses on simplicity, allowing the developers to concentrate on the business problem at hand instead of fighting or configuring the framework.

The only drawback of the REST-style approach is that it's crucial to correctly design the application's data flow and the REST-style architecture. Happily, Play is here and it provides all the tools to do so. The next section outlines how to architect our warehouse enterprise application based on what we've learned.

4.4   *Defining our warehouse enterprise application*

Through the next chapters, we'll design and create our warehouse enterprise application. A warehouse application is an application that manages diverse products. A product is identified by a unique EAN number. Within the warehouse, we want to know how many products there are. We also want to make sure that we can record a product leaving or entering the warehouse. The application must:

- Add products
- Edit products
- View products
- View current product's stock
- Add a certain quantity of product X to this warehouse
- Subtract a certain quantity of product X from this warehouse

Our system is only required to interact with humans; this means we'll serve HTML to our web browser and the client will send back HTML forms.

Following the advice in the previous sections, we can model what our URLs and our web application calls are going to be:

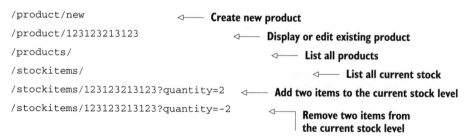

Applying HTTP verbs, we want to expose the following:

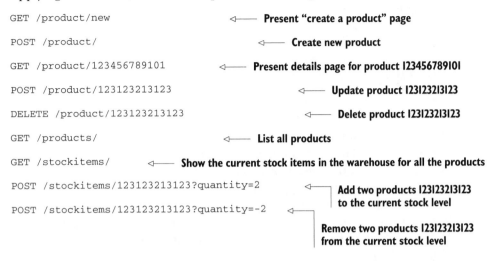

```
GET /product/new              ◄─── Present "create a product" page

POST /product/               ◄─── Create new product

GET /product/123456789101    ◄─── Present details page for product 123456789101

POST /product/123123213123   ◄─── Update product 123123213123

DELETE /product/123123213123 ◄─── Delete product 123123213123

GET /products/               ◄─── List all products

GET /stockitems/             ◄─── Show the current stock items in the warehouse for all the products

POST /stockitems/123123213123?quantity=2    ◄─── Add two products 123123213123
                                                 to the current stock level
POST /stockitems/123123213123?quantity=-2   ◄───
                                                 Remove two products 123123213123
                                                 from the current stock level
```

We can see that the last two rules are a bit different in the sense that the URL takes the quantity parameter. This is because URLs should be idempotent; that is, they always return the same value for a given URL (in mathematics, idempotent means not changed in value following multiplication by itself). With the interface we defined, we're able to split the work between two teams easily. One team can develop the product part while the other one can concentrate on managing the stock items. Other systems (and other teams) can already simulate the use of the interface, as we're only returning simple and agreed-upon data messages.

For example, to create a new product, we would issue the following using our browser:

```
Request URL:/products/ Request Method:POST
Request Body:
------WebKitFormBoundaryllSQqb38u5oy6
Content-Disposition: form-data; name="ean"

1234567891012
------WebKitFormBoundaryllSQqb38u5oy6Kc8
Content-Disposition: form-data; name="name"

Item
------WebKitFormBoundaryllSQqb38u5oy6Kc8
Content-Disposition: form-data; name="description"

A new item
------WebKitFormBoundaryllSQqb38u5oy6Kc8--
```

And we'll get the following back from the server:

```
HTTP/1.1 201 Created
Location: /product/123456789101
Content-Length: 0
```

Now if we want to expose our application as a web service, we'll probably have the following URLs as well:

```
POST /api/v1/product/
GET /api/v1/product/${id}
POST /api/v1/product/${id}
DELETE /api/v1/product/${id}
GET /api/v1/products/
GET /api/v1/stockitems/
POST /api/v1/product/${id}?quantity=${qty}
```

You'll notice that we prefix our calls by a version number that we expose through the /api resource. This is because other systems can then refer to this unique URL without any fear that the version will change. It allows our API to live its own life without impacting the rest of the application. Our application would then interact with other systems. This means we would serve XML, for example, and interpret XML. Note that we could decide to stay with HTTP, but that wouldn't be practical for the other system involved. In the case of a web service, we're only interested in the business data and not *how to represent them*.

This means that if we issue the following:

```
Request URL:/products/
Request Method:POST
Request Body:
<?xml version='1.0' encoding='utf-8'?>
<product ean="123456789101" name="item"
            description="an item"/>
```

The server responds with:

```
HTTP/1.1 201 Created
Location: /product/123456789101
Content-Length: 102
<?xml version='1.0' encoding='utf-8'?>
<product ean="123456789101" name="item"
            description="an item"/>
```

As you can see, this is the same behavior; only the exchange protocol changes. XML is usually easy to transform, and any system can then modify it for other application needs. The big advantage of such an interface is that your application is now able to communicate with others. This means that another application in your enterprise can act as a client and request information from the warehouse application. And because Play is asynchronous by nature, Play applications can request multiple pieces of information at the same time while combining and transforming the results as they're available.

4.5 Summary

In this chapter, we explained what an enterprise application is and how it differs from other applications. We saw different types of architecture that allow enterprise applications to communicate. We identified the upcoming enterprise challenges and quickly saw how Play proposes to address them. We then saw how Play fits into an enterprise environment and, by using the RESTful principles, how enterprise applications can communicate simply and effectively. We also learned how to decompose our applications so that several teams can work in parallel.

We then focused on the application we'll build throughout the book and how to build an interface so that internal and external systems can communicate with it. In the next chapter, we're going to implement this interface. We'll make it concrete by explaining how controllers work in Play.

Controllers—
handling HTTP requests

In this chapter we'll explain in detail one of the key concepts of the Play framework MVC paradigm: the controller. We'll take a closer look at our warehouse web application and at the same time explain how interaction with a web client works in Play.

We'll start by explaining controllers, and from there we'll examine action methods and how we can return results to web clients. We'll then see how to use routes to link HTTP requests to a controller's action method. After that, we'll look at what interceptors are and talk about what scopes are available in Play. All of these concepts are important when processing and responding to client requests.

Let's see how we can accept and process a request from a client. First, we'll introduce the concepts of *controllers* and talk some more about *action methods*.

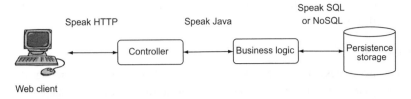

Figure 5.1   Role of the controller

5.1   *Controllers and action methods*

Business data is often stored in a relational database. That means that if you wanted to add a new product to the catalog, you'd have to write some SQL. But that wouldn't be very practical, would it? This is where web applications come to the rescue. Using a web application, the warehouse manager can interact with the database stock level. This is an easier and cheaper solution than learning SQL or having an on-site SQL expert.

But there's still a problem: the web browser can't directly access the data because it doesn't speak SQL. The web browser speaks HTTP. Moreover, the model layer is usually fine-grained, whereas the user usually wants to execute a series of actions in one go. For example, when you add a product, you want to make sure the data describes a valid product and that the product wasn't already created.

This is precisely the role the *controller* plays. The controller connects HTTP requests to the server business logic. It acts as glue between domain model objects and transport layer events. A controller exposes some application functionality at a given address or URI (unique resource identifier). In fact, it exposes the application business logic at a given address: it's our web application's public API. Like the HTTP interface, controllers are procedural and request/response oriented.

Figure 5.1 illustrates the role of the controller in a typical web application.

A controller is one of the central points in Play, as in any MVC framework. It is also the application entry point for you as a developer. As soon as a client (for example, a web browser) issues a request, Play will accept this request and delegate the processing of it to a controller. This is usually where your code comes into action. Figure 5.2 illustrates this lifecycle.

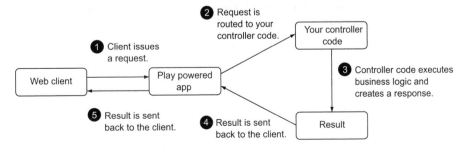

Figure 5.2   Controller lifecycle

While the controller is a central point in any Play application, its actual code resides in its action methods.

5.1.1   Action methods

In Play, a controller is an aggregation of action methods. An action method is a static method that takes some parameters as input and always returns an instance of (a subclass of) the `Result` class. In other words, an action method always takes the following form:

```
public static play.mvc.Result methodName(params...)
```

Note that action methods are static. This is because controllers are effectively singletons, which fits the HTTP approach. Because HTTP doesn't have the concept of an object but is mainly procedural, we shouldn't try to map those object concepts in our controller. You should really think of your action methods as the entry point from HTTP to your application. You could compare them to the `static main()` method of a Java program.

Since an action method mainly serves as an entry point, you shouldn't put too much business logic into your controllers and action methods. Rather, you should do what is necessary to translate an incoming HTTP request to data your business logic understands, hand it off to that business logic, and translate the result into an HTTP response.

When coding static methods, thread safety is usually a concern, but Play will make sure all action methods are thread-safe. You will see that making action methods static has little impact on the way you write code.

For now, imagine that Play queues the incoming requests for a controller in order to process them as fast as possible. Netty and Akka are used under the hood to dispatch and process users' requests as fast as possible in a thread-safe way. But the cool thing about Play is that all this complexity is handled for you, so don't have to worry about it.

We've already created our first controller, `Products`, in chapter 3. Let's examine it.

5.1.2   Examining our controller

In chapter 3, we created a controller class called `Products`. We put it in the `/app/controllers/` folder, which is the default location for all controllers in a Play application. You can change these defaults if you want to, but you should rarely need to do so.

Let's revisit the contents of the controller. In your favorite text editor or IDE, open the file called `Products.java` in the `app/controllers` directory, as shown in listing 5.1.

Listing 5.1 Project directory overview

```
warehouse
    ├─ app
    │    ├─ controllers
    │    │     └─ Products.java          This is where our
    │    ├─ models                       Products controller lives
    │    └─ views
    ├─ conf
    ├─ public
    ├─ test
    └─ db
```

We'll first pick apart the class definition. The following listing shows a reminder.

Listing 5.2 `Products` class definition

```
...
import play.mvc.Controller;
...

public class Products extends Controller {
  ...
}
```

The class definition tells us that we're extending the `Controller` class from Play. That's the only prerequisite for a controller; there is nothing else that makes a controller class "special." Let's move on to the action methods.

The first action method of this controller, `list()`, displays the product items in stock at the warehouse. The following listing shows a reminder.

Listing 5.3 The `list()` action method

```
public static Result list() {
  List<Product> products = Product.findAll();
  return ok(products.list.render(products));
}
```

In this example, the `ok` method constructs a `200 OK` HTTP response containing a response body that is the result of rendering the `list` template. Note how little code this method contains. All it does is delegate data lookup to the model layer (the `models`.`Product` class) and data presentation to the view layer (the `list` template).

As you may recall from chapter 3, we can access the `list` method by requesting the `/products/` URL from our application. The reason why this works is because we've also configured a *route*. We'll learn everything about routing in section 5.3, but first, let's learn a little more about results.

5.2 *Returning results from action methods*

Besides the `list()` action methods, our `Products` controller contains several more action methods. Listing 5.4 shows an overview of their definitions.

Listing 5.4   The action methods in `Products`

```
public class Products extends Controller {

    public static Result list() {
    ...
    }

    public static Result newProduct() {
    ...
    }

    public static Result details(String ean ) {
    ...
    }

    public static Result save() {
    ...
    }

}
```

An action method is a Java method that processes the request parameters and produces a result to be sent to the client. The action method is where the response is processed. Each action method returns a result, represented by a `play.mvc.Result` value, which represents an HTTP response.

5.2.1   *Results*

Let's take a closer look at what our action method returns: a `Result` object. A result is a response to a client request. Since we're creating a web application, it's always an HTTP response. It can be an `OK` with some text body, an error with an HTML error message, a redirect to another page, a 404 page, and so on.

The `Controller` class contains several static methods that generate `Results`. These methods all correspond to an HTTP status code, and they wrap an object that represents the body for the request. An example of this is the `ok()` method that we used to create the `200 - OK` response code. We supplied it with HTML contents from the `list` template, thus generating the `Result` that we returned. Try to find the best response code for any situation.

For example, if a user enters an unknown EAN number as a parameter for the `show` method, we could return:

```
return badRequest("Incorrect EAN: " + ean)
```

This code returns an HTTP error code 400 with the text "`Incorrect EAN: x`" as content.

A more appropriate response would be to answer that we didn't find the product:

```
return notFound("No product with EAN " + ean);
```

This code returns an HTTP 404 error code with the text "`No product with EAN: x`" as content.

5.2.2 Redirect result

Another useful `Result` object is the `Redirect` result object. As its name suggests, it redirects to another action method. For example, using the `Redirect` result, we can redirect the user from the `index` method to the `list` method, allowing our users to see a list of products on the main page.

```
public static Result index() {
  return redirect(routes.Products.list());
}
```
Redirect to the product list action method

The `routes` object is a class that's generated by Play 2 based on your `routes` file. The class only contains static members that allow you to access your controller methods. For now, remember that the `Redirect` result redirects from one action method to another action method. We'll go into more detail in the next section.

THE TODO RESULT There is also a useful `Result` object called `TODO`. As you might have guessed, this `Result` indicates that the action method has not been implemented yet. This is useful when you're developing your application and don't have your action method implementation finished, but still need to return a result. For example, if we have the following action method but our implementation is not ready yet, we can return a `TODO` result:

```
public static Result items() {
  return TODO;
}
```

When an action method returns a `TODO` result, the client will receive a `501 - Not Implemented` HTTP response.

5.2.3 Using results

We are now able to control what status codes we return. But what about the response body? And how does Play know how to set the correct content-type header?

All result methods let you pass a `Content` object as a parameter. The type of content that object contains tells Play what kind of data it is. As it turns out, templates in Play also return `Content`.

In chapter 3, we built our first template, `products/list.scala.html`. The following listing reminds you of what it does.

Listing 5.5 Displaying our stock items

```
@(products: List[Product])
@main("Products catalogue") {

  <h2>All products</h2>

  <table class="table table-striped">
   <thead>
     <tr>
       <th>EAN</th>
       <th>Name</th>
       <th>Description</th>
     </tr>
```

```
    </thead>
    <tbody>
    @for(product <- products) {

      <tr>
        <td><a href="@routes.Products.details(product.ean)">
          @product.ean
        </a></td>
        <td><a href="@routes.Products.details(product.ean)">
@product.name</a></td>
        <td><a href="@routes.Products.details(product.ean)">
@product.name</a></td>
      </tr>
      }

    </tbody>
  </table>

  <a href="@routes.Products.newProduct()" class="btn">
    <i class="icon-plus"></i> New product</a>
}
```

This template prints a list of products and their descriptions. What you need to know is that Play automatically compiles the template when it sees it. The result of this compilation step is a Java class with a `render()` method. By convention, it's compiled into a class with the name `views.html.{name of the template}`. In this case, since we created a template called `list` under the `views/products/` directory, the corresponding class is `views.html.products.list`.

When we render the template, the generated classes contain a `render` method. In Play, all templates are type-safe, which means the `render()` method expects a certain number of parameters of the correct types. In this case, we have to pass the `products` list as a parameter. All this will be explained in more detail in chapter 8.

What matters to us at the moment is to understand how we send HTML from our controller. In chapter 3, we rendered the template and immediately passed it the `ok()` method, like so:

```
public static Result list() {
  ...
  return ok(list.render(products));
}
```

This is the most concise way to render a template and return a `Result` that wraps the rendered content, but we could have also used an intermediary variable, like so:

```
public static Result list() {
  ...
  Html renderedTemplate = list.render(products);
  return ok(renderedTemplate);
}
```

As you can see, the template rendering doesn't simply return a string containing HTML; it actually returns an object of type `play.api.templates.Html`. That class is a subtype of `play.mvc.Content`, which is a type that can be used as a parameter for the `ok()` method (and all result methods, for that matter).

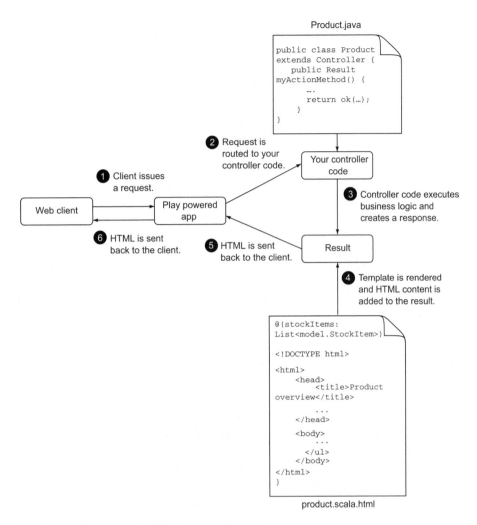

Figure 5.3 Detailed view of the controller lifecycle

You should now have an idea of how templates and results fit into the bigger picture of a Play application. Figure 5.3 shows the place of the controllers and products in the lifecycle diagram.

We've displayed some HTML without much effort; we only changed the provided `Result` object in our action method with some `Content`. Let's do something extra. Let's serve the client with the type of result they're asking for. If the web client asks for text, we'll return some text; if it asks for HTML, we'll return some HTML. This is easy to do with Play:

```
if (request().accept("text/plain")) {                    request() method accesses
    return ok(StringUtils.join(products, "\n"));          the current request
}
return ok(list.render(products));
```

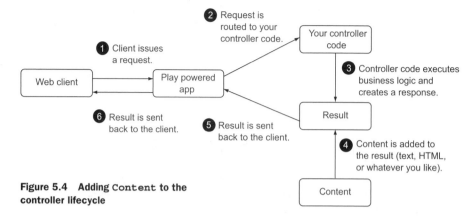

Figure 5.4   Adding Content to the controller lifecycle

We are now able to serve content according to the client's wishes. We added our Content object to the diagram to explain the complete request/response lifecycle in Play, as shown in figure 5.4.

We are now able to respond to a request with some content. Let's take a look at how our code is actually called in response to a request.

5.3 Using routing to wire URLs to action methods

We now know how we can render some content and how to execute business logic. But how do we link the controller method to be executed to the URL that the client invokes?

5.3.1 Translating HTTP to Java code

Remember, our client only speaks HTTP. But the code that we're writing is in Java. We therefore need to translate the HTTP "language" to the Java language. This is the role of the router: translating each incoming HTTP request to an action method call. This way, it exposes the controller's action methods to the client. An HTTP request can been seen as an event, from Play's point of view. The router's role is to coordinate a reaction to such an event (figure 5.5).

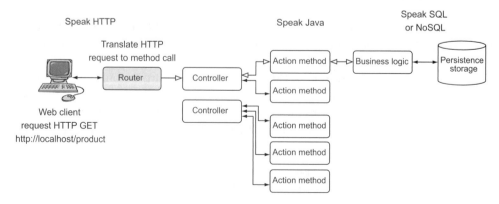

Figure 5.5   Role of the router

Two major pieces of information are contained in the request:

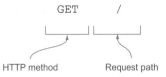

Figure 5.6   Request

- The request path (such as /clients /1542, /photos/list), including the query string (such as id=2)
- The HTTP method (GET, POST, …)

For example, when you enter the URL http://localhost/ in your browser, let's say to view the home page, it issues a request to the localhost server. On the server, the request is then decomposed as shown in figure 5.6.

Let's take a look at another example. To display the first page of a product listing, a URL could be http://localhost/product?page=1. It would decomposed as shown in figure 5.7.

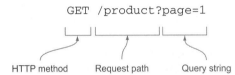

Figure 5.7   Request with query string

The HTTP method can be any of the valid methods supported by HTTP (GET, POST, PUT, DELETE, or HEAD). The request path identifies the resource we're trying to serve. Query strings are optional and are used to provide dynamic parameters. A query string is specified after the ? sign and is always of the form name=value. We assume you know all about what a URL is and what HTTP methods are. If not, please read about them in chapter 3.

Let's get back to our application. We'd like to provide certain functionality, and therefore we should be able to respond to the requests shown in table 5.1.

As you might have guessed, we need to translate each of these requests to a controller and action method. This way, we're translating from an HTTP request to a Java method call. This translation is what we call a *route definition*. Route definitions are contained inside a *routes file*. For our application, the routes file will expose the application functionality just listed.

Table 5.1   List of requests

Method	Request path	Description
GET	/	Home page
GET	/products/	Product list
GET	/products/?page=2	The products list's second page
GET	/product/5010255079763	The products with the given EAN
POST	/product/5010255079763	Update the product details

Routes are defined in the `conf/routes` file, as shown in the following listing.

Listing 5.6   Project directory structure

```
warehouse
    ├─ app
    │   └─ controllers
    │   │      └─ Products.java
    │   ├─ models
    │   └─ views
    │        └─ products
    │              ├─ list.scala.html
    │              └─ details.scala.html
    ├─ conf
    │   └─ routes
    ├─ public
    ├─ test
    └─ db
```

> **The routes file that
> contains the routes
> to your controller's
> action methods**

The routes file isn't just a text-based configuration file; it's actually code that will be compiled into a Java object. The object is accessible in our controllers and is called `routes`. This means that you'll see compile-time errors if a route definition is not valid or if a requested URL doesn't exist in your application, as shown in figure 5.8.

This is convenient, as you know immediately that something is wrong in your application. This is another example of Play 2 employing type safety to make your application more robust. Let's see what other benefits we get from that.

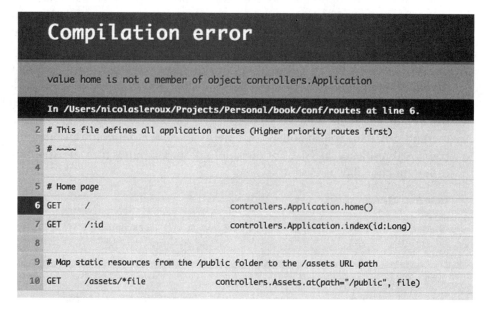

Figure 5.8   An error in the routes file

TYPE SAFETY IN THE ROUTES FILE

Beside the obvious error reporting, another benefit of compilation is that the routes object is accessible from the controllers and templates. This comes in handy when you want to refer from one action method to another, or when you want to link to an action from a template.

An example of using the routes from a controller is redirection. Let's say we have an index method available at http://localhost:9000/ that should redirect the client to the product list method available at http://localhost:9000/product. Using the routes object, you can simply refer to the products method, which is used to do something called *reverse routing*, which is explained in section 5.3.5. But for now, let's focus on the syntax of the routes file.

5.3.2 *The routes files explained*

So, what are routes, exactly? As explained previously, the routes file is where the translation between the HTTP request and your code is performed. Let's take a close look at the routes file syntax. The routes file lists all of the routes needed by the application, and each route consists of an HTTP method and a URI pattern associated with a call to an action method. This is what we call a *route definition*.

Let's see what a route definition looks like for the products home page:

```
GET    /            controllers.Products.index()   ◁─┤  Assume we have a
                                                        Products controller with
                                                        an index action method
```

This means that when a client issues an HTTP request `GET /`, the action method located in the `Products` class should be called. The `Products` class is our code; it's our entry point.

In the routes file, a route definition is composed of the following parts:

- The HTTP method
- The request path
- Optionally, the query string
- The call definition

Figure 5.9 breaks down our example route definition. Figure 5.10 breaks down a route definition that includes the optional query string.

Let's take a look at a more complicated route definition. If we want to have a route definition that displays product details based on the product EAN, we could put the following entries into our route files:

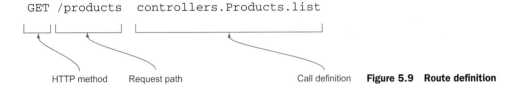

GET /products   controllers.Products.list

HTTP method   Request path   Call definition   **Figure 5.9 Route definition**

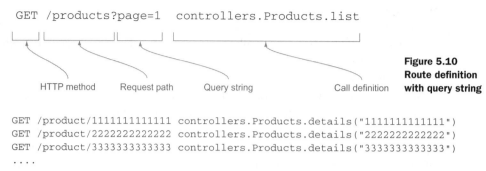

GET /products?page=1 controllers.Products.list

HTTP method   Request path   Query string   Call definition

**Figure 5.10
Route definition
with query string**

```
GET /product/1111111111111  controllers.Products.details("1111111111111")
GET /product/2222222222222  controllers.Products.details("2222222222222")
GET /product/3333333333333  controllers.Products.details("3333333333333")
....
```

But that wouldn't scale very well (not to mention that we'd need to predict future products). We need to have a way to have a dynamic part in our route definition.

5.3.3 *Dynamic path parts*

Part of the path of our route can actually be used as a parameter for our action method. It would look like this:

```
GET     /product/:ean    controllers.Products.details(ean: String)
```

We replaced the part of the path that indicates the ID with a parameter name, indicated by the colon (:). We then reference that parameter in the action method call.

You'll notice that in the action method call, we added the parameter type after the parameter name. For parameters of type String, specifying the type of the parameter is optional, but it's required for every other type.

Every time we request /product/1111111111111 in our browser, the details method on the Products controller is called, with 1111111111111 as the ean parameter. Since our parameter is a String, Play doesn't have to do much. But if our parameter's type had been a Long, for example, Play would make sure the parameter is transformed into a Long. Play is also able to convert to other types such as arrays and dates, and you can even add your own types as well, as we'll show you in chapter 6.

If Play can't convert to the required type, it means that the expected type is not the right one, and you're doing something you should not. You'll see an error screen like the one shown in figure 5.11.

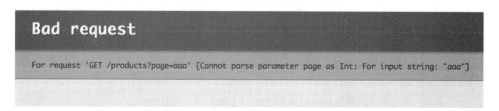

Bad request

For request 'GET /products?page=aaa' [Cannot parse parameter page as Int: For input string: "aaa"]

Figure 5.11   Bad request error screen

> ### A word about simple data binding
>
> Type conversion is handled automatically by Play, so you don't have to handle the conversion between Strings and other types. The automatic conversion is called *binding*. It's binding values from the HTTP requests (which are strings by definition) to a Java type. In chapter 6, we'll explain how Play can bind to other types. Binding is actually part of the translation process from HTTP to your Java code.

This is a really nice feature that allows us to concentrate on the problem at hand. If you were using Servlet or any other framework, you'd probably have to write something along the lines of the following listing.

Listing 5.7 A conventional Servlet method

```
public void doGet(HttpServletRequest request,
  HttpServletResponse response) throws ServletException, IOException {
  try {
    final String id = request.getStringParameter("id");
    final Long idCode = Long.parseLong(id);
     // Process request...
  } catch (NumberFormatException e) {
    final int status = HttpServletResponse.SC_BAD_REQUEST;
    response.sendError(status, e.getMessage());
  }
}
```

Play takes care of this for us. Note that you'll only see the message between brackets (in figure 5.11) while developing. In production, the detailed information is left out. Now let's get back to the discussion about dynamic route parts.

When using this syntax to define dynamic path parts, each parameter will match exactly one path part, which means each part between forward slashes (or the start of the path).

But you might sometimes want more flexibility. If you want a dynamic part to capture more than one request path segment, separated by forward slashes, you can define a dynamic part using the `*id` syntax, which will use the rest of the path as the value for the parameter.

For example, let's say that we want to get the path to our product image. The route definition is as follows:

```
GET   /product/image/*imagePath
            controllers.Products.downloadImage(imagePath: String)
```

If we issue a request like `GET /products/image/29929/paperclip.jpg`, the `imagePath` value will be `29929/paperclip.jpg`.

If you know what regular expressions are, you can also define your own regular expression for the dynamic parts using the `$id<regex>` syntax:

```
GET   /product/$ean<[0-9]{13}>
                    controllers.Products.details(ean: Long)
```

This route definition will only apply if the EAN consists of 13 digits, which is handy in our case, because we know that our product EAN codes consist of 13 digits. Play will return a not found error code if we enter alphanumeric characters as IDs.

As you know, you can also pass parameters with your URL. For example, http://google.com?query=playframework contains a parameter called *query*, with the value "playframework." So how do you specify a parameter like that in your routes file so that you can access it from your action methods? Actually, you don't have to declare it in your routes file at all. You can just use a parameter of the same name in your action method signature:

```
public static Result products(String filter) {
    ...
```

If the action method defines some parameters, *all of these parameter values will be searched for in the request path.* They will either be extracted from the request path as we saw before, or they will be extracted from the query string.

Let's see a more detailed example. Let's say we want to display a list of products. But that's potentially a really large list, so we want to paginate it. To access the first 20 items, we will request the first page; for the next 20, we will request the second page, and so on. The following route definitions can be seen as equivalent, functionally:

```
GET /products/:page controllers.Products.list(page: Int)
GET /products/ controllers.Products.list(page: Int)
```

What is the difference between the two route definitions? The first route definition has the page parameter as part of the actual request path. The client requests the following URL to access the second product list page: http://localhost/products/2. The second route definition doesn't require the page parameter to be part of the request URL. Instead, it's a parameter that the user needs to provide. This is done by requesting the following URL: http://localhost/products/?page=2.

It's interesting to note that http://localhost/products/2 (where "2" is the page number) isn't a good identifier for a resource. The product list for the second page is likely to change over time. Therefore the second definition is to be preferred. For more information about RESTful concepts like this, please refer to chapter 4.

Also notice that Play complains if we don't specify the page parameter in the request URL, as shown in figure 5.12. The error is thrown because Play has no way to tell what the default value for the parameter is. There's a way to find out, though: default values in the routes file.

Bad request

For request 'GET /products' [Missing parameter: page]

Figure 5.12 Bad request error screen for missing parameter

ROUTE WITH DEFAULT VALUE

We can (and should) choose a default value to use if none is specified in the request. For example, for our list of products with pagination, the following syntax will request the first page to be displayed if no first page is specified.

```
GET /products  controllers.Products.list(page: Int ?= 0)
```

Using this syntax, it's impossible to get "Bad request" errors due to missing parameters. When the parameter *isn't* provided, the value specified ("1" in this case) will be used instead. Please note that we're using the `Int` keyword, as it is the Scala representation of an integer. This is the equivalent of the Java `Integer` type.

FIXED VALUE AS PARAMETER

Now let's say that we want the home page to display the first page of our product listing. We can do that using a fixed value as a parameter:

```
GET / controllers.Products.list(page: Int = 0)
```

The value of the `page` parameter will always be 1 on the home page, even if another value is provided using a query string parameter.

Using all these different syntaxes for route definition, it's very possible to construct multiple routes that will match the same URL. What happens then?

CONFLICTING ROUTES

Because many routes can match the same request, if there is a conflict, the first route (in declaration order) is used. For example, in our routes file we have the following route definitions:

```
GET   /products/new        controllers.Products.newProduct()
GET   /products/:ean       controllers.Products.details(ean: String)
```

The bottom line would *also* match on /products/new. But since there is a line matching that URL first, that is the one that is used. Therefore, calls to /products/new will be served by newProduct(), which is exactly what we want. If we were to switch the lines around, the same request would be handled by the details() method, with the value "new" used for the ean parameter, which would cause problems.

We now know enough about route definitions. Let's get back to our application.

5.3.4 *Completing our routes file*

With all we've learned about routes so far, we can finish the routes file for our application's product catalog. Edit the routes file so it contains the routes shown in the following listing.

Listing 5.8 Our current routes file

```
# Home page
GET   /                    controllers.Products.index()
GET   /products            controllers.Products.list(page: Integer ?= 1)
POST  /products/           controllers.Products.save()
```

**These lines changed
from chapter 3**

```
GET   /products/new         controllers.Products.newProduct()
GET   /products/:ean        controllers.Products.details(ean: String)
```

Compared to what we ended with in chapter 3, the first two lines have changed. The first line, which matches the root URL of our application, used to point to `Application .index()`, but it now points to the `index` method of our `Products` controller. Since we now no longer have any routes using the `Application` controller, feel free to delete that class.

The second route still points to our product catalog, but the call to the action method has gained a `page` parameter, which defaults to 1. To get the application to compile and run again, we need to change the action methods to match the routes. The first method, `index`, is new. We want it to show the first page of the product catalog, which we'll do by redirecting to it. Add the following action method to the `Products` class:

```
public static Result index() {
  return redirect(routes.Products.list(0));
}
```

The other change we made in our routes file was that we added the `page` parameter to the product listing. We need to change the action method to match the call in the routes file, or the routes file won't compile. Go ahead and add the parameter to the `list` method in the `Products` class, and fix the call to it on the last line of the `save()` method, like so:

```
public class Products extends Controller {
  public static Result list(Integer page) {
    ...
  }

  ...
  public static Result save() {
    ...
    return redirect(routes.Products.list(1));
  }
}
```

Don't worry about changing the method's implementation; we'll get to that later. For now, it's enough to get our routes compiling again.

So we now know how to link a URL to an action method. But what about the other way around? If we know the action, how do we get a corresponding URL? That is a process called *reverse routing*.

5.3.5   *Reverse routing*

The implementation of our `index` method from the previous section is interesting. It sends an HTTP response that redirects the user to the `list` method. To construct the URL for that method, it uses the `routes` object.

The `routes` object was generated by Play as a result of compiling the routes file. The `routes` object is a singleton object that contains only static methods that return an object of type Action. It's used as a way to reference our action methods from the controller, but it's also used anywhere else we might need it (in our views, for example). Our action methods are added as methods to the object at compilation time, when Play generates the routes object.

The routes object provides what we call *reverse routing*.

Reverse routing, as the name implies, does the opposite from regular routing: it translates from Java to HTTP. Reverse routing is important, as it allows us to get an HTTP request for a given action method.

For example, say you want to be able to point your client to the edit method. Remember, your client only speaks HTTP. You need to return an HTTP call: an HTTP method and a URL. It's as simple as asking the routes object how to access the action method. The routes object returns a play.mvc.Call object. The play.mvc.Call defines an HTTP call, and provides both the HTTP method and the URL. It also makes sure the method call is correctly translated, especially when parameters are part of the action method. For example, the following call:

```
routes.Products.list(4)
```

is translated to:

```
GET /products?page=4
```

You now know everything about how to translate HTTP requests to action methods and vice versa with reverse routing. You should now have a complete picture of how Play operates when a request is received from the client and executed as Java code. Now it's time to see in more detail how to simplify some tedious operations in the controller.

5.4 Interceptors

Let's get back to our warehouse application. From time to time, an exception may occur. But if that happens, we can't spot it. It would be nice if we could just tell Play to send an email with the error whenever an exception occurs in specific controllers or action methods.

Action methods can be easily composed. This means that you can add extra behavior to action methods, and that's what we want to do: we want to catch any exceptions occurring in our action methods and send an email about them. Let's see how it works.

5.4.1 The @With annotation

Play provides an @With annotation, which allows you to compose an action. The @With annotation is used before an action method declaration. It can also be used on the class level—on the controller itself. Declaring the @With annotation on our action method tells Play that a certain action must be performed *around* each execution, meaning before and after. This is also called an *interceptor*, because it intercepts a call to the action method.

The @With annotation takes one parameter: the type of Action we want our code to be composed with. We will build a CatchAction class shortly.

For example, the following code tells Play it must execute the action method using the CatchAction action:

```
@With(CatchAction.class)
public static Result show(Long ean) { .... }
```

Because we specify the annotation on the method level, Play will only use it for this specific action method. If we were to declare it at the class level, the CatchAction would be used for all the controller's action methods:

```
@With(CatchAction.class)
public class Products extends Controller { .... }
```

But what exactly is this CatchAction class? It's where we will put our code that will provide the added functionality. We need to build it. The @With annotation takes an Action object as a parameter. An action object must extend the abstract class play.mvc.Action, which means it must implement the following method:

```
public Result call(Http.Context ctx)
```

The call method is called before the action method execution. From there, the call method must actually call the action method using the delegate object. The delegate object is a reference to the action method of type play.mvc.Action that is marked with the @With annotation. In other words, it represents the original action method.

Let's just go ahead and code our exception interceptor. First, we'll create a fake ExceptionMailer class, to stand in for what would be an actual emailing class, which is not the point of this exercise. Create the file shown in the following listing.

Listing 5.9 /app/utils/ExceptionMailer.java

```
package utils;

public class ExceptionMailer {
  public static void send(Throwable e) {
    System.out.println("Sending email containing exception " + e);
  }

}
```

We'll create our interceptor action by extending the Play.SimpleAction abstract class that Play provides. The Play.SimpleAction class provides everything we need to get started. In the next listing, we'll define our CatchAction, which will catch any exceptions and email them.

Listing 5.10 /app/controllers/CatchAction.java

```
public class CatchAction extends Action.Simple {
  public F.Promise<SimpleResult> call(Http.Context ctx) {
    try {
      return delegate.call(ctx);
    } catch(Throwable e) {
      ExceptionMailer.send(e);
      throw new RuntimeException(e);
    }
  }
}
```

We execute the action

We extend the Action.Simple class that extends the abstract Action class

This is the main method we need to implement

Any exception is caught and sent using our ExceptionMailer class

We can now use our `CatchAction` on our `Products` controller, by annotating the controller with `@With(CatchAction.class)`:

```
...
import play.mvc.With;

@With(CatchAction.class)
public class Products extends Controller {
  ..
}
```

Let's see how our implementation does its trick.

5.4.2 Explaining our CatchAction

The behavior of our custom `Action` is defined by our implementation of the `call` method. That method takes one parameter, the Play *context* object. The context object holds our session, request, response, and flash objects. We'll take a closer look at those concepts in the next section.

In our implementation, the actual call to the action method is done via the `delegate` object, which contains its own `call` method. In case an exception is triggered, we catch it, and our `ExceptionMailer` class sends an email with the exception stack trace.[1]

Now that we know how actions work, let's see some other ways to use them.

5.4.3 Action composition

Once you have one interceptor, you're probably wondering how you can use more of them; for example, a `LogAction` that logs any access to our controllers. We can just add another parameter to the `@With` annotation:

```
@With(CatchAction.class, LogAction.class)
```

If you are familiar with annotations,[2] you can also define your own, to signify that a certain action should be added to an action method. This is a more readable notation,

---

[1] The `ExceptionMailer` code is not relevant at this moment, as the goal is to show you how interceptors work.

[2] Read http://en.wikipedia.org/wiki/Java_annotation if you're not.

and it allows reuse across multiple web applications. For example, an annotation for our `CatchAction` would be:

```
@With(CatchAction.class)
@Target({ElementType.TYPE, ElementType.METHOD})
@Retention(RetentionPolicy.RUNTIME)
public @interface Catch {

}
```

In this example, we define a new annotation called `Catch`, and use the `@With` annotation as usual to indicate which action class it should use. Using our newly defined annotation, we can now annotate our controller as follows:

```
@Catch                                          ⟵─── Our newly defined annotation
public class Products extends Controller { .... }
```

We don't just use our own annotation is for readability purposes; we can also use it to pass extra configuration information. Using the previous example, we could specify if we want to send an email, or if we want to log the exception instead. Let's redefine our catch annotation:

```
@With(CatchAction.class)
@Target({ElementType.TYPE, ElementType.METHOD})
@Retention(RetentionPolicy.RUNTIME)
public @interface Catch {
 boolean send() default true;                   ⟵─── Add this line
 }
```

We've added a `send` parameter to our annotation, with a default value of `true`, specifying whether we want to send an email or just log instead. The parameter value can be accessed via the configuration object in our action. The following listing shows how.

> **Listing 5.11   `CatchAction` using configuration**

```
public class CatchAction extends Action<Catch> {       ⟵┐  We extend
   public F.Promise<SimpleResult> call(Http.Context ctx) {  │  Action rather
   try {                                      ❷ We read the │  than
    return delegate.call(ctx);                  configuration ❶ Action.Simple
   } catch(Throwable e) {                        value
    if (configuration.send)                    ⟵┘
      ExceptionMailer.send(e);                  ⟵─❸ We either send an email...
     else
      e.printStackTrace();                      ⟵─❹ ... or log the error
    }
  }
}
```

In this version of `CatchAction`, we extend the `Action` class directly, supplying a generic type parameter to indicate that we want to use our `Catch` annotation for configuration ❶. The `configuration` object will now be an instance of our `Catch` annotation, meaning we can access the `send` parameter on it ❷. We can then use a simple `if` statement to decide what we want to do ❸ ❹.

We are now able to be notified of any exceptions occurring in our code. This is a trivial example, but think about how you can use interceptors for transactions, security, and for a lot of other interesting examples you can think of.

There's one more important aspect of controllers that we haven't covered yet: scopes.

5.5 About scopes

We saw that by using the controllers and the routes, we're able to retrieve data from the clients and send data back to those clients. We didn't really talk about the lifetime and accessibility of that data. We assumed the data was transmitted each time a communication was made between the server and the client; that really is what's happening.

But as a developer, you don't really want to manage that dataflow. You want to store data for a certain period of time; for example, for the duration of a request or a browser session. You store that data in a certain *scope*. Play supports a number of scopes, for which it stores data for a certain lifetime. They're accessed in a similar way as a Map in Java; you store and retrieve values based on a key.

5.5.1 A bit of history about the scopes

Java EE traditionally defines these scopes:

- Application scope
- Session scope
- Request scope
- Page scope

The *application scope* has an application lifetime: you store data that will stay as long as your application is running.

The *session scope* has a session lifetime: you store data that will stay as long as your browser is open. This is traditionally the JSESSIONID parameter you sometimes see in URLs. The JSESSIONID is also stored in a cookie, so it's always available to the server on consecutive requests. This JSESSIONID is just an ID that points to some server-side storage space. The session scope is usually used to store information about your shopping basket or the fact that you're logged in.

The *request scope* defines data within the lifetime of request: the client makes an HTTP request, and with the request comes some data. That data is stored in the request scope and can only be accessed while that particular request is being processed.

The *page scope* defines data that is accessible in the view only: it can be accessed during the rendering phase. For example, you might want to store the current breadcrumb of your application in that scope, to display the current application path.

The different scopes can be conceptually viewed as shown in figure 5.13.

NOTE Though some Java EE frameworks introduce a *conversation scope*, we don't think this is relevant for our explanation and may be confusing more than anything else.

In a traditional Java EE environment, all the storage happens server-side. This means that each client has a unique ID, and the server uses that unique ID to retrieve the client storage space server-side.

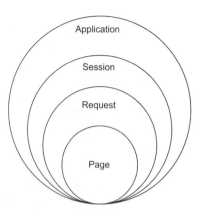

Though this has the advantage of potentially using less bandwidth, it can be problematic when scaling up (adding more servers) since you need to synchronize all the client storage space between the different servers. Another disadvantage is that it makes the servers compute more operations, while the client stays idle. This used to be an advantage, but nowadays web clients are powerful beasts. An iPhone is more powerful, CPU-wise, than any computer older than five years. Moreover, web standards have evolved and added a lot of features to web clients, such as local storage and web workers.

Figure 5.13   In JEE, application scope is the longest lived and page scope is the shortest lived.

5.5.2   *Storing data with Play*

Of course, as you may have guessed by now, Play is a bit different from Java EE frameworks. It's interesting to note that web frameworks from other languages, such as Django, Ruby on Rails, and Symphony, have been following an approach similar to that of Play.

Play defines four scopes:

- Session scope
- Flash scope
- Request scope
- Response scope

Before we start explaining those scopes, *there is a fundamental difference* between Play and the more traditional Java EE frameworks (read: servlet-based frameworks). *Play doesn't hold any data server-side. Data is held either in the client or in the database.* Because of that fact, scaling up is easy with Play. Just add a new server and a load balancer, and you're done. No server-side session replication is needed, so there's no risk of losing data on the server since there is no data to lose. But how does that work? What's Play's secret?

> ### What is a cookie?
>
> A *cookie*, also known as an HTTP cookie, web cookie, or browser cookie, is used by a web server to store data in the client's browser. The browser sends that information back to the server on every request. That information can be used, for example, for authentication, identification of a user session, user preferences, shopping cart contents, or anything else that can be accomplished through storing text data on the user's computer. A cookie can only be used to store text.

Well, really, there is no secret. Play stores the data client-side using cookies. It also encourages developers to think differently, to architect their application differently (following REST principles), and to fully embrace client-side technology.

While a Java EE developer would see the session as a giant cache in which everything is allowed, Play forces developers to think in terms of web development. And that is a good thing, since we happen to use Play mainly to develop web applications. So, no, you can't store your complete object tree in your session. And no, you can't save your last 10,000 database results. In fact, you can "only" store up to 4 KB (maximum cookie size), and you can only store string values. You might see that as a step back, but we'll attempt to explain to you that in fact it's a step forward. But first, let's go back and explain the four scopes in Play.

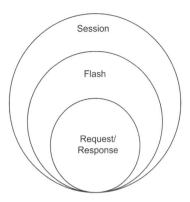

Figure 5.14 In Play, request scope is the shortest lived and session scope is the longest lived.

The four different scopes can be conceptually viewed as shown in figure 5.14.

5.5.3 The context object

First of all, all accessible scopes in Play are stored in a `Context` object. The `Context` object is a final static class that contains the `Request`, `Response`, `Session`, and `Flash` objects. You can access it statically using the `current()` method. From there, you can access all the Play scopes:

```
Context ctx = Context.current();      ◁—— Context object
Request request = ctx.request();      ◁—— Request object
Response response = ctx.response();    ◁—— Response object
Session session = ctx.session();      ◁—— Session object
Flash flash = ctx.flash();            ◁—— Flash object
```

In your controllers, the request, response, session, and flash objects are also available directly, since they are part of the `Controller` class that any controller must extend.

Let's take a look at each of the scopes, starting with the request scope.

The context object and thread safety

If the context object is static, what does that mean for thread safety? The answer is easy. Each `Context` object is associated to the current thread using a `ThreadLocal` object. This ensures that there's no thread-safety problem and that your context object is really your context object and not the one from your neighbor (each thread holds an implicit reference to its copy of a thread-local variable). This ensures that our scope objects are *our* scope objects.

If you didn't follow all of that, just take our word for it: access to the context and scope objects is thread-safe.

5.5.4   *The request scope*

The request scope can't be used to store objects. It is used to access the data of the current request. For example, you can access the values submitted using an HTML form via the request scope.

5.5.5   *The response scope*

The response scope can't be used to store objects. It is used to set the response content type and any extra cookies to send extra information. For example, you can set the response content type to XML with the following code:

```
Context.current().response().setContentType("application/xml");
```

Charset

For text-based HTTP responses, it's important to set the character set (or character encoding) correctly when you set the response content type. Play handles that for you and uses UTF-8 by default.

The charset is used to both convert the text response to the corresponding bytes to send over the network socket, and modify the `ContentType` header with the proper `;charset=xxx` extension.

The charset can also be specified when you are generating the result value, in this case the `ok` result value:

```
public static Result index() {
    response().setContentType("text/html; charset=iso-8859-1");    ◁── Set the charset (encoding) on the response
    return ok("<h1>Hello World!</h1>", "iso-8859-1");    ◁── Our result is using ISO-8859-1
}
```

Using the response object, we can also store extra data on the client, using a new cookie. For example, if we were to save the preferred theme for our application from our controller:

```
response().setCookie("theme","blue");
```

Then, on a next request, from our controller's action method, we could check if the theme was set using the cookie method:

```
public static Result index() {
    if ("blue".equals(cookies("theme").value())){
        // Do something
    }
    ....
}
```

You could also store more information by serializing your data into strings, but remember that you can only store up to 4 KB per cookie. Therefore, save only what you need, which is often entity IDs.

Finally, to discard a cookie, use `discardCookies`:

```
response().discardCookies("theme");
```

As you can see, the response object is rather straightforward.

5.5.6 The session scope

Objects stored in the session scope have a session lifetime: you can store data that will stay as long as the client's browser is open. It's important to understand that sessions are *not* stored on the server but are added to each subsequent HTTP request, using the cookie mechanism. So the data size is very limited (up to 4 KB), and you can only store string values. This means that the `Session` object *should not* be used as a cache! Play does offer a caching mechanism, which you can use instead.

To store a value in the session:

```
Context.current().session().put("x", "myvalue");     ⟵  Store the value myvalue in the session with key x
String value = Context.current().session().get("x");  ⟵  Retrieve the value from the session
System.out.println(value);
```

Print myvalue

From a controller, you can also use the convenience methods provided by the controller:

```
session("x", "myvalue");              ⟵  Store the value myvalue in the session with key x
String value = session("x");          ⟵  Retrieve the value from the session
System.out.println(value);
```

Print myvalue

Why can I only store strings in my Session?

You may argue that a `Session` object that can only store String objects is a regression; we feel that it's the way it should be. By disallowing the storing of complex objects, we're also removing a lot of associated problems of synchronizing the object states and/or any side effects. By storing immutable objects, like Strings, in our session, no side effects can occur.

For example, if we were to store an attached (marked as connected to the DB) database entity in our session, the entity might really well be detached (no longer connected to the DB) the next time we access the object, causing all sorts of troubles. Or the entity may have been modified by a third party since we last accessed it, causing unexpected behavior.

5.5.7   *The flash scope*

Objects stored in the flash scope have a lifetime of exactly two requests. It means that data in the flash scope will service one redirect. This is really useful when you want to retain data after a redirection. To understand this better, let's look at a concrete example.

The client issues the following request:

```
GET /
```

The server renders an HTML page. On the page, we have a form to input a telephone number and a *Submit* button. When the user submits the form, a POST request is made to the server to the following address:

```
POST /phonenumber/
```

Now, once the controller receives the request, it attempts to validate the phone number. In case the validation fails, the server renders the same page with an error message. But if you try to refresh your browser, you're in for a surprise: your browser is asking you if you want to resubmit the data. Why is that? This is because, as far as your client is concerned, its last execution point matches POST /phonenumber. And indeed, the URL that your browser shows is http://localhost:9000/phonenumber.

Figure 5.15 illustrates the problem we just described.

A way to avoid bad surprises is to send a redirect instruction to your client, so it redirects to GET /. But of course, in the meantime, because of the redirect, you lost your error message. This is exactly the use case for which flash scope was invented. Storing the error messages in the flash scope allows you to still have access to your error messages after the redirect.

In Play, the objects in the flash scope are stored in a special cookie that's flushed after the second consecutive request.

Figure 5.16 illustrates the same problem, but uses the flash scope as a solution.

> **NOTE**   The flash scope has been introduced in Java EE 6 and defines the same lifetime as its Play equivalent, but it lives server-side. At the time of this writing, most Java EE web frameworks do not have flash scope.

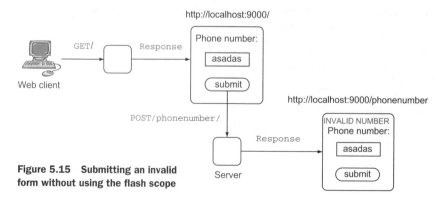

Figure 5.15   Submitting an invalid form without using the flash scope

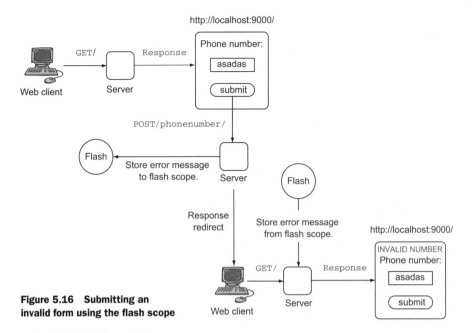

Figure 5.16 Submitting an invalid form using the flash scope

5.5.8 What about security?

Storing data client-side brings some security concerns with it. Because the user has access to this data, it can't be trusted without taking some additional measures. For example, when you store the user's username, there is nothing preventing the user from putting in another username and impersonating a different user.

For this reason, cookies are signed with a secret key so that the client can't modify the cookie data (if they do, the data will be invalidated).

The secret key used to sign the cookie is actually set in your `conf/application .conf` file (see following listing).

Listing 5.12 Project structure

```
warehouse
    ├─ app
    │   └─ controllers
    │       │   └─ Products.java
    │       └─ models
    │           └─ views
    ├─ conf
    │   ├─ routes
    │   └─ application.conf
    ├─ public
    ├─ test
    └─ db
```

application.conf contains the application configuration and the important secret key

If you open the `application.conf` file in an editor, you will find a line starting with `application.secret`:

```
application.secret="FuqsIcSJlLppP8s?UpVYb5CvX1v55PVgHQ1Pk"
```

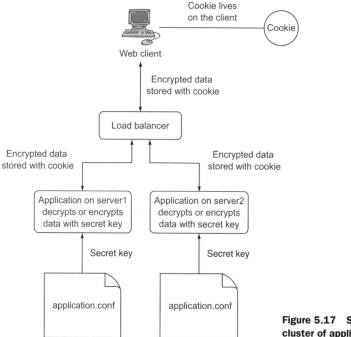

Figure 5.17   Secret key with a cluster of applications

This is the key we're signing our cookies with. It's essential to keep it secret, so be sure you don't divulge your key. This also brings us to another important point: if you're running multiple instances of your application, the secret key needs to be shared between the applications, or one instance won't be able to verify the data that has been set by another instance.

Let's imagine the following scenario. One load balancer and the same application are running on two different nodes: server1 and server2. Each client can be dispatched to either server1 or server2. If server1 and server2 don't share the same key, the clients will need to communicate with the same server every time; otherwise the server can't decipher the cookies. If both server1 and server2 have the same key, they can decipher the same cookies, and neither the client nor the load balancer will need to distinguish between server1 and server2.

Figure 5.17 illustrates the data encryption/decryption flow.

But what about my session timeout?

We can argue that session timeouts were introduced as a technical solution for server-side session storage rather than as a useful feature. Indeed, without this feature, user sessions could only grow on the server, resulting in memory deprivation. But developers are so used to session timeouts that they actually see them as useful functionality.

In Play, there is no technical timeout for the session. It expires when the user closes the web browser. If you need a functional timeout for a specific application, just store a time stamp in the user session and check it against your application needs (max session duration, max inactivity duration, and so forth).

5.6 Summary

We started this chapter by explaining what controllers are. We then looked into the specifics of Play controllers and more particularly the controller's action methods. We learned about routing our clients' requests to our action method code.

Let's pull out some of the key practices to take away from the chapter:

- Use flash scope. Flash scope is ideal for passing messages to the user (when a redirect is involved).
- Use action methods. This is the entry point for your business logic. Keep them short and delegate all business logic to your business models.
- Simple data binding is URL-centric data mapping to your action methods.

We covered how to use interceptors and why they're useful. We implemented a simple interceptor that catches all errors and sends an email.

We've learned a lot about the internals of controllers in this chapter, and in the next chapter we'll build on our knowledge by implementing some nice views to give our warehouse application some visual appeal.

Handling user input

This chapter covers

- Working with forms
- Data binding
- Using body parsers
- Validation
- Handling file uploads

In this chapter, we'll explain in detail how users can interact with our application. This is where we'll enable users to send data to our application. We'll see how to handle different kinds of data and how to customize Play to use our own data types. We'll also explain how to make sure the data sent is correct and, if it's not, how to alert our users.

6.1 Forms

Working with forms in a web application involves two operations: displaying the form and processing the form submission. Forms allow users to send data to the server (our application). In Play, forms are represented by objects that you can manipulate. Play provides useful helpers to handle form submission. Because we don't want users to send just any kind of data, Play makes sure the data is properly formatted and processed. If data isn't well formatted, we need to tell the user what the problem is, so they can correct it and resubmit the form.

In our application, to submit a new product, we created two action methods: the first one, called `newProduct()`, displays the *create a new product* form, whereas the second, `save()`, handles the form submission. First we'll take a closer look at what exactly the action method that shows the empty form does.

As a reminder, figure 6.1 shows the form.

As we've seen, displaying a form involves the following steps:

Figure 6.1   Our "create new product" form

- Creating an action method to display the form template
- Creating the form template
- Creating an action method to handle the form submission

Figure 6.2 illustrates the different steps.

6.1.1   Displaying the new product form

To display a form, we create a `Form` object to represent it. In this case, we want our form to represent a `Product` instance, so we create a form based on the `Product` class (a `Form<Product>`). Our existing `newProduct()` action method does that:

```
...
import play.data.Form;

public class Products extends Controller {
  private static final Form<Product> productForm =
    Form.form(Product.class);
...
  public static Result newProduct() {
    return ok(details.render(productForm));
  }
...
}
```

Create a new form object based on Product

Render a template with our Form as argument

As you can see, we're creating a new `Form` object using the `Form.form()` method. The resulting object holds all the information about our product and can contain additional information that we can use while rendering the form, such as validation

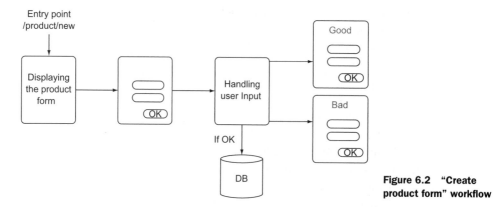

Figure 6.2 "Create product form" workflow

errors, prefilled values, and so on. We'll examine the form object in more detail later in this chapter.

THE ROUTE TO OUR FORM

When we created the `newProduct()` action method back in chapter 3, we also set up a route to it. Here's a reminder:

```
GET /products/new  controllers.Product.newProduct()
```

This route makes the form available at http://localhost:9000/products/new.

ADDING THE VIEW

Also in chapter 3, we created the `product.scala.html` template that renders our HTML product form. The `newProduct()` action method uses it to render a blank product form.

The "new product" form template allows us to collect the information needed to create a new product. It uses HTML input tags to allow the user to input information.

The important thing to realize is that the HTML form is backed by a Play `Form` object. A form object is a *container* object. It contains information about our object model and, potentially, validation error information. In section 6.4 we'll talk extensively about validation.

For now, it's important to know you can access any form field value via a form object, and that you can use it to re-render the original value that was entered by the user if the action method detects a validation error. Our input helpers take care of that for us, so we don't see the code that does it.

The following listing shows the full template for our form.

> **Listing 6.1 The "new product" form template**

```
@(productForm: Form[Product])          Form object passed
@import helper._                       into template by
@import helper.twitterBootstrap._      newInstance()

@main("Product form") {
  <h1>Product form</h1>
  @helper.form(action = routes.Products.save()) {
```

```
<fieldset>
  <legend>Product (@productForm("name").valueOr("New"))</legend>
  @helper.inputText(productForm("ean"))
  @helper.inputText(productForm("name"))
  @helper.textarea(productForm("description"))
</fieldset>
<input type="submit" class="btn btn-primary">
  }
}
```

Access form's name value ⟶

⟵ **Access form's EAN value**

⟵ **Access form's description value**

This HTML template is responsible for rendering the new product page (repeated in figure 6.3).

If your form looks different, please refer back to chapter 3, in which we showed you how to include Bootstrap to make things look a little nicer.

This form is for creating a *new* product and, therefore, it's empty. Let's see how the same template can serve as an *edit* form.

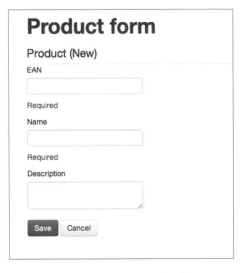

Figure 6.3 The "create new product" form

6.1.2 Displaying the edit product form

In our application, we also want to be able to edit a product. The "edit product form" is more or less the same form as the "create new product" form. The only difference is that we need to prefill some values and update an existing model object. But from a presentation point of view, the two forms are similar.

To turn the create form into an edit form, we perform the following actions:

- Prefill the edit form with the product value
- Display the edit form with the prefilled data
- Handle the user's input

Figure 6.4 illustrates the workflow.

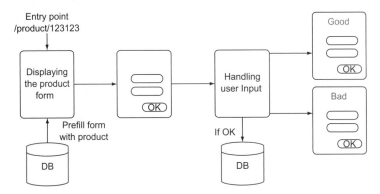

Figure 6.4 "Edit product" workflow

FILLING A FORM WITH INITIAL VALUES

Because we're using a form object in our view, we can decide to prefill the form with some default values. This is exactly what we need to do if we want to edit a product. When we know the unique identifier for the object we want to edit, we can then fetch it from our database so we can use the values in our HTML form. The action method we wrote to accomplish this is shown in the following listing.

Listing 6.2   Displaying a form with preset values

```
public class Products extends Controller {
    private static final Form<Product> productForm =
        Form.form(Product.class);
...
  public static Result details(String ean) {
    final Product product = Product.findByEan(ean);
    if (product == null) {
      return notFound(String.format("Product %s does not exist.", ean));
    }

  Form<Product> filledForm = productForm.fill(product);
  return ok(details.render(filledForm));
  }
...
}
```

We also added the following route in our routes file. The route indicates that every time we access the /products/xxx page, we will in fact render an edit page for the product *xxx*, where *xxx* is the product's EAN number.

```
GET /products/:ean  controllers.Product.edit(ean:Long)
```

Now let's see why the existing products/details.scala.html supports both creating and updating a product. Take a look at the following listing.

Listing 6.3   /products/details.scala.html

```
@(productForm: Form[Product])
@import helper._
@import helper.twitterBootstrap._

@main("Product form") {
  <h1>Product form</h1>
  @helper.form(action = routes.Products.save()) {
    <fieldset>
      <legend>Product (@productForm("name").valueOr("New"))</legend>
      @helper.inputText(productForm("ean"))
      @helper.inputText(productForm("name"))
      @helper.textarea(productForm("description"))
    </fieldset>
  <input type="submit" class="btn btn-primary">
  }
}
```

> If the name field has a value, we show a different legend

> The form helpers take care of rendering the value, if there is one

As you see, the edit product form and the create new product form can use the same template. If the form contains a value for the product's ID, then it's an update; otherwise, we're creating a new product.

We're now able to display a form to create or edit a product. Next, we need to process the data from the submitted form.

6.1.3   Processing form input

After the form is submitted, our action method that handles the form submission transforms the data the browser sent to the server into a `Product` instance and saves it. Finally, it sets a success message in the flash scope[1] and redirects to the page showing all products. The following listing shows `save()`, an action method that processes the form submission.

Listing 6.4   The `save()` action method

```
public class Products extends Controller {
  private static final Form<Product> productForm =
    Form.form(Product.class);

  ...
  public static Result save() {                            ❶ Create a Form
    Form<Product> boundForm = productForm.bindFromRequest();    object from
    if(boundForm.hasErrors()) {                                 the request
      flash("error", "Please correct the form below.");    Detect errors
      return badRequest(details.render(boundForm));        (we'll cover
    }                                                       this later)
                                                ❷ Extract a Product
    Product product = boundForm.get();            instance from the form
    product.save();
    flash("success", String.format("Successfully added product %s", product));

    return redirect(routes.Products.list(1));    Redirect to the "view
    }                                            all products" page
  }
}
```

Save that instance → `product.save();`

First, we're creating the form object with all the information that we have received via HTTP ❶. Then, we check whether the submitted information is valid, and display a message if it isn't.

If everything's in order, we ask the now-populated form object for the `Product` instance ❷ that it contains. The object instance will have its fields populated with the data extracted from the HTTP request. We then save the `Product` instance to our data store. Finally, we present another page to the user, using a redirect to the "all products" page.

Our `save()` action method is also represented in our routes file:

```
POST /products/  controllers.Product.save()
```

---

[1] We introduced the flash scope in the previous chapter, in which we also added the message to our main template.

We've seen how our form submission is processed. Once the form is displayed, the user enters the data and submits the form. The browser will then send a POST request with the form data to our application. The routes file determines that the processing is to be delegated to the save() action method.

We're now able to add or edit a product, but let's see in more detail how our action method managed to transform the HTTP form parameters into a Form object.

6.2   *Data binding*

Play transformed the submitted information into a Java object using a process called *data binding*. Data binding is the process of converting elements of a request into objects. There are three binding types in Play:

- Form binding, which we saw in the previous section
- URL query parameters binding
- URL path binding

Data binding is a simple principle. The HTTP parameters are mapped to their counterpart attributes on the Java object. The mapping is done using the parameter's name. Each time a parameter name matches the name of an object attribute, the object attribute is set to the parameter's value. Figure 6.5 illustrates this binding process.

In Play, *form binding* is primarily done with the help of a Form object, via the bindFromRequest() method. The binding processing is delegated to *Spring Data*, a library that can take a request's body and convert it to the properties of a Java object.

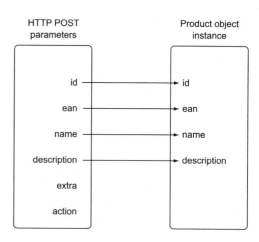

Figure 6.5   The binding process

URL *query parameter binding* consists of taking the URL's parameters (for example, ?x=y) and mapping them onto a Java object. The pattern is derived from the routes file.

For example, if our products had an ID, we could have a route like this:

```
GET /products  Products.edit(id: Long)
```

Which would match the following URL:

```
http://localhost:9000/products?id=12
```

Play will convert the string "12" (query parameters are always strings) to the Long 12.

URL *query path binding* consists of mapping a query path (again, always a string), to another Java type or object. This also happens using the route definitions. For example, when you declare:

```
GET /products/:id  Products.edit(id: Long)
```

and you call:

```
http://localhost:9000/products/12
```

Play will convert the string "12" (the query path) to the Long 12.

Data *unbinding* is the reverse process. We have an object and we want to translate it into a valid URL or form representation. This is notably used in case of reverse routing. For more information about reverse routing, please refer to section 5.3.5.

It's important to note that in Play, each type of binding can be customized and extended. But let's take a step back first, and see how our product form is mapped.

6.2.1 *Binding single values*

Product is defined as the following class:

```
public class Product {
    public String ean;
    public String name;
    public String description;
}
```

To fully understand how binding works, we'll cheat a little and respond to a GET HTTP request to trigger our save() action method, so that we can easily make requests using a browser.

Let's edit our routes file, and add the following line:

```
GET /products/save  controllers.Product.save()
```

We can now invoke our save() action method from the browser, and we should remove this route entry once we're done experimenting (and use the POST /products/ one).

```
http://localhost:9000/product/save?ean=1111111111111&
    name=product&description=a%20description
```

The first line of the save() action method is the most important one:

```
Form<models.Product> productForm =
        form(models.Product.class).bindFromRequest();
```

This creates a new Product instance and then, for each HTTP parameter that matches a property by name, sets the value on that property. For this GET request, a new Product is created and the ean parameter is bound to the ean property, the name parameter is bound to the name property, and so on.

Our product form is filled with the HTTP parameter values from our request. We can then access the newly created Product instance with the following code:

```
models.Product product = productForm.get();
```

And the product object contains the following data:

```
ean: 1111111111111,
name: product,
description=a description
```

As you can see, it matches with the parameters we supplied in our URL. It's a simple and predictable mechanism. It's now trivial to map back and forth from HTTP parameters to objects.

It works well for simple types such as `String`, `Integer`, `Long`, and so forth. Play also provides support for more complex types such as `Date` and for multiple values that must be mapped to an array or `List` object.

For dates, you can annotate your model with the `@play.data.format.Formats`
`.DateTime` annotation to indicate how to transform the HTTP parameter into a `Date` object:

```
@Formats.DateTime(pattern = "yyyy-MM-dd")
public Date date;
```

Here, if we use the date HTTP parameter with a year, month, and day date format, Play will be able to transform the string into a `Date` object using a form data binder called `Formatter`. For example, calling

```
http://localhost:9000/product/save?date=2021-10-02
```

results in a `Date` object when bound to a `Form` object.

Play provides some built-in `Formatter`s, namely `DateFormatter`, `AnnotationDate-Formatter`, and `AnnotationNonEmptyFormatter`. `DateFormatter` attempts to convert parameters to `Date`s with a date format of `yyyy-MM-dd` whenever a `Date` object is required. `AnnotationDateFormatter` is used in conjunction with the `@DateTime` annotation and allows you to specify a date format. The `AnnotationNonEmptyFormatter` is used in conjunction with the `@NonEmpty` annotation and prints an empty string instead of a `null` value.

All the built-in `Formatter`s are located in the `play.mvc.data.Formats` class.

Next, let's see how binding multivalued parameters works.

6.2.2   *Binding multiple values*

This is a common use case: the user selects multiple values from a list of possible values, and we have to store them. To illustrate this use case, let's define a new scenario. We want to be able to tag our product with a certain label. For example, we can tag a product with the words *metal* or *plastic*. Each product can have zero or more tags, and each tag can be applied to multiple products. Figure 6.6 illustrates this relationship.

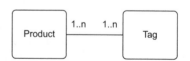

Figure 6.6   Product–Tag relationships

We first need to define our new model. Let's create a `Tag` model class. We create a new file in the `app/models` directory.

> **Listing 6.5   Project directory structure**

```
warehouse
    ├─ app
    │   ├─ controllers
    │   │   └─ Products.java
    │   ├─ models
```

```
|       |    ├─ Product.java
|       |    └─ Tag.java
|       └─ views
├─ conf
|       └─ routes
├─ public
└─ test
```

Our new Tag
entity class

It's a relatively simple class; it holds a tag name. The following isting shows our new class.

Listing 6.6   /app/models/Tag.java

```
package models;

import play.data.validation.Constraints;
import java.util.*;

public class Tag {
  public Long id;
  @Constraints.Required
  public String name;
  public List<Product> products;

  public Tag(){
    // Left empty
  }

  public Tag(Long id, String name, Collection<Product> products) {
    this.id = id;
    this.name = name;
    this.products = new LinkedList<Product>(products);
    for (Product product : products) {
      product.tags.add(this);
    }
  }
}
```

We also need to modify our `Product` class to link the `Tag` class. We use a `List` so that each product can hold multiple tags. This is easily done by adding the following line to our `Product` class (`/app/models/Product.java`).

```
public List<Tag> tags = new LinkedList<Tag>();
```

We now need to create some tags. In order to do that, we'll fake some `Tag` objects in the same way that we created some test `Products`. We'll show you how to use a database as a backing store in chapter 7. For now, let's stick with a static list of tags. In the `Tag` class, add the lines shown in the following listing.

Listing 6.7   Adding mock data to `Tag.java`

```
public class Tag {

  private static List<Tag> tags = new LinkedList<Tag>();

  static {
    tags.add(new Tag(1L, "lightweight",
      Product.findByName("paperclips 1")));
```

The lightweight tag
is added to product
names matching
paperclips I

```
    tags.add(new Tag(2L, "metal",
      Product.findByName("paperclips")));
    tags.add(new Tag(3L, "plastic",
      Product.findByName("paperclips")));
  }

  public static Tag findById(Long id) {
    for (Tag tag : tags) {
      if(tag.id == id) return tag;
    }
  return null;
  }
...
}
```

◁ The metal tag is added to all the products (they all match paperclips)

◁ The plastic tag is added to all the products (they all match paperclips)

We now have our tags ready to be used. Next we need to modify our view so we can tag our products. Because we want to keep things simple, we'll use a predefined set of tags rather than dynamically generate the list of check boxes. Let's add the following code snippet to our products/details.scala.html.

```
<div class="control-group">
<div class="controls">
<input name="tags[0].id" value="1" type="checkbox" > lightweight
<input name="tags[1].id" value="2" type="checkbox" > metal
<input name="tags[2].id" value="3" type="checkbox" > plastic
</div>
</div>
```

We've added some HTML input elements of type checkbox. For the binding process, the important part of these input elements is the id attribute. The [] notation tells Play that we want to bind the check boxes to the product's tag collection (in our case, the List<Tag>). Once the form is submitted, Play will automatically create a new List, with new Tag objects for each checked box, and with the ID specified in the value attribute. For example, if we select "lightweight" and "plastic," Play will create a new List with two new Tag objects during the binding process. The first tag object will have its ID set to 2 and the second one to 3. Figure 6.7 illustrates exactly that.

Now that we have our form ready with the check boxes, let's see how our product form looks (figure 6.8).

We need to modify our Products controller's save method slightly, to take our tags into account. We need to save our relationship between the product and the tags. But

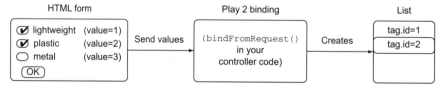

Figure 6.7   Binding HTML check boxes

our tag objects do not yet correspond to the `Tag` objects that we have in our datastore; they are new objects with only the ID set. We need to modify our action method to look up the tag, and set it. This can easily be done in our controller, as the following listing shows.

Listing 6.8 Product save method with tag relationship

```
public class Products extends Controller {
...
  public static Result save() {
    ... (binding and error handling)

    Product product = boundForm.get();

    List<Tag> tags = new ArrayList<Tag>();
    for (Tag tag : product.tags) {
      if (tag.id != null) {
        tags.add(Tag.findById(tag.id));
      }
    }
    product.tags = tags;
    product.save();
    ... (success message and redirect)
  }
}
```

We now need to display the tags when displaying a product. For this, we need to update our view so the correct tag check boxes are selected when a tag is present. We have already seen (in section 6.1.2) how our product prepopulates our product form:

```
productForm = productForm.fill(product);
```

This also loads the product's associated tags, so the action method doesn't need to be changed. Our goal can easily be achieved with a bit of code in our view. When rendering the view, we need to add a `checked` attribute to each check box if its associated tag is present in the `productForm`. The following line of code does exactly that:

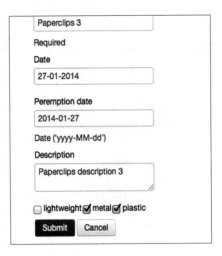

Figure 6.8 Edit product form with tags

```
@for(i <- 0 to 2) { @if(productForm("tags[" + i + "]").value!=null
   && productForm("tags[" + i + "]").value == "1") { checked }}
```

Because our product's associated tags might contain between zero and three tags, we need to iterate through them (the `for` loop in our code). If the tags contain the value

1, then we preselect the check box. Don't worry if you don't fully understand this line; we'll take a closer look at template syntax in chapter 8.

We now need to apply this code for each check box we're displaying:

```
<div class="control-group">
  <div class="controls">
    <input name="tags[0].id" value="1" type="checkbox"
    @for(i <- 0 to 2) {
      @if(productForm("tags[" + i + "].id").value=="1"){ checked }
    }> lightweight
    <input name="tags[1].id" value="2" type="checkbox"
    @for(i <- 0 to 2) {
      @if(productForm("tags[" + i + "].id").value=="2"){ checked }
    }> metal
    <input name="tags[2].id" value="3" type="checkbox"
    @for(i <- 0 to 2) {
      @if(productForm("tags[" + i + "].id").value=="3"){ checked }
    }> plastic
  </div>
</div>
```

Again, in chapter 8, we'll see how we can refactor all this code to make it less repetitive and verbose.

We now can deal with related tags for our product. More importantly, we're now able to map back and forth from check boxes or select fields to our object model.

Let's see what happens if we want to bind a type that Play doesn't know about yet.

6.2.3 *Custom data binders and formatters*

As we have seen in the previous section, Play is able to bind most of the usual types automatically. But what about special types? Play allows you to define your own binder or your own formatter. There are three different ways of binding objects. You can bind objects via the URL or via URL parameters, and it's also possible to use a custom formatter that will transform your object when submitting a form.

PATH BINDERS

When requesting a URL with a named parameter in it, Play already performs some kind of binding. For example, in our application, we have:

```
/product/1111111111111
```

where 1111111111111 is our product EAN number. Internally, Play binds this value to the product's EAN number. This is done when declaring our URL in the route file (see chapter 5):

```
GET /product/:ean  Product.details(ean: String)
```

Play looks for the ean type and converts it into the proper type.

In our case, it binds a string to another string. But Play can also deal with values such as primitives and primitive wrappers, based on information in the routes file. If we have the following route:

```
GET  /product/:ean   Product.details(ean: Int)
```

Play would make sure to convert

```
/product/1122334455
```

into an `Integer` with the value 1122334455. If we were to use aabbcc1122334455, Play would yield an error, because it can't convert aabbcc1122334455 into an `Integer`.

Therefore, there is a mechanism that allows Play to transform part of a URL (our URL parameter, a string) into an object. This means that we could, for example, automatically load and bind our `Product` objects based on the EAN number that is used in our URL.

Whenever we call

```
/product/1111111111111
```

we can have the matching product object passed to our controller, and we can have a details action method that looks like this:

```
public static Result details(Product product)
  Form<models.Product> productForm = form(models.Product.class);
  productForm = productForm.fill(product);
  return ok(edit.render(productForm));
}
```
The product should automatically be looked up using the product's EAN key

Figure 6.9 illustrates what we want to achieve: automatic binding of our `Product` object based on our EAN product number.

Play allows you to define your own binder for URL paths. This is called a *bindable path* in Play. In order to provide our own custom URL path binder, we need to create a new class that implements the play .mvc.PathBindable interface, and our implementation must reference itself as a generic type argument:[2] if we create a class called ProductBinder, we have to implement play.mvc.PathBindable <ProductBinder>.

Because we want to bind the Product entity to the EAN number that is used in our URL, we need to implement the play.mvc.PathBindable interface on our Product class.

Open your editor and edit the Product .java class from the models directory.

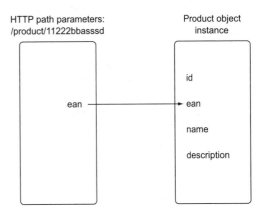

Figure 6.9   The binding process

---

2 This might change in the next version of Play.

Listing 6.9   Project directory structure

```
warehouse
      ├─ app
      │    ├─ controllers
      │    ├─ models
      │    │    ├─ Product.java
      │    └─ views
      ├─ conf
      ├─ public
      └─ test
```

**The class that we
need to edit**

The code is simple; all we need to do is implement three methods. Like we said, our
`Product` class implements the `play.mvc.PathBindable` interface and references itself
(we have the class declaring a `Product`, and `play.mvc.PathBindable` references Product via the use of generics). The three methods we need to implement to satisfy the
interface are:

- `T bind(String key, String txt)`
- `String unbind(String key)`
- `String javascriptUnbind()`

The `bind` method indicates how to bind our product from the URL. The `unbind`
method tells Play what to display when a `Product` is referenced from the view, for
example, in case of reverse routing (see chapter 5). In our case, we should display the
product's EAN number. The method `javascriptUnbind` is used for Ajax calls. We also
want to use the product's EAN number for that.

  Let's add our three new methods. The `bind` method performs a lookup in the
database, using the EAN number. The EAN number is passed via the `txt` parameter.
That is the EAN number as it appears in the URL. The unbinding process is simple and
consists of returning our `Product` instance's EAN number. The following listing shows
our implementation.

Listing 6.10   `Product` class that is `PathBindable`-aware

```
...
import play.mvc.PathBindable;
import play.libs.F.Option;

public class Product implements PathBindable<Product> {

  ...

  @Override
  public Product bind (String key, String value) {
    return findByEan(value);
  }

  @Override
  public String unbind(String key) {
    return this.ean;
  }

  @Override
```

**We're telling Play
that we're defining
a new Binder to
bind URL paths**

**Binding—we're looking in
the DB for a product with an
EAN number equal to the
one passed in our URL**

**Unbinding—we're
returning our raw value**

```
   public String javascriptUnbind() {
     return this.ean;
   }
 }
```
JavaScript unbinding—
we're returning our raw value

We now need to change our routes file to modify our `Product.edit()` route. Edit the routes file located in your `conf` directory.

Let's replace

```
GET /product/:ean  controllers.Product.details(ean: String)
```

with

```
GET /products/:ean  controllers.Products.details(ean: models.Product)
```

This is how we tell Play that we want to use our object. The automatic binding between the `Product` object and the EAN number in our URL path will be performed by the methods we have implemented.

We now need to change our `Products` controller with the following method:

```
public class Products extends Controller {
...
  public static Result details(Product product) {
     Form<Product> filledForm = productForm.fill(product);
     return ok(details.render(filledForm));
  }
...
}
```
The new edit method binds
directly to a product

Now that we've changed the method signature, we need to update its callers too. At this point, we only have one caller. In the products list template, `products/list .scala.html`, change the following line

```
<a href="@routes.Products.details(product.ean)">
```

to

```
<a href="@routes.Products.details(product)">
```

and we're done! We can now automatically bind a URL to an instance of `Product`. Calling http://localhost:9000/products/111111111111 will show the product with EAN 111111111111. This simplifies the code for our controllers and centralizes the program logic that turns a path parameter into a `Product` instance. Any action method that requires a `Product` can now accept it as a parameter directly.

QUERY STRING BINDERS

Up to this point, we've seen that we can bind the URL path to our model objects. We can do exactly the same for URL parameters (the query string part of a URL). Let's take our product example. This time, we're going to bind to a `Product` object when we pass the product's EAN as a query parameter:

```
http://localhost:9000/products?ean=1
```

When Play encounters this URL, it should look up the `Product` in the database, based on the provided EAN. In order to achieve that, we have to implement the `play.mvc.QueryStringBindable` interface, similar to how we implemented `Path-Bindable` earlier. Because we want to look up `Product` objects, we'll implement the interface on our `Product` model class.

Edit the `Product` model class.

Listing 6.11   Project directory structure

```
warehouse
    ├─ app
    │   ├─ controllers
    │   ├─ models              ┐  The Product class
    │   │   └─ Product.java   ◁┘  we're going to edit
    │   └─ views
    ├─ conf
    │   └─ routes
    ├─ public
    └─ test
```

This time, we need to change it to implement the `play.mvc.QueryStringBindable` interface. Like `PathBindable`, this interface provides three methods we need to implement:

- `Option<T> bind(String key, Map<String,String[]> data)`
- `String unbind(String key)`
- `String javascriptUnbind()`

The `bind` method gives us access to the query parameters, both values and associated keys, and must return an `Option` object of type `T`. In our case, `T` is type `Product`. `Option` is the class that allows us to say that either we return something or we return nothing, giving a nicer alternative to returning `null`. The `data` parameter of the `bind` method gives us access to the query parameters. It's represented by a `Map` object that contains the query parameter names with their corresponding values.

Like before, `bind` indicates how to bind our product from the URL parameters, `unbind` tells Play what to display when a `Product` is referenced from the view, and `javascriptUnbind` is to support JavaScript. In our case, the logic is based on the `id` property of our `Product` class.

Let's implement the required methods in the `Product` model class. Please note that this is a simple example, and so it doesn't check for null values or other possible errors.

Listing 6.12   Product class that is `QueryStringBindable`-aware

```
...
import play.mvc.PathBindable;
import play.mvc.QueryStringBindable;

public class Product
    implements QueryStringBindable<Product> {

    ...
```

┐ We're telling Play that we're
│ defining a new Binder to
◁┘ bind query parameters

```
@Override
public Option<Product> bind(String key, Map<String, String[]> data) {
  return Option.Some(findByEan(data.get("ean")[0]));
}

@Override
public String unbind(String key) {
  return this.id;
}

@Override public String javascriptUnbind() {
  return this.id;
  }
}
```

◁┐ **Binding on the product ID number—database lookup based on the product EAN**

◁┐ **Unbinding—return our product EAN**

◁┐ **JavaScript unbinding— return our product EAN**

We need to declare a new route in our routes file that links the URL call to our controller. Open the `routes` file (located in your `conf` directory), and add the following route:

```
GET /products/  controllers.Product.details(ean: models.Product)
```

We're ready to accept URLs such as `/products?ean=1`. Modify the `details` method on the `Products` controller, if you haven't already done so in the previous section.

> **Listing 6.13 Project directory structure**

```
warehouse
    ├── app
    │    ├── controllers
    │    │    └── Products.java
    │    ├── models
    │    │    └── Product.java
    │    └── views
    ├── conf
    │    └── routes
    ├── public
    └── test
```

◁┘ **The Products controller we need to modify**

The edit method becomes the same as when we used the path binder:

```
public static Result details(Product product){
  Form<Product> filledForm = productForm.fill(product);
  return ok(details.render(filledForm));
}
```

◁┐ **The new edit method binds directly to a product**

As you can see, we can manipulate the `Product` object straight from our controller methods. This is quite nice if you want to reduce the size of your controller code. We can now automatically bind URL parameters (id, in our case) to an instance of `Product`. Calling http://localhost:9000/products?ean=1 shows the product with id 1.

FORM FIELD BINDERS

Another form of binding occurs when a form is submitted or displayed. Values are mapped back and forth between the `Form` object and the forms in the views. Inside the form object, the data is stored as objects, but on the client side we can only display their string representations. This is why customized form field binders can be useful.

Form field binders in Play are also referred to as *formatters*, because they format data to and from controllers.

Formatters, both predefined and custom, are always used to map `Strings` to objects. You can register a `Formatter` using the `register()` method of `play.data` `.format.Formatters`. Let's do that now with a custom formatter for dates, by extending the `SimpleFormatter` class. We have to register the formatter at application startup in the `Global` object (or a class that extends `GlobalSettings` and overrides the `onStart` method). For that we need to create a `Global.java` file in the app folder. The `Global` object is part of Play and defines methods that are called during the application lifecycle (`onStart`, `onStop`, `onError`, and so forth). The `Global.java` file content is shown in the following listing.

> **Listing 6.14 Registering a `DateFormatter` class**

```
import play.*;
import play.libs.*;
import java.util.*;
import models.*;
import play.data.format.Formatters;
import play.data.format.Formatters.*;
import java.text.ParseException;
import java.text.SimpleDateFormat;
import java.util.Date;
import java.util.Locale;

public class Global extends GlobalSettings {

    public void onStart(Application app) {
        Formatters.register(Date.class,
                    new SimpleFormatter<Date>() {
          private final static String PATTERN = "dd-MM-yyyy";

          public Date parse(String text, Locale locale)
              throws java.text.ParseException {
            if(text == null || text.trim().isEmpty()) {
              return null;
            }
            SimpleDateFormat sdf =
              new SimpleDateFormat(PATTERN, locale);
            sdf.setLenient(false);
            return sdf.parse(text);
          }

          public String print(Date value, Locale locale){
            if(value == null) {
              return "";
            }
            return new SimpleDateFormat(PATTERN, locale)
                      .format(value);
          }
        });
    }
}
```

Our Global object is part of Play's lifecycle

Register our new Formatter, extending the SimpleFormatter abstract class and specifying that the formatter applies to Date objects

The onStart method is called when Play starts our application

Create a Date object based on our date-format-binding process

Create a string representation of our Date object based on our date-format-unbinding process

Because we're extending the `SimpleFormatter` class, we have to implement two methods: the `parse()` method and the `print()` method. The `parse()` method converts a `String` to a `Date` object (the binding process), whereas the `print()` method converts a `Date` to a `String` (the unbinding process). An incoming date string, such as 11-02-2008, will now be converted to a `Date` object representing that date. Similarly, an outgoing `Date` object will be converted to a "dd-MM-yyyy"-formatted string.

As you can see, this is straightforward to declare. Now every time we encounter a `Date` object, Play knows how to bind a date and send it back as `String`. But there are cases when you don't want the formatting to be global, or you want the date format to be enforced and/or different.

If we were to add a date to our product, the user would have to enter the date as 21-01-2012 in a product details input field using the formatter we defined earlier. Similarly, the date will be shown as 21-01-2012 in the details form. In our object model, however, it will be a `Date` and not a `String`; the formatter handles the conversion between `String` and `Date`.

For example, what if you want to have multiple date representations? For example, suppose you want the user to input 11-02-08 on the main page and 11/02/08 on the login screen. Play allows you to control the binding behavior with annotations, including custom annotations. Let's transform our date formatter into an annotation-based formatter by creating the following:

- An annotation
- A formatter that extends Play's `AnnotationFormatter`

Let's start with our annotation:

> **Listing 6.15 The `DateFormat` annotation, `/app/utils/DateFormat.java`**

```
package utils;

import play.data.Form;
import java.lang.annotation.*;

@Target({ElementType.FIELD})
@Retention(RetentionPolicy.RUNTIME)
@Form.Display(name = "format.date", attributes = {"value"})
public @interface DateFormat {
    String value();
}
```

Indicates the annotation applies to fields only

The annotation is to be applied at runtime

This Play annotation indicates that the i18n name is format.date which has a value parameter—this is used to display a validation error message in case of binding failure

The value will be our date format

The annotation is simple and is mainly a holder for our date format. The `Display` annotation defined on the `DateFormat` annotation holds metadata for Play. When a date can't be bound because of an incorrect date format, Play uses that metadata to display an error message on the form. The annotation tells Play to use the `format.date` message key and that `value` can be used as a parameter for the message.

Let's now define our formatter. We have to indicate that we want an annotation formatter. This is done by extending `Formatters.AnnotationFormatter`.

Listing 6.16 The `AnnotationDateFormatter` class

> **Extends Formatters.AnnotationFormatter so we're annotation aware—the Formatter applies to DateFormat annotation and to Date object**

```
public static class AnnotationDateFormatter
    extends Formatters.AnnotationFormatter<DateFormat,Date> {

    public Date parse(DateFormat annotation, String text,
                                            Locale locale)
        throws java.text.ParseException {
        if(text == null || text.trim().isEmpty()) {
            return null;
        }
        SimpleDateFormat sdf = new
            SimpleDateFormat(annotation.value(), locale);
        sdf.setLenient(false);
        return sdf.parse(text);
    }

    public String print(DateFormat annotation, Date value,
                                        Locale locale) {
        if(value == null) {
            return "";
        }
        return new SimpleDateFormat (annotation.value(), locale)
                    .format(value);
    }
}
```

> **Create a Date object based on our date format value annotation-binding process**
>
> **We're taking the date format from our annotation**
>
> **Create a string representation of our Date object based on our date format annotation-unbinding process**
>
> **We're taking the date format from our annotation**

Because we're extending the `Formatters.AnnotationFormatter` abstract class, as before with the `SimpleFormatter` class, we have to implement two methods: the `parse()` method and the `print()` method. And as before, the `parse()` method binds the date string representation to a concrete `Date` object, whereas the `print()` method does the exact opposite. But this time, the `Formatters.AnnotationFormatter` is annotation aware, and our `print()` and `parse()` methods take an extra parameter: our `DateFormat` annotation. We use it to access the configured pattern.

As we've seen in the previous section, we need to register our `AnnotationDate-Formatter` in our `Global.java` class. Listing 6.17 shows how to do that.

Listing 6.17 Registering our `AnnotationDateFormatter` in the `Global.java` file

```
public class Global extends GlobalSettings {

    public void onStart(Application app) {
        ...
        Formatters.register(Date.class, new AnnotationDateFormatter());
    }
}
```

Register our
AnnotationDateFormatter

Now we can now annotate any object property on a model class to indicate that we want to bind and unbind `Date` from a `Form` object using the following syntax:

Listing 6.18 Object model using the `DateFormat` annotation

```
public Person {
    @DateFormat("MM-dd-yyyy")
    public Date birthDate;
}
```

Now in our view, each `Person`'s birth date will be displayed as MM-dd-yyyy. When submitting a form, the `birthDate` attribute will contain a `Date` object with the expected date. Note that in practice, the example we've seen is already part of Play. You don't need to code it and you can use the `@DateTime` annotation defined in the `play.data.format.Formats` class.

6.3 Body parsers

We've looked at request body data mapped to form objects and vice versa, but we haven't explored how the raw request bodies are processed. This step is the job of body parsers.

Each incoming HTTP `POST` and `PUT` request contains a body. This body may be single part or multipart, and may contain XML, JSON, binary data, or any other type as specified in the request's `Content-Type` header. A body parser will parse the body (hence the name) into a Java object. Further operations, such as formatting, can then take place. Figure 6.10 illustrates this process.

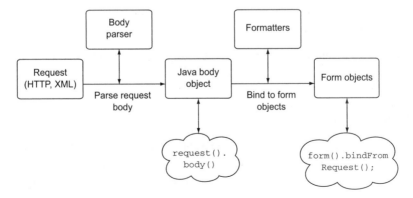

Figure 6.10 Body parser interaction with an incoming request

Body parsers "decode" the request and transform it into objects that can then be used by the other Play components. Because a JSON body is parsed differently to an XML body, Play uses pluggable body parsers. Different content types, therefore, have specific body parsers that can translate arbitrary incoming data into something Play can understand.

Using body parsers, it's possible to directly manipulate the object obtained from a request. The interaction is done through a body-parser API.

6.3.1 *The body-parser API*

All body parsers must generate a `play.mvc.Http.RequestBody` value. This value can then be retrieved via `request().body()`. The following listing shows how to use the API.

Listing 6.19 Accessing the request body

```
public static Result index() {
    RequestBody body = request().body();           ◁  Accessing the
    return ok("Here is the body we received: " + body);   request body
}
```

You can specify the `BodyParser` to use for a particular action using the `@BodyParser.Of` annotation. This means that we can tell Play to use a specific body parser to parse the request and then access the body request to read the value. Listing 6.20 shows an example in which we're specifying a JSON body parser and reading the result via the `body.asJson()` method.

Listing 6.20 Specifying a specific body parser to use

```
@BodyParser.Of(BodyParser.Json.class)
public static Result index() {                          We output the
    RequestBody body = request().body();                JSON value on
    return ok("We expected to get json: " + body.asJson());  ◁─ the console
}
```

All body parsers will give you a `play.mvc.Http.RequestBody` value. From this body object you can retrieve the request body content in the most appropriate type. In our previous example, we used the `asJson()` method. But if we'd used an XML body parser, we would've used the `asXML` method.

> **REQUESTBODY METHODS MAY RETURN NULL** `RequestBody` methods such as `asText()` or `asJson()` will return `null` if the parser used can't handle that content type. For example, in an action method annotated with `@BodyParser.Of(BodyParser.Json.class)`, calling `asXml()` on the generated body will return `null`.

Some parsers can provide a more specific type than `Http.RequestBody` (a subclass of `Http.RequestBody`). You can automatically cast the request body into another type using the `as()` helper method. An example is shown in the following listing.

Listing 6.21 Using the `as()` helper method

```
@BodyParser.Of(BodyLengthParser.class)
public static Result index() {
  BodyLength body = request().body().as(BodyLength.class);
  return ok("Request body length: " + body.getLength());
}
```

> Using as() to
> automatically bind
> the request body to
> a BodyLength class

If you don't specify a body parser, Play will use the Content-Type header to determine which built-in parser to use:

- text/plain—String, accessible via asText()
- application/json—JsonNode, accessible via asJson()
- text/xml—org.w3c.Document, accessible via asXml()
- application/form-URL-encoded—Map<String, String[]>, accessible via asFormUrlEncoded()
- multipart/form-data—Http.MultipartFormData, accessible via asMultipartFormData()
- *Any other content type*—Http.RawBuffer, accessible via asRaw()

Please note that if the requested body type isn't available, the method will return null. The following listing shows an example of how the asText() method can be used.

Listing 6.22 Using the `body.asText()` method

```
public static Result save() {
  RequestBody body = request().body();
  String textBody = body.asText();

  if(textBody != null) {
    return ok("Got: " + text);
  } else {
  return badRequest
    ("Expecting text/plain request body");
  }
}
```

Text-based body parsers (such as text, JSON-, XML-, or URL-encoded forms) use a maximum content length because they have to load all the content into memory. There is a default content length limit of 100 KB.

> **OVERRIDING THE DEFAULT MAX CONTENT-LENGTH** The default content size can be defined in application.conf: parsers.text.maxLength=128K.

You can also specify a maximum content length via the @BodyParser.Of annotation, for example to only accept 10 KB of data:

```
@BodyParser.Of(value = BodyParser.Text.class, maxLength = 10 * 1024)
public static Result index() {
  ...
}
```

Custom body parsers must be written in Scala, because they process incoming data incrementally using Scala's Iteratee I/O.

But Play has body parsers for typical web content types such as JSON and binary data, and these can be reused to create body parsers in Java.

Now that we understand how to receive and transform data, we need to be able to ensure the data is valid.

6.4   Validation

We've seen how we can translate user data to our own object model and vice versa. But we also need to ensure the data is valid in the context of our application by meeting certain criteria. For example, some fields might be mandatory. The binding process can't guarantee that data is valid. Play allows you to define constraints to catch invalid submitted data. It also provides detailed feedback to the client in the case of invalid data. In this section we'll see how we can define constraints on the data the user inputs.

6.4.1   Using the built-in validators

Play validates the data once it is bound to the domain model. Play uses JSR-303[3] and Hibernate validators for this step. Defining constraints is as simple as annotating the object model. For example, ensuring that the user inputs an EAN number in our product form is as simple as adding the `@Required` annotation on the `Product` object:

```
import play.data.validation.Constraints.*;
...

public Product extends Model {
  ...
    @Required                          Indicates this
    public String ean;                 field is required
}
```

To ensure the user input complies with the constraint defined by the annotation, we need to check the `hasError` method on our `Form` object. Validation occurs immediately after binding and registers errors in the form as they are found. The validation process sets any validation errors to the `Form` that was bound. Validation errors contain the relevant i18n error message key, the field name, and a potential parameter list to display with the error message. Listing 6.23 shows the `save` method seen in section 6.1.3, with the validation check added.

Listing 6.23   Save action method with validation

```
public static Result save() {
  Form<models.Product> productForm =            Create a Form
  form(models.Product.class).bindFromRequest();  object from the
                                                 current request
  models.Product newProduct = productForm.get();
                                                 Bind the Product
                                                 object from the form
```

---

[3] JSR-303 is a Java specification that defines a metadata model and API for JavaBean validation based on annotations; see http://jcp.org/en/js/r/detail?id=303.

If a validation error occurred

```
if (productForm.hasErrors()) {
    return ok(edit.render(productForm));
} else {
    newProduct.saveOrUpdate();
    return redirect(routes.Product.all());
}
}
```

Rerender our form

Save or update our current Product object

Redirect to our "view all products" page

As you can see, validating a form is straightforward.

Play comes with a lot of commonly used validations, and these are detailed in table 6.1.

Table 6.1   Built-in Play validation annotations

Name	Description
@Required	A Play-specific validation indicating the field must be non-null or, in the case of `Strings` and `Collections`, not `null` and not empty. Works with any object.
@Min	Indicates the minimum this number should be; for example, `@Min(1)`.
@Max	Indicates the maximum this number should be; for example, `@Max(2)`.
@MinLength	Defines a minimum length for a string field.
@MaxLength	Defines a maximum length for a string field.
@Pattern	Checks if the annotated string matches the regular expression pattern.
@ValidateWith	Uses a custom validator (see section 6.4.3).
@Email	Checks whether the specified string is a valid email address.

Play uses an implementation of the JSR-303 specification,[4] better known as *Bean Validation*, to perform the validation. The standard also comes with its own set of validation annotations that covers most common use cases.

Table 6.2 shows some built-in annotations that come with Bean Validation. They can all be found in the `javax.validation` package.

Table 6.2   Built-in Hibernate validation annotations

Name	Description
@Null	Indicates that the field should be `null` (but it can be empty).
@NotNull	Indicates that the field cannot be `null`.
@NotEmpty	Checks if the string is not `null` nor empty.
@AssertTrue	Asserts that this field is a Boolean that resolves to `true`.

---

[4] Hibernate Validator, to be precise.

Table 6.2   Built-in Hibernate validation annotations *(continued)*

Name	Description
`@AssertFalse`	Asserts that this field is a Boolean that resolves to `false`.
`@Min`	Indicates the minimum this number should be; for example, `@Min(1)`.
`@Max`	Indicates the maximum this number should be; for example, `@Max(2)`.
`@DecimalMin`	Indicates the minimum this decimal number should be; for example, `@Min(1.1)`.
`@DecimalMax`	Indicates the maximum this decimal number should be; for example, `@Max(4.2)`.
`@Size`	Indicates range this number should be in; for example, `@Size(min=2, max=4)`.
`@Digits(integer=, fraction=)`	Checks whether the property is a number, having up to `{integer}` digits and `{fraction}` fractional digits.
`@Past`	Checks whether the annotated date is in the past.
`@Future`	Checks whether the annotated date is in the future.
`@Pattern(regex=)`	Checks if the annotated string matches the `{regex}` regular expression pattern.
`@Valid`	Performs validation recursively on the associated object.
`@Email`	Checks whether the specified string is a valid email address.
`@Length(min=, max=)`	Validates that the annotated string is between `{min}` and `{max}` (inclusive).

These annotations are self-explanatory, but further information can be found in the documentation for Bean Validation (http://beanvalidation.org).

6.4.2   *Partial validation*

A common use case is having multiple validation constraints for the same object model. Because we're defining our constraint on the object model, it's normal to have multiple forms that refer to the same object model. But these forms might have different validation constraints. To illustrate this use case, we can imagine a simple wizard in which the user inputs a new product in two steps:

1   The user enters the product name and submits the form.
2   The user enters the product EAN number and the description.

We could validate the product's name during step 2, but displaying an error message for the product name at that point would be weird. Fortunately, Play allows you to perform partial validation. For each annotated value, we need to indicate at which step it applies. We can do that with the help of the `groups` attribute from our annotations. Let's change our `Product` model class to do that:

```
public Product extends Model {
    public interface Step1{}          ◁— Define first step
    public interface Step2{}             ◁— Define second step

    @Required(groups = Step1.class)   ◁— This constraint only applies to first step
    public String name;
    @Required(groups = Step2.class)   ◁— This constraint only applies to second step
    public String ean;
}
```

We now need to indicate which step we're at. This is done when binding from the request, specifying `Step1`:

```
// We re//strict the validation to the Step1 "group"
Form<Product> productForm =
    form(Product.class, Product.Step1.class).bindFromRequest();   ◁
if(filledForm.hasErrors()) {
...
```

> **When binding, tell validator we're only interested in constraints that apply to first step**

We can do the same for `Step2`. This is useful if the model object is used on different forms and has different validation constraints.

6.4.3 *Creating a custom validator*

Play gives you the ability to add your own validators. This is useful if you need to perform custom validation. You can implement your own validator in different ways:

- Using ad hoc validation—this method is the quickest and simplest one
- Using `@ValidateWith` and defining your own `Validator` class
- Defining a new JSR 303 annotation and defining a new `Validator` class

We'll take a closer look at each of these approaches, starting with ad hoc validation.

AD HOC VALIDATION

You can define an ad hoc validation by adding a `validate` method to your model object. Play will invoke the `validate` method of every object model. For example, to validate our EAN number, we can add a `validate` method on our `Product` object model. The `validate` method must return a `String` or `null`. If it returns a `String`, it must either contain the validation error message or the i18n key for one. A `null` return value indicates there are no errors.

An EAN is a 13-digit number. Our `validate` method must check that the `String` EAN variable contains exactly 13 digits. Listing 6.24 shows you how to do that.

Listing 6.24   EAN number ad hoc validation adding the `validate` method

```
public Product extends Model {
  ...
  public String ean; public String validate() {
    String pattern = "^[0-9]{13}$";
    Pattern regex = Pattern.compile(pattern);
    return name !=null &&
      regex.matcher(name).matches()?null:"Invalid ean number";
  }
}
```

The validate method returns null in case of success, or the error message otherwise

This regex pattern means "a number character, 13 times"

Return the error message if the input doesn't match; null otherwise

The `validate` method is not practical if you have several attributes to validate, but it's the easiest and quickest way to add simple validation constraints. Let's take a look at how we can do more complex validation.

PLAY @VALIDATEWITH

Using `@ValidateWith`, we can have fine-grained control over validation. Let's use the EAN number as an example again. First, we need to annotate the `ean` attribute with the `@Constraints.ValidateWith.ValidateWith` annotation. The `@ValidateWith` method takes a class as parameter: the class that will do our custom validation.

We need to implement a class that extends the Play `Constraints.Validator` class. In our `Validator` class, we need to implement the `isValid` and `getErrorMessageKey` methods. `isValid()` tests the field's validity, and `getErrorMessageKey()` returns the i18n message key for the error message. The following listing shows how to validate the EAN number using `@ValidateWith`.

Listing 6.25   EAN number validation using the `@ValidateWith` annotation

```
package models;

import play.data.validation.Constraints;
...

public class Product implements PathBindable<Product>,
    QueryStringBindable<Product> {

  public static class EanValidator
      extends Constraints.Validator<String> {

    @Override
    public boolean isValid(String value) {
      String pattern = "^[0-9]{13}$";
      return value != null && value.matches(pattern);
    }

    @Override
    public F.Tuple<String, Object[]> getErrorMessageKey() {
      return new F.Tuple<String, Object[]>("error.invalid.ean",
```

Our custom validator class must extend the Play abstract Validator class

Our implementation of the isValid method

Return true if the string has exactly 13 digits

```
        new Object[]{});
    }
}
```
← **getErrorMessageKey returns i18 message key and potential argument values**

```
...
    @Constraints.Required
    @Constraints.ValidateWith(value=EanValidator.class,
      message="must be 13 numbers")
    public String ean;
...
}
```
← **Indicates we want to validate using our custom validator class**

Using @ValidateWith, we now have a custom, fine-grained, reusable validation mechanism. This approach to validation is Play-specific, but using the JSR-303 standard, there is a way to specify validation logic in a more portable way. Let's see how that works.

JSR-303 CUSTOM ANNOTATION AND VALIDATOR

This approach is the JSR-303 standard way to add custom validation. It's not specific to Play and could be used in other, non-Play applications. This approach requires two steps:

- Define an annotation and reference a Validator class
- Define the Validator class that is referenced by our annotation

Let's define an @EAN annotation that will be used to make sure our EAN number has exactly 13 digits. We need to declare a new annotation and annotate that with the @javax.validation.Constraint annotation later. The @Constraint annotation references a Validator class that we need to implement next. The following listing shows you how to create the annotation.

Listing 6.26 Custom JSR-303 EAN annotation

```
@Constraint(validatedBy = EanValidator.class)
```
← **Indicate that it is a validation annotation that should use the EanValidator class to validate the value annotated by this annotation**

```
@Target( { FIELD })
```
← **Our annotation targets the field value**

```
@Retention(RetentionPolicy.RUNTIME)
```
← **We always compute the annotation at runtime**

```
public @interface EAN {

  String message() default "error.invalid.ean";
```
← **The default error message— can be overwritten when setting the annotation**

```
  Class<?>[] groups() default {};
```
← **The groups we want to apply the annotation to during partial validation— see section 6.4.2 for more on partial validation**

```
  Class<? extends Payload>[] payload() default {};
```
← **Payload is a standard JSR-303 property currently not used by Play**

```
}
```

We now need to define a `Validator` that will hold the business logic to validate our EAN number. Our validator has to implement the JSR-303 `ConstraintValidator` interface, and we need to implement the `isValid` method. The `isValid` method returns a Boolean that indicates whether the value is valid. The following listing shows the `Ean-Validator` implementation.

Listing 6.27 Custom JSR-303 validator

```
public static class EanValidator extends Constraints.Validator<String>
  implements ConstraintValidator<EAN, String> {                        ⟵─┐
    final static public String message = "error.invalid.ean";
    public EanValidator() {}
                                          The ConstraintValidator class
                                          identifies our validator; it extends
                                          Play's Constraints.Validator class.

    @Override
    public void initialize(EAN constraintAnnotation) {}     ⟵  This is called
                                                               when the validator
                                                               is initialized
    @Override
    public boolean isValid(String value) {
      String pattern = "^[0-9]{13}$";
      return value != null && value.matches(pattern);       ⟵  The business
    }                                                           logic—if regular
                                                                expression doesn't
                                                                match, it isn't valid
    @Override
    public F.Tuple<String, Object[]> getErrorMessageKey() {
      return new F.Tuple<String, Object[]>(message,
          new Object[]{});
    }
  }
}
```

We can now annotate our `Product` object model with the `@EAN` annotation:

```
public Product extends Model {
...
  @EAN
  public String ean;
}
```

And our EAN field will automatically be validated. As you can see, it's easy to add new validation logic to our object models. Play allows you to validate your objects with your own custom validation code, so you can validate against a database if you wish to.

6.4.4 *Displaying the validation errors on the form*

Nice—we can now validate our forms. But we also need to present the cause of the validation errors to our users. This is trivial to do; the error messages are stored in our `Form` object. By passing the `Form` object to our views, we can easily display the error messages. For example, in our controller's `save()` action, we check the form for errors and pass it along to the view:

```
Form<Product> boundForm = productForm.bindFromRequest();
if (boundForm.hasErrors()) {
  return ok(details.render(productForm));
}
```

We're passing our product form to the view ◁┘

In our view, we can access the form object and display the errors. We can access the error message using the `errors()` method on the form or on a specified field. If you want to display all the validation errors, iterate over the form errors using the `errors()` method:

```
<p>Please fix the following errors<ul>
@for(error <- productForm.errors() ) {
  <li>@error.message</li>
}
<ul></p>
```

If you want to access the errors per field, then you can use the `errors()` method on the field value. For example, if we want to access the potential validation error for the product name field:

```
@productForm("name").errors()
```

This returns a list. But using the built-in `mkString` method to join strings, we can have a comma-separated list of errors per field using the following code:

```
@productForm("name").errors().mkString(", ")
```

For our current form, there's no need to use these methods, because the form helpers already include errors. But there's no magic to the form helpers; they render the errors using exactly this technique, as you can see in the following listing, which shows the template for the field helper.

Listing 6.28 Source code for the field helper template

```
@(elements: views.html.helper.FieldElements)

@import play.api.i18n._
@import views.html.helper._

@**************************************************** *
Generate input according twitter Bootstrap rules *
****************************************************@

<div class="clearfix @elements.args.get('_class)
  @if(elements.hasErrors) {error}"
  id="@elements.args.get('_id).getOrElse(elements.id + "_field")">
  <label for="@elements.id">@elements.label(elements.lang)</label>
  <div class="input">
    @elements.input
    <span class="help-inline">
      @elements.errors(elements.lang).mkString(", ")
    </span>
    <span class="help-block">
```

```
      @elements.infos(elements.lang).mkString(", ")
    </span>
  </div>
</div>
```

We now know how to validate and to report any validation errors back to the user. We're now able to submit any user inputs, process them, and reject any invalid data. Let's see about a more complicated type of input: file uploads.

6.5   *File uploads*

It's time to go back to our current application. There's something missing that could make our paperclips more identifiable; we need to visually recognize them. Let's add a picture. For that we need to modify the `Product` object model slightly: see the following listing.

Listing 6.29   Adding a picture to the `Product` object model

```
public class Product {
...
  @Constraints.Required
  @Constraints.ValidateWith(EanValidator.class)
  public String ean;
  @Constraints.Required
  public String name;                         Add this line—
  public String description;                  a byte array will
  public byte[] picture;                      hold our picture

...
}
```

We now need to give our users a chance to upload a picture for a product; we need to add an HTML input file element to our form. To do that, we need to edit the existing `product.scala.html` template that we created in section 6.1.1, add an HTML file input element, and display a picture if one exists using an HTML `img` element. We also need to change the form encoding type to send multipart data.

The form now looks like the one shown in the following listing.

Listing 6.30   "Product create" form with picture uploading

```
@(productForm: Form[Product])
@import helper._
@import helper.twitterBootstrap._

@main("Product form") {
  <h1>Product form</h1>
  @helper.form(action = routes.Products.save(),          The HTML form is
    'enctype -> "multipart/form-data") {                 now multipart
  <fieldset>
    <legend>Product (@productForm("name").valueOr("New"))</legend>
    @helper.inputText(productForm("ean"))
    @helper.inputText(productForm("name"))
    @helper.textarea(productForm("description"))          Our input file
    @helper.inputFile(productForm("picture"))             HTML element
```

```
@if(!productForm("picture").valueOr("").isEmpty()) {
<div class="control-group">
  <div class="controls">
    <img
      style="position:relative; left:50px;height:80px"
      src="/picture/@productForm("ean").value">
  </div>
</div>
}
...
  }
}
```

The img HTML tag used to display the picture

Once the form is submitted, we need to save the picture sent by the user. Unfortunately, because of the way HTTP file uploads work, Play is unable to bind the file directly to the picture field, so we'll need to modify our save() method on the Product controller.

In order to obtain the file that was uploaded by the user, we need to access the part of the HTTP body that holds the file. We've seen how we can use the body-parser API to do that in section 6.3.1; we call request().body().asMultipartFormData().

Once we access the body, we can request the file and convert it to a byte array. Then we can save our product and the associated picture to the datastore. We could also access the filename and its content type through the FilePart object that we obtain from the multipart body, but we currently have no need for that in our application.

The following listing shows how to read and save the file.

Listing 6.31 Obtaining and saving uploaded files

```
import static play.mvc.Http.MultipartFormData;
...
public static Result save() {
  Form<Product> boundForm = productForm.bindFromRequest();
  if(boundForm.hasErrors()) {
    flash("error", "Please correct the form below.");
    return badRequest(details.render(boundForm));
  }
  Product product = boundForm.get();
  MultipartFormData body = request().body().asMultipartFormData();
  MultipartFormData.FilePart part = body.getFile("picture");

    if(part != null) {
    File picture = part.getFile();
      try {
        product.picture = Files.toByteArray(picture);
      } catch (IOException e) {
        return internalServerError("Error reading file upload");
      }
    }
```

Binds form as a multipart form so we can access submitted file

Requests picture FilePart—this should match the name attribute of the input file in our form (for example, input name=picture)

Get file →

A utility method copies file contents to a byte[]

```
List<Tag> tags = new ArrayList<Tag>();
for (Tag tag : product.tags) {
  if (tag.id != null) {
    tags.add(Tag.findById(tag.id));
  }
}
product.tags = tags;
product.save();                                    Save product
flash("success",                                   as usual
    String.format("Successfully added product %s", product));
return redirect(routes.Products.list(1));
}
```

We're now able to save our product and the associated picture to our datastore. If you wanted to store the file some other way, such as on the filesystem, you could easily write code that does that; once you have the `File` object, it handles like any other file.

Now, we still need a way to *display* the product picture on our form. This is easily done by adding a new method on our `Product` controller. Let's add a `picture()` method. This method takes an EAN number, uses it to look up the matching product in the database, and uses the image byte array to generate a `Result`.

The following listing shows how the `picture()` method is implemented.

Listing 6.32 Our picture method

```
public static Result picture(String ean) {
  final Product product = Product.findByEan(ean);
  if(product == null) return notFound();
  return ok(product.picture);
}
```

As usual when we implement a new action method, we need to edit our `routes` file to link the picture method to a URL. To request a picture for a product, we want to call the /picture/ean URL. We add the following line to our routes file:

```
GET /picture/:ean  controllers.Products.picture(ean:  String)
```

In our `product.html.scala` file, we already added the image:

```
@if(!productForm("picture").valueOr("").isEmpty()) {
  <img src="@routes.Products.picture(productForm("ean").value)"/>
}
```

We're now able to display our product picture. Figure 6.11 shows what you should now see in the application.

Now that we're able to handle file uploads, we've covered all aspects of handling user input!

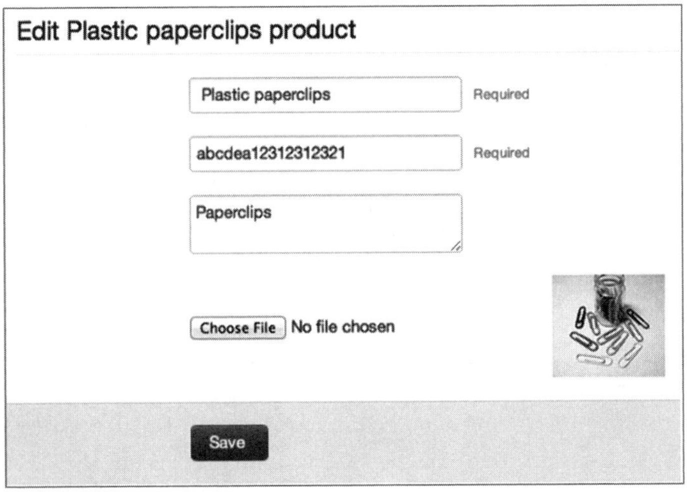

Figure 6.11   Our paperclip picture

6.6   *Summary*

This chapter has been dense, and we saw a lot. We learned how to handle user input—from a simple form submission to a more complex file submission. We also learned how all this was possible through the use of body parsers. We saw in detail how the Play binding process transforms user-submitted data into data that our application can understand. We also learned how we could extend that binding process; we know how to customize and create our own binders.

Once we were ready to process user data, we saw how to validate that data. We also saw how we could create our own validator if needed. We then saw how to handle invalid data and to report those errors back to the user. We finished the chapter with a concrete example of how to handle file submission. We're now able to handle any data type, process it, and validate it when needed. In the next chapter, we'll see how to model our warehouse application.

Models and persistence

This chapter covers

- Defining data models
- Persisting data
- Mapping your model using JPA annotations
- Loading initial data
- Querying data using Ebean

In the previous chapters, we covered the basic requirements for our paper clip warehouse application. Until now, we've been faking data storage by maintaining static `Lists` in memory. Now it's time to start saving our data in a database. We'll take a closer look at our data model, and learn more about the role of a data model in a Play application.

First things first?

Although it seems to be convention in most application frameworks to start with the data model, Play doesn't dictate where you start developing your application; if you want to start developing your views or controllers first, Play won't fight you. Feel free to work in any order you like!

We'll start this chapter by developing the data model as Java classes, extending the application we created last chapter. Then we'll make it possible to store data in a relational database using the persistence facilities that come with Play.

But first, we'll expand our data model.

7.1 Modeling the real world in code

The most basic requirement of our warehouse application is keeping track of what stock items are in our warehouse and what kind of product each item is. A common trick for creating a data model is to take a use case, and write down all the nouns and the relationships between these nouns. If we apply the requirements from chapter 4, we get the model shown in figure 7.1.

A data model can be seen as a representation of a real-world concept in code. Object-oriented languages are quite suitable for this. A key aspect of objects is that they group data and behavior in a single entity. For our current data model, we're only interested in grouping data; there's no behavior we want to capture yet. Java-Beans are exactly this kind of object; they model state, but not behavior. They're a collection of private fields, accessible through instance methods called *getters* and *setters*.

A typical JavaBean is a pretty dumb piece of code, with tons of unnecessary boilerplate code. If you think about it, most JavaBeans are private fields with simple getters and setters. JavaBeans are so full of boilerplate code that they can mostly be generated by any IDE worthy of the name.

7.1.1 The reasons for getters and setters

The main reason Java classes, and JavaBeans in particular, are often given getter and setter methods is to encapsulate data and hide the internal representation of an object.

The difference between calling a `getName()` method on a `Person` object and accessing its `name` field directly is the difference between asking a person for their name and accessing their birth certificate and reading the name on it. The former

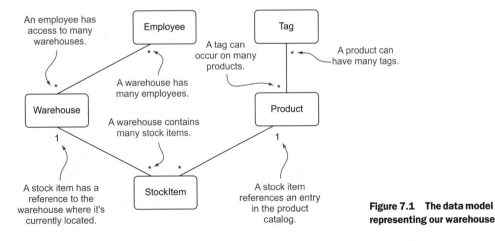

Figure 7.1 The data model representing our warehouse

gives the person whose name we want to know a lot more control than the latter, and the latter is also possibly exposing a lot more information than that person might choose to give. Also, we might destroy the birth certificate. It doesn't even matter whether we do it unintentionally or on purpose.

Now consider a person wearing a name tag: the name is there, clearly visible to everyone, not giving any more information than that, and it's not modifiable. The fact that the person *has* a name also isn't exposing anything about the person we don't already know; a person always has a name, you could say it's part of their public inter-face. In this case, asking the person for their name seems silly. This situation is similar to having a `Person` class with a `name` field that is marked both `final` and `public`.

Let's see what all this looks like in code. The following listing shows the situation when using a getter.

Listing 7.1 Person with `getName()`

```java
public class Person {
    private final String name;              ⟵── A private name field

    public Person(String name) {
        this.name = name;
    }

    public String getName() {               ⟵── The corresponding getter
        return name;
    }
}
String name = new Person("John Doe").getName();   ⟵┘ "Asking" the Person
                                                     object for its name
```

In this example, we define a field, but access to it is delegated through the `getName()` method. We "ask" the `Person` for its name, using the getter method.

The following listing shows the same class, but implemented using a public field.

Listing 7.2 Person with a public name property

```java
public class Person {
    public final String name;               ⟵── A public name field

    public Person(String name) {
        this.name = name;
    }
}
String name = new Person("John Doe").name;   ⟵┘ Reading the
                                                name directly
```

In this example, we expose the field directly, and now the client reads the `name` field directly. We've achieved the same result as in the previous example, but with less code.

The problem with providing public field access to object properties is that we don't get to change our minds. Once we expose a field, it's part of that object's public API, and we should support it forever, or risk breaking client code that depends on it. For example, if we introduce a public `name` field, and later decide we want to "lie" about the name of our `Person`, we can't, because its internal state is exposed for the world to see, and our client code depends on it being there. This is why it's common to see Java classes with private fields, and corresponding getters that return the values of the fields, as a way of future-proofing the class's API.

Another good reason for getters and setters is that they're part of the JavaBeans[1] specification, which offers a standardized way to expose private properties through methods. Many tools require this, including Ebean, which we'll cover later in this chapter. Tools that depend on the JavaBean convention won't work on classes without getters and setters.

Although the case for getters and setters is strong, the downside is that they generate a lot of noise; a simple field with both a getter and a setter requires around seven extra lines of code (depending on your code-formatting convention). Although this may not seem like much, the noise adds up if you have a class with lots of fields; plus you have to remember to generate or write the correct method whenever you introduce a new field. Wouldn't you rather focus on something else?

7.1.2 Let Play eliminate some noise for you

Play helps you eliminate all this boilerplate code in which you'd normally write a simple getter and setter, and it allows you to use public fields whenever you don't require special logic you'd put in a getter or setter.

Don't worry: tools you use still get to use your model classes like JavaBeans. Play uses a cool trick called *bytecode enhancement* to add getters and setters right after your original code is compiled, and then it silently rewrites all your client bytecode to use the generated getters and setters. If you change from field access to getters/ setters, or the other way around, you'll find your code no longer compiles. This is because the bytecode enhancement takes place *after* your class is compiled, which means it has to compile first.

This means that if you ever change your mind about using getters and setters, you'll have to rewrite your client code. Fortunately, all IDEs will help you do that automatically, and if you do happen to miss an occurrence, you'll get a compile-time error informing you. It's not that big a deal, as long as it's in

> **Pay no attention to the man behind the curtain**
>
> The bytecode enhancement Play uses to transparently add getters and setters is an example of Play "magic"; there are things going on behind the scenes that are not immediately obvious from looking at the code, but the effects are there. It's arguable whether this is a desirable situation, but in practice it turns out that the pros often outweigh the cons.
>
> There used to be a lot more "magic" like this in Play 1.x, but in Play 2, this is the only thing that was carried over from Play 1. You don't have to use it if you don't want to; you can create your own getters and setters, and Play won't touch your classes.

---

[1] Visit http://docs.oracle.com/javase/tutorial/javabeans/ for more information.

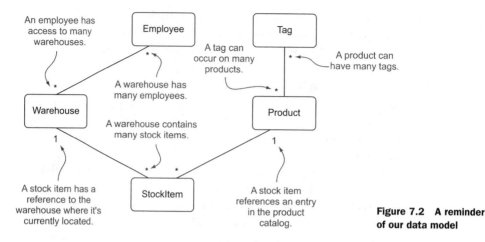

Figure 7.2 A reminder of our data model

your application. Do think long and hard about choosing either approach if you ever decide to export and reuse a class *outside* of your application, such as when writing a Play module or sharing your data model between applications. Breaking a public interface is not cool.

7.1.3 *Creating our classes*

Because we have the basic relational model, let's fill in the details directly in Java. See figure 7.2 for a reminder of what our complete model looks like.

We already created the Product and Tag classes in previous chapters, but the other classes are new. Create the classes as in listing 7.3 in the models package under the application we created last chapter:

Listing 7.3 Our basic data model, represented in classes

```java
public class Product {
  public String ean;
  public String name;
  public String description;
  public byte[] picture;
  public List<Tag> tags;

  public String toString() {
    return name;
  }
}

public class Tag {
  public Long id;
  public String name;
  public List<Product> products;
}

public class Warehouse {
  public String name;
  public List<StockItem> stock = new ArrayList<>();
```

An EAN is an international product number

Note that these fields are relationships

```java
  public String toString() {
    return name;
  }
}

public class StockItem {
  public Warehouse warehouse;
  public Product product;
  public Long quantity;

  public String toString() {
    return String.format("%d %s", quantity, product);
  }
}
```

> **Note that these fields are relationships**

Your application directory should now look like the following.

```
warehouse
        ├── app
        │      ├── controllers
        │      ├── models
        │      │       ├── Product.java
        │      │       ├── StockItem.java
        │      │       ├── Tag.java
        │      │       └── Warehouse.java
        │      └── views
        ├── conf
        ├── public
        ├── test
        └── db
```

Congratulations, you have a full data model! Don't worry too much about the output to the browser yet; we'll talk about view templates in chapter 8.

Now that we have our data model and we know how to use it in our controllers and views, it's time to start thinking about storing the data we collect.

7.2 *Persistence and Object-Relational Mapping (ORM)*

Having all this data is useful, but currently all data we build up during a request is lost as soon as we finish handling a request. Therefore, we'll want to *persist* this data. We'll be using a tool called *Ebean* to save our objects to a database. Although other options are available, a database is the most common solution.

7.2.1 *About relational databases*

The term *database* deserves a little explanation. Although a database is technically any kind of data store, when developers say "database," they usually mean a *relational* database, which is a specific kind of database. I'm sure you've used one before, but here's a quick recap so we're on the same page.

The most defining aspect of relational databases is that they store their data in tables, which have columns of specific data types and contain rows of data. Contrary to what the name suggests, relational databases don't model relations between tables.[2]

---

[2] The name comes from the mathematical concept of *relations*, which we're just calling *tables*.

There are a few tricks that most databases implement to help cope with the lack of these relations. For example, you can enforce that the value of a certain column is present in another table's identifying column (its *primary key*), which you can use to keep your data consistent when using JOIN clauses while querying for data. This relationship isn't strong, however, because the records aren't *actually* linked together; it's a trick to look up data that's related. It happens to be a trick the database is optimized to perform.

An object hierarchy, on the other hand, *does have* relationships between its entities. One object can "have" other objects, and that relationship can go both ways (a warehouse has stock items, but a stock item has a warehouse as well). Another concept from the object-oriented world, which you generally won't find in a database, is *inheritance*. Inheritance is a different kind of relationship. Uniting these two different views on data structures is a challenge when using an object-oriented language with a relational database.

7.2.2 *Bridging the relational world and the OO world*

Although there are mismatches between the OO world and the relational world, it's not impossible to map objects to databases and vice versa. This process is called *Object-Relational Mapping (ORM)*. There are many tools that offer ORM for Java, but the standardized one is the Java Persistence API (JPA). Another well-known tool for this is Hibernate, and Hibernate can also serve as a JPA implementation. If you've done anything database-related in Java, you've probably used these, or you've at least heard of them.

> **Summarizing the relations between databases and object models**
>
> - (Relational) databases and object models are fundamentally different.
> - They can be mapped onto each other; this is called *Object-Relational Mapping*, or ORM.
> - The most common Java standard for this is JPA.
> - Because of some mismatches between Play and JPA, Play comes with Ebean instead (discussed later in this chapter).

JPA allows you to use annotations to specify the mapping of classes and fields to tables and columns, respectively. It also allows you to define relationships between classes. Any class mapped to the database is referred to as an *entity*, and we'll be using this term from now on. In addition to mapping entities, JPA also specifies an API for saving and updating entities, managing transactions, and querying the database for entities.

JPA has more or less become the default persistence API in the Java ecosystem, particularly in the JEE world. Although Play doesn't prevent you from using JPA and/or Hibernate (or any other persistence solution, for that matter), it isn't the default solution. This is because a big part of the JPA spec is based on managing entity state, such as across requests, which is something Play has no use for, due to its stateless nature. Instead Play comes with a different ORM framework: Ebean. Ebean is the default persistence solution for Play 2.0 and 2.1.

7.2.3 Introducing Ebean

Ebean is an ORM framework that takes a different approach to managing entities than most other ORM tools, such as JPA. The main difference—and this is what makes it a good match for Play—is that it has a *sessionless* API. Don't worry too much about what that means for now, but if you've used JPA before, you'll notice that you'll spend a lot less time on managing entity state. If you haven't used JPA before—congratulations, you won't ever have to worry about what it means to "refresh an entity," or what the difference is between "attached" entities and "detached" entities.

There's one aspect of JPA that Ebean borrows: the annotations for mapping entities. When using Ebean, you map entities exactly the same way as with JPA. Let's see how this works.

> **REUSE YOUR EXISTING JPA ENTITY CLASSES** Because Ebean uses regular JPA annotations, you can easily reuse existing model classes. This can be extremely useful when you're writing a Play version of an existing JEE application.

7.3 Mapping basic entities

> **SKIP AHEAD IF...** If you already know how to map entities using JPA, you could skip ahead to the next section. Take a look at the code samples to get up to speed with the data model.

When mapping classes to the database, you have to instruct the ORM tool, Ebean in this case, what data in the object model goes where in the database. You do this by mapping *classes* to *tables* and *fields* to *columns*. You also need to flag a class as an *entity*, telling the tool that this is a class you want to use as part of the data model you're mapping. We'll do all this using annotations from JPA (found in the `javax.persistence` package).

In addition to mapping the class, it's a good idea to let our entity class extend Play's `Model` class. The `Model` class will take some of the work off your hands, adding some convenience methods to the entity, which we'll discuss later in this chapter.

Anything stored in a database also needs some way to *identify* it. This is called its *primary key*. Although we could use a field on the entity that's guaranteed to be unique (this is called a *natural key*), such as the EAN field on our `Product` class, it's often considered good practice to have a field specifically for this purpose (called a *synthetic key*). Therefore, we'll introduce a `Long` field called `id` to our entities, and annotate it with `@Id` to indicate that we want to use it as the identifier for the class.

Let's start with the simplest case, one without relationships: the `Product` class. As you can see in figure 7.3, the class itself owns no relationships.

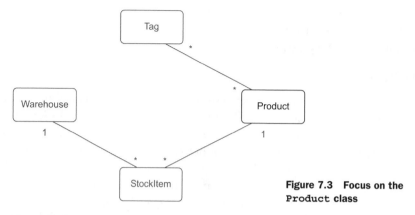

Figure 7.3   Focus on the Product class

To map the Product class like figure 7.3, make the changes as shown in listing 7.4.

Listing 7.4   Mapping the Product class

```
import javax.persistence.*;
import play.db.ebean.Model;

@Entity
public class Product extends Model {

        @Id
        public Long id;

        public Long ean;
        public String name;
        public String description;
        }
```

Add this annotation to flag this class as an entity

Extend Model class for convenience

Introduce the id field

… and that's all there is to it. We're going to try it out in a minute, but first, let's configure Play to use a database and tell Ebean where to look for entities.

7.3.1   Configuring Ebean and the database

We'll use H2, a lightweight DBMS that comes bundled with Play. The nice thing about H2 is that it has an "embedded" mode, which means it will load itself on demand, in the same JVM as Play runs in. It can also create databases in memory on demand, making it ideal for use during development, when you want to experiment with the database and don't care about the data being kept around.

Play's configuration contains default settings for using H2 and Ebean, but they're commented out because not all applications require persistence. Open up the file conf/application.conf in your application's directory, and find and uncomment the following lines:

```
db.default.driver=org.h2.Driver
db.default.url="jdbc:h2:mem:play"
db.default.user=sa

    ...

ebean.default="models.*"
```

Tell Play's DB system to use H2

Enable Ebean for our models package

Note that we're using the `db.default` namespace but we could have specified any other namespaces. Play supports connections to multiple databases. All you need to do is to specify different namespaces (such as `db.acceptance.driver`, `db.test.driver`, and so forth).

Before we test if everything works, let's review what we're doing. In the beginning of the chapter, we defined our data model using Java classes, which represent our real-world concepts in code. This allows us to build a representation of the warehouse state in the JVM memory. Now we want to store our data in something more durable; we want to *persist* it in a database. Where Java uses objects and method calls, databases store data in tables and are accessed through SQL. To bridge the gap between the Java and SQL worlds, we're *mapping* our classes to the database, using a kind of tool called ORM. Our ORM tool of choice is Ebean.

The database server (also called a DBMS) we'll use while developing our application is H2. This is because of the flexibility it offers, which is also the reason it comes bundled with Play. When moving your app to production, you're probably going to swap it out with another DBMS, such as MySQL, PostgreSQL, or Oracle, which are the most well-known options. Ebean has support for most major DBMSs, but if you're worried about compatibility, be sure to check the Ebean documentation.

Figure 7.4 illustrates the architecture we described.

Okay, now (re)load the page at http://localhost:9000/show, and see if it worked. Unfortunately, you'll probably see a page that looks like figure 7.5.

Whoa. What happened? Well, although it may not look like it, this is Play being helpful. When we defined a database connection, we told Play to connect to an H2 database, which will be automatically created upon connection.[3] But what was not automatically created was the database *schema*: that is, its structure—the tables and column definitions. Play generated an SQL script for that, and is now offering to run it for you. The script is located in the `conf/evolutions/default/1.sql` file. This is called database *evolution*, and we'll see later how this allows you to create incremental versions of your database schema. The *default* folder matches the database configuration we specified earlier. For now, go ahead and click *Apply this script now!* You should be greeted by the same default welcome page we saw back in figure 1.3.

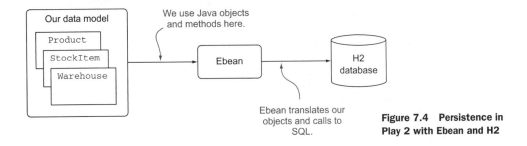

Figure 7.4 Persistence in Play 2 with Ebean and H2

---

[3] This is an H2 feature, not a Play feature. This will probably not happen with other DBMSs.

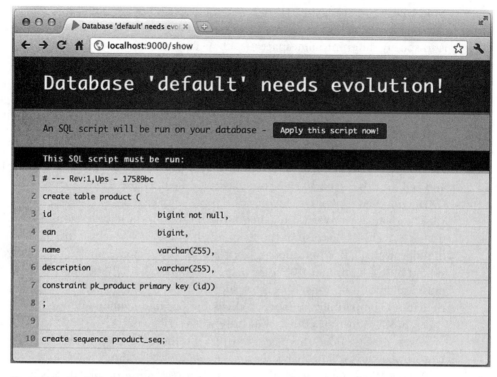

Figure 7.5   Play offering database evolution

7.3.2   *Inspecting the H2 database*

Presumably, we now have a database with a table in it. But how can we check? The H2
database comes with a web application that allows you to interact with the database
easily, called the *H2 console*. Play has made it easy to start this web application. To start
it, enter the h2-browser command on the Play console. Your browser should open on
the H2 browser page. If not, check your Play console; you should see output similar to
the following listing.

Listing 7.5   Starting the H2 console

```
[Warehouse] $ h2-browser
Web Console server running at http://192.168.1.191:8082
  (only local connections)
TCP server running at tcp://192.168.1.191:9092
  (only local connections)
PG server running at pg://192.168.1.191:5435
  (only local connections)
```

Copy the first URL from the output, and paste it into your web browser.

We can see the table here,
including its columns.

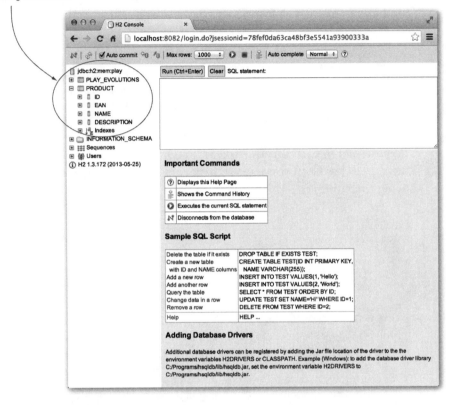

Figure 7.6   H2 console showing the database schema

The web application you now see is the H2 web console. It gives you a UI to the H2
database server. The default connection settings should be OK,[4] so click *Connect*. You
should see a page like that shown in figure 7.6.

If you look at the left side, you'll see our newly created product table, including the
columns we defined as properties in the `Product` entity class.

Now that we know we have a database with a table matching our entity's scheme,
let's put something in it.

7.3.3   *Saving our first entities*

Saving an entity is easy, because of the model class. We already have all the code we
need! We even have a little too much. The `save()` method we created in chapter 3 is
overriding the `save` method on the `Model` class. Go ahead and remove the `save`
method from the `Product` class.

---

[4] It should match the connection string in `application.conf`.

Now, as a reminder, here are the relevant parts of the `Products.save()` action method. This, as you'll remember, is the method responsible for saving `Product` instances from our web forms.

```
public static Result save() {
  ...
  Product product = boundForm.get();
  ...
  product.save();                          ❶ Call save() directly
  ...                                         on our instance
  return redirect(routes.Products.list());
}
```

Because we removed our own `save()` method, we're now using the one provided by the `Model` class ❶. If you wanted to, you could be more explicit about what exactly is doing the saving:

```
...
Product product = boundForm.get();
Ebean.save(product);

return redirect(routes.Products.list());
...
```

> ### Preventing model anemia
>
> The `Model` class provides some common database-related methods in an effort to prevent you from ending up with something Martin Fowler has dubbed an *Anemic Domain Model*.[5] An anemic domain model is a model that has no behavior (methods) or state (fields, data). This is often considered an anti-pattern, because the whole point of object-oriented programming is to couple behavior and state.
>
> By providing the database operations with the entity classes, it becomes possible to do a database operation *anywhere you have an entity instance*, without having to "hunt" for some other object or class that provides that functionality. It's important to remember that this doesn't have to stop with the behavior provided by the `Model` class. When aiming for rich model classes, it's a good idea to add any functionality that operates on your entities to the entity classes themselves, rather than to a controller or utility class.
>
> Ultimately, it's your choice whether you want a rich data model or one that serves as a container for data, but it's wise to make that choice consciously.

Now let's see if everything works as expected. Go to the "create product" form in your browser, at http://localhost:9000/products/new, and create a new product. Next, go to the H2 browser, and click the product table in the database. Next, click the *Run* button to execute a "select all" query on that table. The result should be one row, representing the product you persisted, as seen in figure 7.7.

---

[5] See http://www.martinfowler.com/bliki/AnemicDomainModel.html for more information.

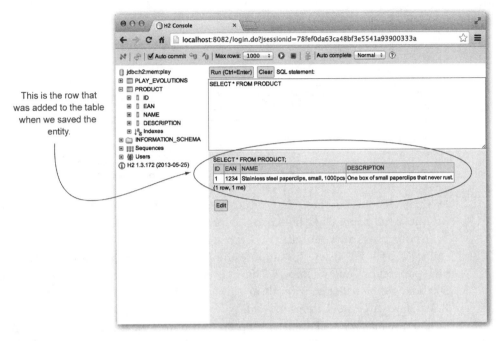

Figure 7.7   H2 console showing the contents of the product table

If everything seems to have worked, we can move on to the next entity, which will have a relation to the Product class we created.

7.4 *Mapping relationships*

Let's start working on our StockItem class. Figure 7.8 shows a reminder of its role in the model.

In our model, the StockItem class has two relationships: one to Product and one to Warehouse. Let's ignore the warehouse for now, and focus on the reference to

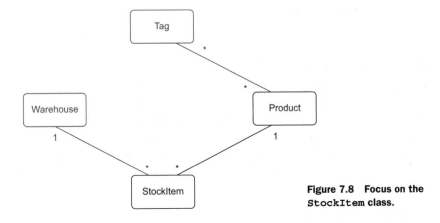

Figure 7.8   Focus on the StockItem class.

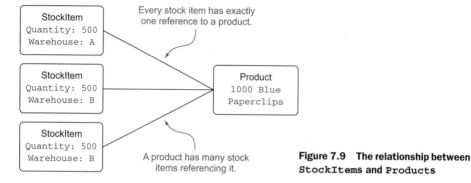

Figure 7.9 The relationship between StockItems and Products

Product. In our warehouse's product catalog, we'll store many[6] different kinds of products: red paper clips, blue paper clips, and so on.

In our physical warehouse, we'll store many batches of those products, which we call *stock items*. For example, suppose the product catalog has an entry "Box of 1000 blue paperclips," and we know we have three pallets of these paper clips, each holding 500 boxes. One pallet is currently in warehouse A, and the other two are in warehouse B. We have three stock items in total.

Each *individual* stock item will represent the stock of exactly *one* product from the product catalog. This means the stock items have a "many-to-one" relation to their product. The opposite is also true; each product is potentially referenced by *many* stock items, so the product has a "one-to-many" relationship to the stock items. This concept is illustrated in figure 7.9.

In a relational database, a one-to-many relationship is usually modeled as a column on the "many" side (in this case, the stock item) pointing to the ID of a record on the "one" side (such as the product). Whenever a stock item is retrieved from the database, that ID can be used to retrieve the correct row from the product table, if needed. The ID used to point to the primary key of another table is called a *foreign key*. This is illustrated in figure 7.10.

7.4.1 *Mapping a one-to-many relationship*

Now let's map the StockItem class. Add the @Entity annotation to the StockItem class, have it extend Model, and give it an id field. In the previous example, the Product class, we didn't add any annotations to the fields of the class. This is because all its fields can be stored in the database directly; there's no relationship involved. In the StockItem class, we have only one such field: the quantity field, which is a Long that maps neatly to the SQL number type, which Ebean can automatically map.

The other fields are our own Product and Warehouse classes. We need to tell Ebean that they are references to other entities, and *what kind* of relationships they have. Let's focus on the StockItem for now. As we saw before, StockItem has a *many-to-one*

---

[6] Let's assume "many" means "more than one."

stock_item		
id	product_id	quantity
1	1	500
2	1	500
3	1	500

The product_id column links the stock items to a product using the product's ID.

Product			
id	ean	name	description
1	1234567891231	1000 Blue paperclips	These blue paperclips...
2	1234567891232	1000 Red paperclips	These red paperclips...
3	1234567891233	1000 Green paperclips	These green paperclips...
4	1234567891234	1000 Yellow paperclips	These yellow paperclips...

Figure 7.10 The one-to-many database relationship

relationship to `Product`. Therefore, we flag this field with the `@ManyToOne` JPA annotation, as shown in the following listing.

Listing 7.6 Mapping the `StockItem–Product` many-to-one relationship

```
import javax.persistence.ManyToOne;

@Entity
public class StockItem extends Model {

  public Warehouse warehouse;          ← Ignore this relation for now; we'll map it later

  @ManyToOne
  public Product product;
  public Long quantity;
}
```

Time to persist our product, this time including its `StockItem` member. We'll assume that when we create a product, it isn't present yet in the warehouse, so we'll create a `StockItem` with a quantity of 0. In our `Products.save()` method, create a `StockItem`, and call the `save()` method on it. See the following listing.

Listing 7.7 Saving the `StockItem` and its relationship

```
...
StockItem item = new StockItem();
item.quantity = 0L;
item.product = product;

product.save();
item.save();          ←— Add this line
...
```

Reload a page in the browser, and Play will offer to update your database for you. Go ahead and apply the update.

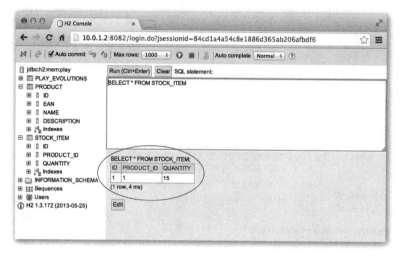

Figure 7.11   Looking at the stock item table in the H2 console

BE CAREFUL WHEN APPLYING EVOLUTIONS ON PRODUCTION DATABASES   Play's evolution mechanism checks your database schema against the schema it expects, and offers to make changes to the database if the two don't match. This can involve removing columns or even entire tables, causing *loss of data*. Be careful when applying evolutions on a database that has data you care about!

When we create a new product, we should also have a new table for our stock items, containing a single row with the stock item we saved. Let's check it out in the H2 console; you should see results similar to figure 7.11.

Now that we've seen how to map a one-to-many relationship, what about the other side, many-to-one? Well, the Product class is a good candidate for this. When we have an instance of StockItem, we can already tell what product it's for. But when we have a Product, we can't tell which stock items reference it. To do this, we have to make the relationship *bidirectional*.

7.4.2   *Making the one-to-many relationship bidirectional*

Mapping the "many" side of a bidirectional many-to-one relationship doesn't affect anything in the database; the information about the relationship is already stored in the table that makes up the "one" side of the relationship (see figure 7.12).

warehouse				Address					
id	name	address_id		id	street	number	postalcode	city	country
1	Warehouse A	1		1	Heemraadssingel	70	3021DD	Rotterdam	Netherlands
2	Warehouse B	2		2	Rue Traibout	64	75009	Paris	France
3	Warehouse C	3		3	Sand Hill Rd	2550	94025	Menlo Park	United States

Figure 7.12   A one-to-many database relationship

This means that all you need to do to retrieve stock items belonging to a certain product is write a query to include the stock items that have the product's ID stored in their *product_id* column.

Let's tell Ebean how to retrieve the `StockItem` objects. First, we need a field to store these in, so add a `List<StockItem>` field to the `Product` class. All we need to do now is mark it as a *one-to-many* relation, as we did with the many-to-one field on `StockItem`: annotate it with `@OneToMany`. Because the `StockItem` class is the side that persists the relationship, we need to indicate what property on the `StockItem` class holds the relationship we're mapping. We do this using the `mappedBy` attribute on the annotation, as in the following listing.

Listing 7.8 Making the `Product–StockItem` relationship bidirectional

```
import javax.persistence.*;
...

@Entity
public class Product extends Model {

  @Id
  public Long id;
  public Long ean;
  public String name;
  public String description;

  @OneToMany(mappedBy="product")
  public List<StockItem> stockItems;
}
```

Now whenever you retrieve a `Product` instance from the database, you'll have access to its `stockItems` as well.

The relationship between `Warehouse` and `StockItem` is another example of a one-to-many relationship. Let's go ahead and implement it as in the listings ahead. The `StockItem` class should look like the following listing.

Listing 7.9 `StockItem.java`

```
import javax.persistence.*;
...

@Entity
public class StockItem extends Model {

  @Id
  public Long id;

  @ManyToOne
  public Warehouse warehouse;

  @ManyToOne
  public Product product;

  public Long quantity;

}
```

And the `Warehouse` class should look like the following listing.

Listing 7.10 `Warehouse.java`

```java
import javax.persistence.*;
...

@Entity
public class Warehouse {

  @Id
  public Long id;

  public String name;

  @OneToMany(mappedBy = "warehouse")
  public List<StockItem> stock = new ArrayList<>();

  @Override
  public String toString() {
    return name;
  }
}
```

Our `Warehouse` class doesn't store a lot of information about the warehouse. Let's do something about that.

7.4.3 *Giving our warehouse an address*

Let's add a little more information to our warehouse. We need to know where on the planet it is, so that we know where our items are: we need an address. We could add a bunch of properties to the warehouse class, like in the following listing.

Listing 7.11 Adding address properties to `Warehouse`

```java
@Entity
public class Warehouse {

  @Id
  public Long id;

      public String name;

      public String street;
      public String number;          ┐ Together, these
      public String postalCode;        properties form
      public String city;            ┘ an address
      public String country;

      @OneToMany
      public List<StockItem> stock = new ArrayList<StockItem>();
}
```

Although this would solve our problem, it also adds a lot of properties to the `Warehouse` class that make up a single property of the warehouse: its address. Therefore, it's nicer to give the address its own class. Create the `Address` class as in the following listing.

Listing 7.12 `Address.java`

```
public class Address {

  public Warehouse warehouse;

      public String street;
      public String number;
      public String postalCode;
      public String city;
      public String country;

}
```

And then add an `address` property to the `Warehouse` class, as in the following listing.

Listing 7.13 `Warehouse.java`

```
@Entity
public class Warehouse {

  @Id
  public Long id;

      public String name;                     The address is neatly
                                              encapsulated in its
      public Address address;              ◁── own class

      @OneToMany
      public List<StockItem> stock = new ArrayList<StockItem>();
      }
```

Figure 7.13 shows these classes in a diagram.

Now to map this new relationship. The classes `Warehouse` and `Address` have a *one-to-one* relationship: a warehouse has exactly one address, and an address belongs to exactly one warehouse. When looking at the database, a one-to-one relationship is indistinguishable from a one-to-many relationship; it's mapped by a foreign key column on one table, pointing to the primary key column on another table, as illustrated in figure 7.14.

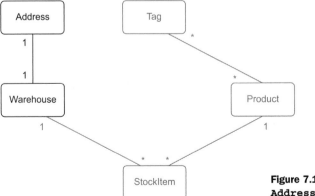

Figure 7.13 The `Warehouse` and `Address` classes in the data model

warehouse			Address					
id	name	address_id	id	street	number	postalcode	city	country
1	Warehouse A	1	1	Heemraadssingel	70	3021DD	Rotterdam	Netherlands
2	Warehouse B	2	2	Rue Traibout	64	75009	Paris	France
3	Warehouse C	3	3	Sand Hill Rd	2550	94025	Menlo Park	United States

Figure 7.14 A one-to-many database relationship

But there's a decision to be made while mapping a one-to-one relationship: we need to pick the *owning side* of the relationship. When we mapped the many-to-one relationship, it was clear that the table on the "many" side had to point to the primary key on the "one" side. It's impossible to do it the other way around, because a database field may not contain multiple values. In the case of a many-to-one relationship, we call the "many" side the *owning* side of the relationship; it's the side where the relationship is stored.

In the case of a one-to-one relationship, it's unclear what the owning side should be; both sides are capable of storing the relationship. Therefore, *we* have to indicate which side gets to be the owning side. When the relationship is unidirectional (say, on the warehouse only), it's sufficient to mark the field in question with the @OneToOne annotation. When the relationship goes both ways, the fields on both sides should be mapped with @OneToOne. To indicate which side is the owning side, add the mappedBy parameter to point at the owning field. After we map our classes, they look like this:

Listing 7.14 `Warehouse.java`

```
@Entity
public class Warehouse {

  @Id
  public Long id;

  public String name;

  @OneToMany
  public List<StockItem> stock = new ArrayList<StockItem>();

  @OneToOne
  public Address address;

}
```

Listing 7.15 `Address.java`

```
@Entity
public class Address {

  @Id
  public Long id;

  @OneToOne(mappedBy="address")
  public Warehouse warehouse;
```

```
    public String street;
    public String number;
    public String postalCode;
    public String city;
    public String country;
}
```

In this case, we've picked the `Warehouse` class as the owning side of the relationship. In the database, the relation between `Warehouse` and `Address` is stored as shown in figure 7.15.

Go ahead and create and persist a few warehouses with addresses, and check the database to see if everything goes as planned. Everything works the same as with the one-to-many relationships.

> **ALWAYS SET BOTH SIDES OF A RELATIONSHIP** To make sure a relationship between two entities is persisted, it's always sufficient to set the field on the owning side of the relationship, and persist the owning entity. If the relationship is bidirectional, the other entity in the relationship is now *inconsistent*; it might still be pointing at the entity it previously had a relationship to, or it might not be aware of its new relationship. Therefore it's best to always set both sides of the relationship.

Now there's one more relationship we have to map: that between `Product` and `Tag`.

7.4.4 Mapping the product–tag relationship

Let's look at our `Product` and `Tag` classes. Figure 7.16 shows where they fit in the data model.

In our situation, a single employee has access to many tags. This also means that a particular tag could be linked to many products. In our Java class hierarchy, this is represented by two `List`s: a `List<Product>` on `Tag`, and a `List<Tag>` on `Product`. You can see this in listings 7.16 and 7.17.

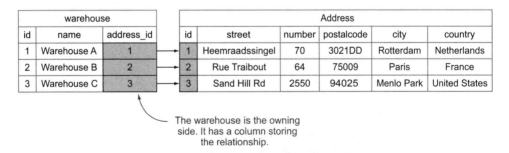

warehouse				Address					
id	name	address_id		id	street	number	postalcode	city	country
1	Warehouse A	1		1	Heemraadssingel	70	3021DD	Rotterdam	Netherlands
2	Warehouse B	2		2	Rue Traibout	64	75009	Paris	France
3	Warehouse C	3		3	Sand Hill Rd	2550	94025	Menlo Park	United States

The warehouse is the owning side. It has a column storing the relationship.

Figure 7.15 A one-to-one database relationship

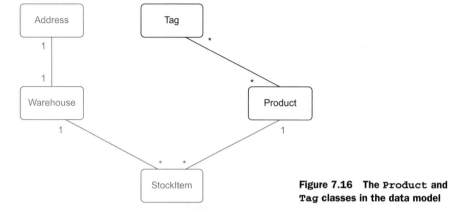

Figure 7.16 The Product and Tag classes in the data model

Listing 7.16 Tag

```
@Entity
public class Tag {

  @Id
  public Long id;

  public String name;

  public List<Product> products;
}
```

Listing 7.17 Product.java

```
@Entity
public class Product extends Model {

  @Id
  public Long id;
  public Long ean;
  public String name;
  public String description;

  @OneToMany(mappedBy="product")
  public List<StockItem> stockItems;

  public List<Tag> tags;
}
```

Because both sides of the relationship can contain many instances of the other side, this type of relationship is called a *many-to-many* relationship. There's a problem when we want to map this relationship to the database: because there's no way to store multiple values in a single database column, and both sides are many-valued, there is no place to store a foreign key to store the relationship.

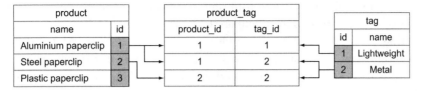

Figure 7.17   A many-to-many database relationship

The answer is adding an extra table to store all the relationships between our two entities. This looks like figure 7.17.

Time to map our Java classes. The annotation to map many-to-many relationships is @ManyToMany. Because we're mapping a bidirectional relationship, we also need to designate one side as the owning side and tell the other side which property is the owning property, using the mappedBy attribute like before.

```
@Entity
public class Product {

    ...

    @ManyToMany
    public List<Tag> tags;

    ...

}

@Entity
public class Tag {

    ...

    @ManyToMany(mappedBy="tags")
    public List<Product> products;

    ...

}
```

It's important to note that any changes in this relationship are *only* saved when the *owning* side is saved: Product, in this case.

Now that we have our entire data model mapped to the database, let's see how to retrieve objects from the database. This is called *querying* the database.

7.5   *Querying for objects*

As Java developers, we don't *want* to write SQL queries to retrieve our data from the database. We know it's what's used to communicate with the database, but we don't want to deal with messy, untyped string concatenation. We'd rather use some nice, object-oriented, type-safe APIs to express what we want to do. Luckily, that's what Ebean provides.

We've already seen some of this kind of functionality when we were saving objects to the database; whenever we call save(), what happens behind the scenes is that

Ebean translates this method call into one or more SQL INSERT statements, which is how you store a new record in a database table using SQL.

Next, we want to do a similar thing for *querying* the database: ask the database for data, based on some criteria. In the most simple case, query the database for an object based on its ID. This is something you'd do when you know exactly what object you want to access.

Now we're going to be querying our database for some test data, so we'd best have something interesting in it. If you're in a DIY mood, go ahead and create and persist a few object hierarchies with some interesting test data. If you're feeling lazy, like all good programmers, you could switch to the application for this chapter from our sample code archive. We've set it up so it preloads a bunch of test data using the evolutions mechanism. Run the application, and it will populate the database on the first request.

We should now have a nice batch of test data loaded into our database. Let's get to work.

7.5.1   *Retrieving by ID*

Let's retrieve a Product based on ID. We should have one in our database by now, so let's look at the H2 console to find an ID for the product we saved last. Open the H2 console, and click the product table. It will populate the text area on the right side of the window with an SQL query that selects all rows from the product table. Click *Run* and look at the results. Note the ID for the last row; in our examples we'll be assuming it's 1.

Okay, now to use the database. Finding an entity based on its ID is so common that Ebean has a dedicated static method for it: Ebean.find(clazz, id). As you can tell from the parameters, all we need to tell it is the class of the object we want to find (Product) and its ID (1). In our case, we're looking up products based on their EAN numbers. Let's see how we can do a database lookup using the EAN number.

7.5.2   *Using the Finder API*

Remember how, in section 7.3.3, we added the save() method to the Product class itself, by extending the Model class? Wouldn't it be nicer to have that for find() as well? It would be trivial to add a static method to the Product class that delegates to the Ebean.find() method, but Play already provides an even better option for you: the Model.Finder class, which provides a complete querying API for any entity.

You'll need to instantiate it, so let's add a field to the Product class to obtain a Finder instance for Products. Add the following method to the Product class:

```
public class Product extends Model {
...
  public static Finder<Long, Product> find =
    new Finder<>(Long.class, Product.class);

...
}
```

As you can see, the constructor for `Finder` takes two parameters, both `Class` objects. The first parameter tells the `Finder` what type the ID field for the entity is, and the second parameter is the type of the entity we want to query for. We can use the find object to look up our products by their ID:

```
Product.find.byId(1L);
```

Moreover, we'll use our find object to look up products based on their EAN numbers.

If you remember chapter 6, we implemented our `Product` object lookup based on the EAN product number. The following listing shows the relevant code in the `Product` model class.

Listing 7.18   Our current `Product` model class EAN lookup

```
...
import play.mvc.PathBindable;                                    Tell Play that we're
import play.libs.F.Option;                                       defining a new Binder
                                                                 to bind URL paths
public class Product implements PathBindable<Product> {   ◁

  ...

  @Override                                                      Binding—look in the DB
  public Product bind(String key, String value) {               for a product with an EAN
    return findByEan(value);                                     number equal to the one
  }                                                        ◁     passed in our URL

  @Override
  public String unbind(String key) {             Unbinding—return
    return this.ean;                             our raw value
  }                                         ◁

  @Override
  public String javascriptUnbind() {             JavaScript unbinding—
    return this.ean;                             return our raw value
  }                                         ◁

}
```

As you can see, all we're left to do is to provide a correct implementation for the `findByEan` method. Our new implementation is shown in the following listing.

Listing 7.19   Updated `findByEan` implementation

```
public class Product {
  ...                                                            Database lookup to
  public static Product findByEan(String ean) {                 find product based
    return find.where().eq("ean", ean).findUnique();   ◁        on EAN
  }
  ...
}
```

The findByEan method implementation is pretty straightforward. We're issuing a database query to select the unique product where an EAN number matches the one given as an argument.

Save all files, and load http://localhost:9000/details/111111111111 in your browser. You should see the information for the product you saved earlier.

The controller save() action method from our Products controller needs to slightly change, because we now need to differentiate when creating and updating a new product. The following listing shows the new implementation.

Listing 7.20 New save() implementation

```
public static Result save() {
    MultipartFormData body = request().body().asMultipartFormData();
    Form<Product> boundForm = productForm.bindFromRequest();
    if(boundForm.hasErrors()) {
      flash("error", "Please correct the form below.");
      return badRequest(details.render(boundForm));
    }
    Product product = boundForm.get();
    MultipartFormData.FilePart part = body.getFile("picture");
    if(part != null) {
      File picture = part.getFile();
      try {
        product.picture = Files.toByteArray(picture);
      } catch (IOException e) {
        return internalServerError("Error reading file upload");
      }
    }

    List<Tag> tags = new ArrayList<Tag>();
    for (Tag tag : product.tags) {
      if (tag.id != null) {
        tags.add(Tag.findById(tag.id));
      }
    }
    product.tags = tags;
    if (product.id == null) {            ⟵ Check if it's a newly
      product.save();                        created product
    } else {                             ⟵── Create product
      product.update();
    }                                    ⟵── Update product
    flash("success",
      String.format("Successfully added product %s", product));
    return redirect(routes.Products.list(1));
  }
```

The new implementation checks if it's a new product. If it's a new product, the product doesn't have a database ID yet. We therefore use the save() method to create the product. If the product has an ID, we use the update() method.

Because we're now using the product ID, we also need to update our details.scala.html template to reflect that fact. In our form, add the following input field:

```
@helper.form(action = routes.Products.save()
                , 'enctype -> "multipart/form-data") {
  ...
<input type="hidden"
    value="@productForm("id").valueOr("")" name="id"/>
  ...
}
```

This hidden input field, which we added in chapter 6, is used to pass on the product ID to our controller from our view and vice versa. It also means that the ID field is empty for new products, since the id property is not present then.

Save all files, and load http://localhost:9000/product/new in your browser.

Fill in the information to create a new product and observe that you have created a new product without specifying a tag. Now update that same product and you'll see the updated product, still without a tag. We'll look at how to deal with tags in the next section.

In any case, we won't be needing the mock data store anymore, so go ahead and delete the set of products, the static initializer, and the remove() method from the Product model class.

Change the delete() action method from the Products controller to call the product.delete() method:

```
public static Result delete(String ean) {
    ...
    product.delete();
    return redirect(routes.Products.list(1));
}
```

We can also clean up the Tag model class a little. Go ahead and remove the static data store and its initializer. The findById() method will break, so reimplement it to use the database:

```
public class Tag extends Model {

  public static Finder<Long, Tag> find() =
    new Finder<>(Long.class, Tag.class);

  public static Tag findById(Long id) {
    return find().byId(id);
  }
...
}
```

As you can see, we added the find object for Tag as well. We're going to need a find() method on all of our entities soon, so go ahead and add one to the StockItem and Warehouse classes, too.

In our current application, after an application restart, you probably noticed that updating tags on products doesn't work anymore and that you get an error. This is because we're referencing Tag objects that don't exist in the database anymore but are referenced by our view.

7.5.3 *Loading initial data*

We have established that we need to load data at application startup. Play allows you to load data in two ways:

- Evolution scripts
- `onStart()` method on the `Global` Java class called at application startup and a YAML data file

EVOLUTION SCRIPTS

We have seen in section 7.3.1 that Play generates a database script to create our schema. All we need to do then is to add data to this script. Another alternative is to create a file called `2.sql` in the `conf/evolutions/default/` directory and to add an SQL insert to add our data at application startup. An evolution SQL script has a specific format as the following listing shows.

Listing 7.21 Evolution script structure

```
# --- Initialize tags

# --- !Ups                                          ◁──┐ Ups: SQL script
insert into tag(id,name) values (1, 'lightweight');     │ that is applied at
insert into tag(id,name) values (2, 'metal');           │ application startup
insert into tag(id,name) values (3, 'plastic');

# --- !Downs                                        ◁──┐ Downs: SQL script
                                                        │ that is applied at
SET REFERENTIAL_INTEGRITY FALSE;                        │ application shutdown

delete from tag;
```

Evolution scripts are used to create database schemas and to populate initial data to your application. They are also used to perform schema updates between different versions of your application. Evolution scripts contains two parts: SQL that is executed at application startup and SQL that is executed at application shutdown.

Evolution scripts are called *sequentially* (`1.sql`, `2.sql`, and so on); at application startup the SQL defined in the *Ups* section is applied, and at application shutdown the `Downs` section is applied.

You can easily prepopulate your database with existing products by adding SQL insert statements in your evolution script in the *Ups* section.

YAML DATA FILE

We have seen in chapter 6 section 6.2.3 that Play provides a way to include custom code during application startup using the `onStart()` method of the `Global` class. This class is instantiated automatically and the `onStart()` method is called when our application is starting.

We will use this same technique to load a file that contains our tag catalog. Our catalog will be written in YAML. *YAML* is a human-friendly data serialization standard for all programming languages.

Edit the file `Global.java` located in the `app` directory and modify the `onStart()` method as shown in the following listing.

Listing 7.22 The new `onStart()` method on the `Global` class

```
...
import com.avaje.ebean.*;
import models.*;

public class Global extends GlobalSettings {
...
  public void onStart(Application app) {
  ...
  InitialData.insert(app);
  }
  static class InitialData {
    public static void insert(Application app) {           If we have no tags
      if(Ebean.find(Tag.class).findRowCount() == 0) {  ◁─┘ in the database...
      Map<String,List<Object>> all =
        (Map<String,List<Object>>)Yaml.
                        load("initial-data.yml");    ◁   ...load the
      Ebean.save(all.get("tags"));        ◁─┐             data from the
      }                                     │             initial-data.yml file
    }                              Insert our tags
  }                                in the database
 }
}
```

The `InitialData.insert()` method is straightforward: we insert our data in the database if the data isn't yet there. Play provides a utility class to load the YAML file, making it extra easy. It's now time to create our YAML file. Create an `initial-data.yml` file in the `conf` directory. Play by default makes the `conf` directory part of the classpath. It means that files located in this directory can be loaded without specifying their full path. The `initial-data.yml` content is shown in the following listing.

Listing 7.23 The `initial-data.yml` file

```
tags:

    - !!models.Tag
        id:         1
        name:       lightweight

    - !!models.Tag
        id:         2
        name:       metal

    - !!models.Tag
        id:         3
        name:       plastic
```

Please note that the file doesn't contain tabs, but spaces. The spaces and the punctuation before are important. Using the file we're defining a `tags` collection that contains a `model.Tag` object. Each object contains an `id` and a `name`. The `tags` collection is referenced and saved through Ebean with the following line:

```
Ebean.save(all.get("tags"));
```

We know how to load initial data at application startup, which is pretty useful. You can now safely tag products, as the tags are now referenced in the database. You'll now need more powerful ways to query the database. Let's see what else Ebean and the Finder class have to offer.

7.5.4 *Creating more complex queries*

Databases are good at *searching* for data on any criteria you want. As mentioned before, SQL is the language used when searching for data in an RDBMS. A downside of SQL when used in an object-oriented environment is that it's based on a relational view of the world; it's not compatible with object-oriented programming, which is the whole point of our ORM exercise.

JPA and Hibernate (and some other solutions) get around this issue by defining a different query language, which looks a lot like SQL but allows you to query classes and objects rather than database tables and columns.

Creating queries like that using Java would mean using strings to form them. If we want to compose a query dynamically, which is an OO sort of thing to do, we'd need to concatenate strings; things would get messy and confusing fast, which means our code would get hard to read or, worse, buggy. Working with strings is not something you want to do; among other things, it's tedious, messy, and error-prone, and the compiler can't help us at all. It's not nice to do in a type-safe world.

An alternative to constructing database queries is a *criteria*-based API. A criteria-based API allows you to use object composition to construct a query object that will construct and execute an SQL query for you. This means you don't have to deal with messy strings; you get to construct objects to tell the database what you want instead. Let's see how that works.

> **WE'LL STOP SHOWING YOU TWO APIS NOW**   Until now, we've been showing you how to use both the Ebean API and Play's Finder class. From this point forward, we'll stop showing you both and use only the Finder. Everything you can do through the Finder class you can do through Ebean directly, so if you prefer to do things that way, read through the Ebean documentation to learn how to do things using the Ebean API. It's not particularly different, and the concept is exactly the same.

When querying the database, you specify the following *clauses*:

- *What* data you want
- One or more *criteria* that data must satisfy
- The *order* of the data
- *How much* data you want (that is, pagination)

Not all of these parts are required. If you omit any of these clauses, defaults are used instead. Here's an example query, in plain English, that we could ask the database:

- Give me all StockItems...
- ... that have a *quantity of 300 or more...*

- … with *higher quantities first…*
- … but *ten* items is enough.

Using the Ebean API, a query is constructed exactly like this—clause by clause. Let's build up this example query. First, add the following `toString()` to the `StockItem` class, so that stock items are a little easier to identify when we print objects later:

```
public class StockItem {
  ...
  public String toString() {
    return String.format("StockItem %d - %dx product %s",
        id, quantity, product == null ? null : product.id);
  }
}
```

We need a point of entry for our code to run. This is a good time to create a new controller, `StockItems`. Go ahead and create it, as we created `Products` back in chapter 3. Also add an `index()` action method, and create a route to it, so you can access it at the `/stockitems/` URL. The following listing shows our class and method.

Listing 7.24 `StockItems` controller, `/app/controllers/StockItems.java`

```
package controllers;

import play.mvc.*

public class StockItems extends Controller {

  public static Result index() {
    return TODO;
  }
}
```

And here is the route line:

```
GET    /stockitems/              controllers.StockItems.index()
```

Now we'll use our new action method, `StockItem.index()`, to run our code. Start off with the following query:

```
public class StockItems extends Controller {

  public static Result index() {
    List<StockItem> items = StockItem.find().findList();      The query is
    return ok(items.toString());                              executed here
  }
}
```

Here, we're executing a query and rendering the results as text. In this query, we've only told the database *what* we want to find: `StockItems`. We did that when we instantiated the `Finder` object, by passing in the `StockItem` class. Listing 7.25 shows a reminder.

> **Listing 7.25   The `find` method on `StockItem`**

```
...
public static Finder<Long, Product> find() {
  return new Finder<Long, Product>(Long.class, Product.class);     ⟵
  }
...
```
**Construct a Finder that finds
StockItem objects**

When we run this code, we'll get a complete list of all stock items in the database. Go ahead and load http://localhost:9000/stockitems/ in your browser. You'll see output similar to this:

```
StockItem 1 - 300x product 1
StockItem 2 - 200x product 1
StockItem 3 - 500x product 1
```

FILTERING OUR SELECTION

Let's see what the next clause in the English version of our query is:

- Give me all *StockItems*...
- ... *that have a quantity of 300 or more*...
- ... with *higher quantities first*...
- ... but *ten* items is enough.

We want to add *criteria* to our query to narrow the list of results down to the objects we're interested in. To do this, we'll use the `where()` method on our `Finder` objects, followed by the criteria we want our results to match.

In this case, we want to specify a "greater than or equal" criterion, which we can do with the `ge()` method. The criterion needs to know two things: what field it applies to, and what its target value is. We want to apply it to the `quantity` field, and the target value is 300, so we pass those values in. Our method now looks like this:

```
public static Result index() {

  List<StockItem> items = StockItem.find()
      .where()
      .ge("quantity", 300)
      .findList();

  return ok(items);
}
```

Reload the page in the browser, and the list should now only contain stock items with quantities of 300 or more:

```
StockItem 1 - 300x product 1
StockItem 3 - 500x product 1
```

Many more criteria are available; browse the documentation for the Ebean `Query` class for a full list.

Let's see what's next for our query:

- Give me all *StockItems*...
- ... that have a *quantity of 300 or more*...
- ... *with higher quantities first*...
- ... but *ten* items is enough.

The list is now more or less randomly ordered. Well, it's sorted by ID, but because we didn't specify an order, the database is free to return items in any order it wants. Never trust in the default sort behavior; it might change if you switch database vendors (like when taking your app to production).

ORDERING

Let's specify an order clause. This is done using the orderBy method, specifying the field we want to order on: quantity, in our case.

```
public static Result index() {

  List<StockItem> items = StockItem.find()
      .where()
      .ge("quantity", 300)
      .orderBy("quantity")
      .findList();

  return ok(items);
}
```

Refresh the page, and our list should be ordered now:

```
StockItem 3 - 500x product 1 StockItem 1 - 300x product 1
```

There's one more thing to add to our query:

- Give me all *StockItems*...
- ... that have a *quantity of 300 or more*...
- ... with *higher quantities first*...
- ... *but ten items is enough.*

The list of results can get big, so let's get the first ten items. We need to set the maximum number of results, using the setMaxRows() method:

```
public static Result index() {

  List<StockItem> items = StockItem.find()
      .where()
      .ge("quantity", 300)
      .orderBy("quantity")
      .setMaxRows(10)
      .findList();

  return ok(items);
}
```

Reload the page, and our list should be trimmed:

```
StockItem 3 - 500x product 1
```

Using the `setMaxRows()` method, we can implement *pagination*: splitting a big list of data over multiple pages. Using `setMaxRows()`, we determine how many items we want, but not where to start. The database will therefore always return the *first* set of items. If we want to request the second page of data, we can use the `setFirstRow()` method to specify where we want to start.

Using these two methods, one could implement pagination. Ebean makes it even easier and doesn't require you to calculate the pagination parameters. Let's see that in more detail.

PAGINATION

Table pagination is a feature that most web applications require. It's easy to perform using Ebean. Let's take our product listing as an example. Right now, our `Products` controller is calling the `findAll()` method on our `Product` object model. Let's define a `find()` method that takes a page number as an argument, as shown in listing 7.26.

Listing 7.26 `find()` method with pagination support

```
public static Page<Product> find(int page) {        ◁──  Find page now returns
    return                                                a Page object
            find.where()
                .orderBy("id asc")          ◁── Order by ID ascending
                .findPagingList(10)         ◁── Define size of page
                .setFetchAhead(false)       ◁──  Do we need to pre-fetch data?
                .getPage(page);             ◁── The current page number, start at 0
    }
```

This query paginates all products and will return a maximum of 10 products ordered by ID. It offsets the results according to the `page` parameter. We now need to change our `Product` controller `list()` method as follows:

```
public static Result list(Integer page) {
    Page<Product> products = Product.find(page);
    return ok(list.render(products));
}
```

And because we now pass to our `list.scala.html` view a `Page` object, we need to slightly change it as well. The following listing shows the relevant changes.

Listing 7.27 list.scala.html view

```
@(currentPage: com.avaje.ebean.Page[Product])    ◁──  Pass the Page object as an
...                                                    argument to our template
<tbody>
    @for(product <- currentPage.getList()) {     ◁──  Return current list of
        <tr>                                          products for current page
...
    </tr>
    }
...
<div id="pagination" class="pagination">
    <ul>                                         ◁──  Handy method to
    @if(currentPage.hasPrev) {                        determine if we have
                                                      a previous page
```

```
      <li class="prev">
       <a
href="@routes.Products.list(currentPage.getPageIndex-1)">
&larr; </a>
      </li>
    } else {
      <li class="prev disabled">
       <a>&larr;</a>
      </li>
    }
    <li class="current">
       <a>@currentPage.getDisplayXtoYofZ(" - "," / ")</a>
    </li>
    @if(currentPage.hasNext) {
       <li class="next">
        <a
href="@routes.Products.list(currentPage.getPageIndex+1)">
 &rarr;</a>
       </li>
      } else {
       <li class="next disabled">
         <a>&rarr;</a>
       </li>
      }
    </ul>
</div>
...
```

Link to our previous page (current page index -I)

Method to display current page and total number of pages

Method to determine if we have a next page

Link to our next page (current page index+I)

As you probably noticed, the Page object contains useful methods that make pagination child's play. Those methods are used in our view to link to the next and previous pages.

7.6   Using JPA instead of Ebean

When developing a new application, you should definitely consider using Ebean; it's a better match for Play, given its stateless and explicit nature. But there are a few good reasons to use JPA instead. For example, you might be more familiar with it, or have legacy code you want to include, or you might just think it's cooler. Play won't stop you. In fact, Play is even nice enough to include supporting features for it. We won't go into the details of using JPA with Play (you're probably already familiar with it, if you decide you want to use it). Here's how you can set up your JPA app to use Play.

7.6.1   Configuring Play

There are two steps to enabling JPA support in Play: exposing the data source to JNDI and adding JPA dependencies to the dependencies list.

First, open up your application.conf file, and add database configuration as usual (see section 7.3.1). Also add the jndiName property to your database configuration, and configure a default persistence unit name for JPA like so:

```
db.default.driver=org.h2.Driver
db.default.url="jdbc:h2:mem:play"A
```

```
db.default.jndiName=DefaultDS
jpa.default=defaultPersistenceUnit
```

Remember what JNDI name and persistence unit name you use; you'll need these when you define the persistence unit (next section). Also, if you've already enabled Ebean, be sure to remove or comment out all lines starting with ebean to disable it again.

Next, we're going to switch out the Play Ebean module for Play's JPA module. Open up project/Build.scala, and replace javaEbean with javaJpa, so that the appDependencies list looks like the following listing.

Listing 7.28 JPA appDependencies

```
val appDependencies = Seq(
  javaCore,
  javaJdbc,
  javaJpa
)
```

The only thing left to do is to add a dependency on our JPA implementation. Hibernate is a good choice if you're looking for one, but you're free to pick any JPA implementation you want. Find the artifact ID for your implementation of choice, and add it to the dependencies list. Here's the example for Hibernate:

```
val appDependencies = Seq(
  javaCore,
  javaJdbc,
  javaJpa,
  "org.hibernate" % "hibernate-entitymanager" % "3.6.9.Final"
)
```

When you next start your application, JPA will be available. You still need to configure JPA itself; it needs a persistence unit, as usual.

7.6.2 *Adding Persistence.xml*

There are no special steps needed to configure JPA for a Play application. Like with all JPA projects, JPA requires a persistence unit, declared in persistence.xml. In Play, you need to put this file in the conf/META-INF directory. Listing 7.29 shows an example persistence.xml file, to correspond to the H2 DefaultDS data source we configured in the previous section.

Listing 7.29 persistence.xml

```
<persistence xmlns="http://java.sun.com/xml/ns/persistence"
  xmlns:xsi="http://www.w3.org/2001/XMLSchema-instance"
  xsi:schemaLocation="http://java.sun.com/xml/ns/persistence
    http://java.sun.com/xml/ns/persistence/persistence_2_0.xsd"
  version="2.0">

  <persistence-unit name="defaultPersistenceUnit"
      transaction-type="RESOURCE_LOCAL">
    <provider>org.hibernate.ejb.HibernatePersistence</provider>
      <non-jta-data-source>DefaultDS</non-jta-data-source>
```

```
        <properties>
          <property name="hibernate.dialect"
                value="org.hibernate.dialect.H2Dialect"/>
        </properties>
      </persistence-unit>
    </persistence>
```

Now your JPA application should be good to go. Everything will work as with any other JPA application, but there are some support classes in Play that will make your life easier.

7.6.3   Built-in JPA helpers

Here's a small list of features that will help you when using JPA in a Play application:

- *Bootstrapping JPA*—The JPA plugin takes care of initializing JPA for you.
- *Obtaining an* EntityManager—You can obtain an entity manager at any point in your application by calling play.db.jpa.JPA.em().
- *Wrapping action methods in a transaction*—Annotate any action method with @play.db.jpa.Transactional to automatically wrap everything you do in that action in a transaction.

7.7   Summary

In this chapter, we've created a basic data model for our warehouse application, and we've seen how we can use Ebean to persist our objects to a database. We've introduced the principle of ORM, and basic JPA mapping principles have been explained, along with the basic relationship types:

- One to many
- Many to one
- One to one
- Many to many

There's a lot more to JPA mapping than these relationship types, such as mapping class inheritance or embeddable objects, but those subjects are beyond the scope of this book. The Ebean documentation has a pretty good introduction to most features, but read the Java EE tutorial from Oracle if you want to know everything about JPA mapping.

We've also seen how to use Ebean and Play's Finder API to retrieve objects from the database once stored. The most simple form of this is retrieving an object by its ID, but we've also seen how to create more complex queries using Ebean's Query API.

Throughout this chapter, we've been using convenience classes and methods provided by Play, as well as learning some best practices when creating an object model with Play.

Perhaps the most important piece of advice in this chapter is to put *behavior* on your model classes. Most other frameworks discourage this, creating DAO layers instead. Play is different, and it helps you create non-anemic object models by making it easy to do it "right." The most important examples of this are the `Model` and `Finder` classes; you can provide nice and clean APIs by extending or instantiating them.

In the next chapter we'll build on our knowledge by implementing some nice views to give our warehouse application some visual appeal.

Producing output
with view templates

This chapter covers

- An introduction to Scala templates
- The Scala template syntax
- Reusing template code and components
- Performing common tasks

We've seen how to structure and store data and business logs using models, and how to use controllers to bridge the gap between the Java world and the HTTP-based web.

We've covered the *M* and the *C* in MVC, but what about the *V*, the view layer? We need a view layer to present all the work our application does to the client, whether that is a browser or another system using our API.

When developing an application with Play, one of the options for creating output is using *templates*. You've probably used a templating system of some kind before, but you'll find that the Scala template engine, the default template engine that comes with Play, is a little different. As we've demonstrated in earlier chapters, Scala templates are compiled into classes and are completely type-safe.

In this chapter we'll show you everything you need to know to use Scala templates in your Play application to create your views. But Scala templates are not your *only* option. At the end of the chapter, we'll show you some alternative template engines.

But first, we'll dive deeper into how Scala templates work, and why they're the default option, even for Java applications.

8.1   *The benefits of compiled, type-safe templates*

Even when developing a Play 2 application in Java, your default option for templating is the Scala template engine. This may be surprising, because you explicitly chose to use Java over Scala.

First of all, don't be afraid; you don't have to learn Scala to use the templating engine. Much like any other templating system, you can just learn how to do certain things, such as iterating over a collection or making an if/else decision, without having to know how it works or what the syntax means. Also, a lot of the Scala syntax is very similar to Java; the following snippet of code is valid syntax for calling a method with a parameter on an object in both Java and Scala:

```
catalog.getProduct(ean);
```

The use of the Scala language is not the only thing that sets the Scala templating engine apart from other templating systems. The way most conventional templating systems work is that you write a template file in a custom syntax, and you call the template engine with the filename of that template. The template engine then loads that file and evaluates it.[1] This is when it'll detect custom instructions, often called *tags*, which describe the template structure. These are usually instructions such as loops, if/else structures, or including or extending some other template file.

After the template structure is parsed, the template engine will start generating output, at which point it'll have to evaluate the dynamic parts of the template, the *expressions*. These expressions resolve the values that serve as input for the template tags, or just output some variable. These expressions are often in some dedicated expression language, such as the *Unified Expression Language* found in JEE frameworks, or some dynamic language such as Ruby or Groovy.

One of the downsides of this approach is that this expression-evaluation work has to be repeated every time the template is rendered. *Every single time.* That's still wasteful.

Another downside is that most expression engines are *dynamically typed*, meaning that there's no way to guarantee what kind of object will end up in your templates, and therefore the compiler can't warn you ahead of time when you're trying to do something that can't work. Any mistake you make in that regard will show up as a runtime exception, and you have to hope to run into it before the mistake makes it into production.

---

[1] The way this evaluation works differs per template system. JSP and Groovy templates, for example, get compiled into actual bytecode.

The following listing is an example of a Groovy template—the dynamically typed, templated language used in Play 1.

Listing 8.1 Play 1.x Groovy template

```
<h1>Products</h1>

<table class="table table-striped">
    <thead>
      <tr>
        <th>Name</th>
      </tr>
    </thead>
    <tbody>
    #{list products, as:'product'}              ❶ Loop over
      <tr>                                          products
        <td>${product.name}</td>                 ❷ Show name
      </tr>                                          property
    #{/list}
    </tbody>
</table>
```

This template is a simple example; it takes the `products` variable, iterates over it, and outputs the `name` property for every member. This template seems to make two assumptions. First of all, at ❶, we're trying to iterate over the `products` variable, implying that it is actually a collection of some kind. Second, at ❷, the `name` property of every member is accessed, which means that the members of the `products` collection are of some class that *has* a `name` property.

Now, suppose that we don't know about these assumptions, and pass in a `List<String>` for `products` instead (containing, for example, the product names). We start the application, and everything seems to be fine. But things go wrong when we try to access the template; the template engine can't find the `name` property, resulting in the error shown in figure 8.1.

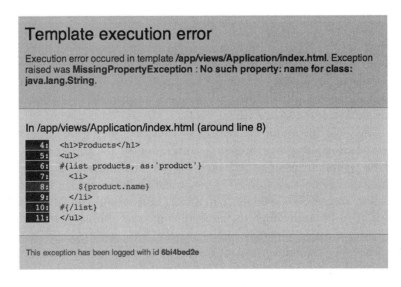

Figure 8.1 Runtime template error in Play 1

The problem here is that the mistake wasn't discovered until runtime because the template engine had no way of knowing what types to expect and what values it would actually get passed. Although the problem in this example happens every time, and thus will probably be caught before it makes it into a production system, it's very possible that more subtle mistakes won't be caught until they cause trouble.

Scala templates avoid all these problems. Instead of being *evaluated* at runtime, they get *compiled* beforehand, including all the expressions. Because all this work is done before the template is used to render a page, when it does the actual rendering, it renders very fast. After all, all the hard work has been done already. It's like running plain code!

In addition to the better performance, Scala templates are type-safe. Try to pass the template an object of a different type than expected, and the code that's trying to call the template function won't compile. Try to use a method that's not available for the class of a given object, and the template itself won't compile.

Take a look at listing 8.2, which shows the Play 2 version of our example template.

Listing 8.2   A type-safe Scala template

```
@(products: List[Product])                          ①  Parameter definition

<table class="table table-striped">
    <thead>
      <tr>
        <th>Name</th>
      </tr>
    </thead>
    <tbody>
    @for(product <- currentPage.getList()) {
      <tr>
        <td>@product.name</td>
      </tr>
      }
    </tbody>
</table>
```

Aside from some minor syntax differences, this template looks almost the same as its Groovy version, with one important addition: at ① we define the *parameter* for this template, and we specify a type. This way, the template "knows" what kind of values it has available, and the compiler refuses to compile if we provide a value of the wrong type or attempt to use it the wrong way.

Although all these forced checks and error messages may seem restrictive, they actually result in an application of higher quality; after all, it's harder to mess things up, because the compiler will scream at you if you get anything wrong.

As an added bonus, because your code now makes it clear what kind of objects the templates expect, your tools can be more helpful. For example, your IDE now has the information it needs to autocomplete expressions in your template, as well as to tell you what arguments your template's render method expects. IDE support for this is already pretty decent—and improving rapidly.

Although compiled templates and type safety are nice, they don't explain why the template language is in *Scala*. After all, Java itself has those features, so why not use Java instead? The answer is that Scala has some features that aren't available in Java, or that make the code less verbose. For example, the Scala compiler does a lot more *type inference* than Java,[2] saving a lot of type declaration.

Now that we know the *why*, let's take a look at the *how*: the actual template syntax.

8.2 Scala template syntax

Scala template syntax is not very complicated: there's just text and Scala code, and a way to distinguish between the two. Of course, things get more complicated if you don't actually know Scala already. Don't worry, we'll show you everything you need to know to use Scala templates. The most basic thing to remember about Scala templates is that the @ symbol switches to Scala context; everything that follows is Scala code until the logical end of the expression. We'll show you how that works in a bit, but first, let's take a look at how you *define* a Scala template.

8.2.1 Template definition

As we showed you in earlier chapters, Scala templates get compiled to classes, which you can call from your Java code. The compiled classes will end up in a view package, and they will all contain a method called render. What parameters this method takes depends on the template parameters that are defined at the top of the template itself.

Template parameters are just function parameters, and like method parameters in Java, they require a name and a type. In Scala, the name comes first, followed by a : and then the type. Templates can have zero, one, or more parameters, which are separated by commas, and they should all be placed at the top of the template file, between braces preceded by the @ symbol. The following snippet shows the parameters for a template which has a products parameter of type List<Product> and a count parameter of type Integer.

```
@(product: List[Product], count: Integer)
```

As you can see, the type parameter for the List is a little different from the regular Java syntax: where Java uses angled brackets, as in List<Product>, Scala uses square brackets, which means that you have to write List[Product] instead. The only difference is the syntax; the meaning is still the same.

Now that we know how to define template parameters, we can take a look at the actual body of a template.

8.2.2 Template body

A Scala template body consists of plain text (which can be anything, such as HTML, JSON, XML, or CSV) mixed with Scala code. The text will get copied straight to the output, whereas the Scala code implements the template's logic and dynamic parts. The

---

[2] This means the compiler knows what type an object is, without it being stated in the source code.

only thing the templating engine introduces is a symbol to denote Scala code: the @ character. For example, consider this snippet from our list template from back in chapter 3, shown in the following listing.

Listing 8.3   list.scala.html

```
<table class="table table-striped">
    <thead>
      <tr>
        <th>EAN</th>
        <th>Name</th>
        <th>Description</th>
        <th>Date</th>
        <th></th>
      </tr>
    </thead>
    <tbody>
    @for(product <- products) {                        A Scala
                                                       "for" loop
      <tr>
        <td><a href="@routes.Products.details(product)">
          @product.ean
        </a></td>
        <td><a href="@routes.Products.details(product)">
        @product.name</a></td>
        <td><a href="@routes.Products.details(product)">
        @product.name</a></td>
        <td>@product.date.format("dd-MM-yyyy")</td>        A Scala
        <td>                                              function call
          <a href="@routes.Products.details(product)">
          <i class="icon icon-pencil"></i></a>
<a onclick="javascript:del('@routes.Products.delete(product.ean)')">
          <i class="icon icon-trash"></i></a>
        </td>
      </tr>
      }

    </tbody>
</table>
```

Outputting Scala values →

As you can see, most of the template consists of plain HTML that will just be copied to the output when this template is rendered. We've marked the parts that are Scala code. These parts are what make your template dynamic.

The most interesting part of this snippet is the for statement. In this form, this Scala for expression is equivalent to a regular Java for/in loop; it takes a collection and repeats the code in its body for every member of that collection. But in this case, the body *isn't code*, it's just text. The loop behaves as you might expect, though; the body is repeated for every entry in products.

The body of the for loop itself also contains some Scala expressions. These Scala expressions are evaluated, and the resulting value is included in the template output. For security and compatibility reasons, all expressions are HTML escaped. This means that any and all characters that are invalid as HTML text are properly escaped for display in an HTML document. If you ever wish to display the raw, unescaped value of an expression in the output document, you can wrap it using @Html():

```
// boldName = "<b>world</b>"
Hello @Html(boldName)!
```

As stated before, Scala expressions start with the @ character. But when does an expression end and the regular text begin again?

8.2.3 Expression scope

In the case of this `for` loop, the scope of the Scala expression is clear: the expression starts at the beginning of the line and, because it contains a block, ends at the end of the block, designated by the closing curly brace.

The situation is less clear with inline expressions, such as a function call to `routes.Products.show()` to generate the value for the product link's `href` attribute, or value references that make up most of the link's text. In those cases, the template engine is smart enough to recognize an expression and outputs the first value it finds. As a consequence, this syntax only works for simple expressions. Consider the text for our product links (described in section 8.3). The breakdown into expression and plain text is shown in figure 8.2.

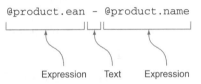

Figure 8.2 Link text, broken down

Here, the template engine knows where the Scala expression ends, and continues to consider the rest of the line as text up until the next @ character.

Sometimes a simple expression is not enough; you might want to output some value that requires a little modification first. In that case, you can still use the @ syntax, but you should wrap the expression in braces as well, as shown in figure 8.3.

This style of syntax allows you to write a more complicated expression by being explicit about where it ends. Now if you wanted to, you could write a more verbose, multistatement expression by using curly braces instead of regular braces, as shown in figure 8.4.

This style of syntax allows you to write very complex expressions if you ever need them.

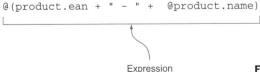

Figure 8.3 A multitoken statement

```
@{desc = product.ean + " - " + product.name; desc}
```

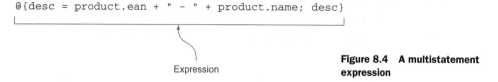

Expression

Figure 8.4   A multistatement expression

> **AVOID COMPLEX TEMPLATE CODE**   Although the template syntax allows you to, think long and hard about what you're doing when you feel you need to write a multistatement expression. Templates are *not* the place to put complex logic, and anything more than a single expression is pushing it. Consider placing this logic in the model or controller layer, keeping the template logic simple and readable.

There are two aspects of the syntax that we haven't covered yet: escaping and commenting. Escaping is simple; the only character that you'll need to escape when you want to use it in a template is the @ character. Simply use two instead:

```
My Twitter username is: @@targeter
```

To escape some template code, use the following syntax:

```
@* This is a comment. *@
```

This works across lines as well, making it possible to use ScalaDoc (http://docs.scala-lang.org/style/scaladoc.html) to document your templates:

```
@**
 * A product listing.
 *
 * @param products The products to list
 *@
```

This covers all of the syntax there is to Scala templates. One way of looking at it is that there's little syntax; escape to Scala mode or just plain text. Another way of looking at it is that you have the entire Scala language at your disposal.

Of course, there's a lot more to templates than just this, so let's look at some things that you will do a lot when using Scala templates.

8.3   *Your basic building blocks*

Like we promised you before, you won't actually have to learn Scala to write templates. But you will need to know how to perform some basic tasks, such as looping, making decisions, and importing classes. Let's start with looping and iteration.

8.3.1   *Iterating*

Scala (and, by extension, Scala template syntax) doesn't have an equivalent of Java's conventional "for" loop. But it *does* have an equivalent to Java's "for-each" loop, allowing you to iterate over the members of a collection.[3] We've seen an example of this

---

[3]   Actually, a Scala *sequence*, but we'll just keep calling them collections or iterables.

already: in section 5 of chapter 3 we used it to loop over the products list. As a reminder, the following listing shows the relevant template code:

Listing 8.4 Looping over the `products` list

```
<dl>
@for(product <- products) {                          ← Looping over the products
  <dt>
    <a href="@routes.Products.show(product.ean)">                     Calling a
      @product.ean - @product.name        ←                          routing
    </a>                                        Outputting            function
  </dt>                                         product
  <dd>@product.description</dd>           ←     details
}
</dl>
```

As you can see, this syntax looks a lot like the familiar Java for-each loop, but with the colon replaced by a left-arrow. Also, because of a Scala feature called *type inference*, we don't have to declare the type of the product variable; the compiler is smart enough to figure out that if you have a list of `Product` objects, the variable should also be `Product` itself.

Scala `for` loops[4] have some other useful features. For example, they can loop over a map. Suppose we have a `Map<Long, Product>`, mapping EAN codes to a `Product` instance. You could rewrite listing 8.4 as shown in listing 8.5.

Listing 8.5 Looping over a `Map`

```
@(eanMap: Map[Long, Product])
<table class="table table-striped">
// We'll skip the irrelevant parts
                                                  Iterating over a Map
@for((ean, product) <- eanMap) {             ←    instead of a List
  <tr>
    <td><a href="@routes.Products.show(ean)">
      @ean</a></td>
    <td>@product.name</td>                  ←  Both an "ean" and
    <td>@product.description</dd></td>         a "product" value
  </tr>                                         are available
}
</table>
```

This way of looping over a map also allows us to do iteration with an index value, which we don't have by default because there's no conventional for loop to maintain an incrementing variable for us. To get the index variable for the entries in our list, we'll use the `zipWithIndex` method that Scala provides for us. The `zipWithIndex` method converts the `Set[Product]` into a `Map[Product, Int]>`, where the value of the map is the index. That would allow you to write a template such as that seen in listing 8.6.

---

[4] Actually, they're *comprehensions*, but for our purposes they might as well be loops.

Listing 8.6   Iteration with index variable

```
@(products: Set[Product])
<table class="table table-striped">
// We'll skip the irrelevant parts

@for((product, i) <- products.zipWithIndex) {

<tr>
   <td>@i</td>
   <td><a href="@routes.Products.show(ean)">
     @ean</a></td>
    <td>@product.name</td>
    <td>@product.description</dd></td>
</tr>
}
</table>
```

The Scala `for` syntax has more features than this, but these techniques should be enough for most templates you'll write. Let's move on to making decisions in templates using if/else statements.

8.3.2   *Making decisions*

Of course, Scala has if/else statements, and they're available from Scala templates. As an example, we'll expand the products list template to show a friendly message when no products are available (see the following listing).

Listing 8.7   If/else statements

```
@if(products.isEmpty()) {
  <p>No products found.</p>
} else {
  <dl>
    // List products here.
  </dl>
}
```

As you can see, `if` statements are pretty straightforward, and exactly the same as in Java. But we could make the `if` statement a little shorter; in Scala, the period before the method call is optional, as are the parentheses. We could rewrite the condition as seen in the following listing.

Listing 8.8   More concise statements

```
@if(products isEmpty) {
  <p>No products found.</p>
} else {
  <dl>
    // List products here.
  </dl>
}
```

Now that we know how to create a template, let's find out how we can reuse template code, to keep us from repeating ourselves.

8.4 Structuring pages with template composition

Just like your regular code, your pages are compositions of smaller pieces that are in turn often composed of even smaller pieces. Many of these pieces are reusable on other pages; some are used on all of your pages, whereas some are specific to a particular page. There is nothing special about these pieces; they're just templates by themselves. In this section we'll show you how to construct pages using reusable smaller templates.

8.4.1 Includes

We've only shown you snippets of HTML and never a full page. Let's start to expand our proof-of-concept application from the previous chapters into a proper application. We'll start by creating a proper HTML document for the catalog page that lists the products we have in our catalog, as in figure 8.5.

The code for the `list` action in the `Products` controller remains the same as in our previous chapters, except that it uses a different template:

```
public static Result list(Integer page) {
    Page<Product> products = Product.find(page);
    return ok(views.html.catalog.render(products));
}
```

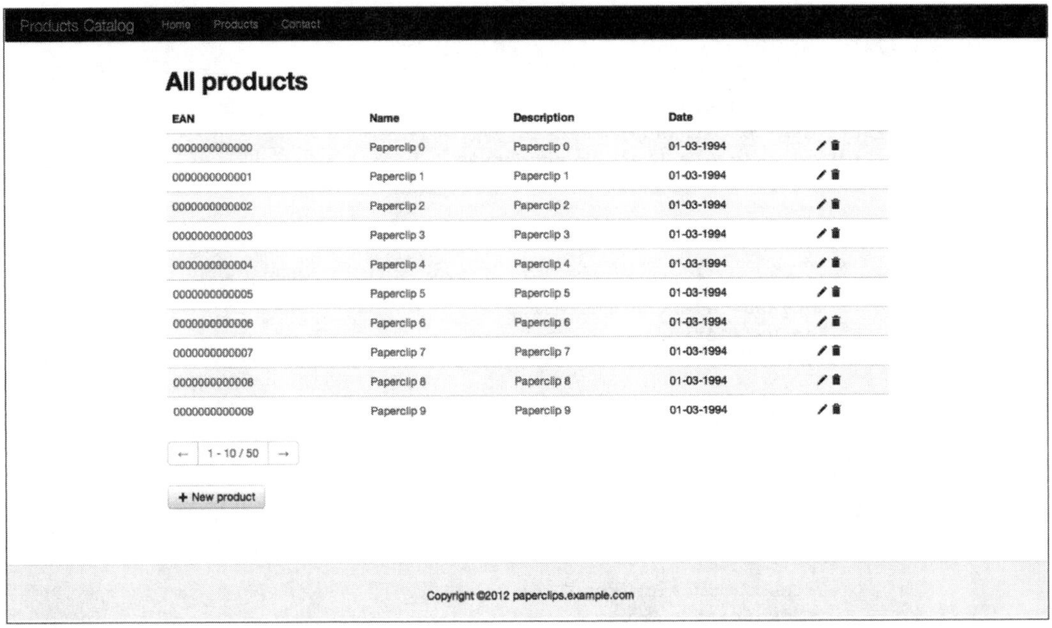

Figure 8.5 The catalog page

To create the template, create a file called catalog.scala.html directly under the views directory. Use the content shown in the following listing.

Listing 8.9 Full HTML for the catalog page, /app/views/catalog.scala.html

```
@(currentPage: com.avaje.ebean.Page[Product])
<!DOCTYPE html>

<html>
  <head>
    <title>paperclips.example.com</title>
    <link href="@routes.Assets.at("bootstrap/css/bootstrap.min.css")"
     rel="stylesheet" media="screen">
    <link href="@routes.Assets.at("stylesheets/main.css")"
     rel="stylesheet" media="screen">
    <link rel="shortcut icon" type="image/png"
     href="@routes.Assets.at("images/favicon.png")">
    <script src="@routes.Assets.at("javascripts/jquery-1.9.0.min.js")"
     type="text/javascript"></script>
  </head>
  <body>
    <div class="navbar navbar-inverse " id="navigation">
     <div class="navbar-inner">
        <div class="container">
         <a class="brand" href="@routes.Products.index()">
    log</a>
         <ul class="nav">
           <li><a href="@routes.Products.index()">Home</a></li>
           <li><a href="@routes.Products.list()">Products</a></li>
           <li><a href="">Contact</a></li>
         </ul></div>
     </div>
    </div>
    <div class="container">
      @if(flash.containsKey("success")){
        <div class="alert alert-success">
        @flash.get("success")
        </div>
      }

      @if(flash.containsKey("error")){
        <div class="alert alert-error">
        @flash.get("error")
        </div>
      }

    <h2>All products</h2>
   <script>
     function del(urlToDelete) {
        $.ajax({
          url: urlToDelete,
          type: 'DELETE',
          success: function(results) {
            // Refresh the page
            location.reload();
```

```
          }
        });
      }
  </script>
  <table class="table table-striped">
   <thead>
     <tr>
       <th>EAN</th>
       <th>Name</th>
       <th>Description</th>
       <th>Date</th>
       <th></th>
     </tr>
   </thead>
   <tbody>
   @for(product <- currentPage.getList()) {

     <tr>
       <td><a href="@routes.Products.details(product)">
         @product.ean
       </a></td>
       <td><a href="@routes.Products.details(product)">
        @product.name</a></td>
       <td><a href="@routes.Products.details(product)">
        @product.name</a></td>
       <td>@product.date.format("dd-MM-yyyy")</td>
       <td>
         <a href="@routes.Products.details(product)">
           <i class="icon icon-pencil"></i></a>
<a onclick="javascript:del('@routes.Products.delete(product.ean)')">
           <i class="icon icon-trash"></i></a>
       </td>
     </tr>
     }

   </tbody>
  </table>
  <div id="pagination" class="pagination">
          <ul>
              @if(currentPage.hasPrev) {
                  <li class="prev">
<a href="@routes.Products.list(currentPage.getPageIndex - 1)">
&larr; </a>
                  </li>
              } else {
                  <li class="prev disabled">
                      <a>&larr;</a>
                  </li>
              }
              <li class="current">
  <a>@currentPage.getDisplayXtoYofZ(" - "," / ")</a>
              </li>
              @if(currentPage.hasNext) {
                  <li class="next">
  <a href="@routes.Products.list(currentPage.getPageIndex + 1)">
&rarr;</a>
```

```
                </li>
            } else {
                <li class="next disabled">
                    <a>&rarr;</a>
                </li>
            }
        </ul>
    </div>
  <a href="@routes.Products.newProduct()" class="btn">
    <i class="icon-plus"></i> New product</a>
    </div>
    <footer class="footer">
      <div class="container">
        <p>Copyright ©2012 paperclips.example.com</p>
      </div>
    </footer>
  </body>
</html>
```

Now we have a proper HTML document that lists the products in our catalog, but we did add a lot of markup that isn't the responsibility of the catalog action. The catalog action doesn't need to know what the navigation menu looks like. Modularity has suffered here, as has reusability. In general, the action method that is invoked for the request is only responsible for part of the content of the resulting page. On many websites, the page header, the footer, and the navigation are shared between pages, as shown in the wireframe in figure 8.6.

Here, the boxes *Header, Navigation,* and *Footer* will hardly change, if at all, between pages on this website. On the other hand, the content box in the middle will be different for every page.

In this section and the next, we'll show you some techniques that you can use to break up your templates into more maintainable, reusable pieces.

The HTML fragment that renders the navigation area lends itself well to being extracted from the main template and into a separate template file. From the main catalog template, then, we include this navigation template. We start with creating a file, `views/navigation.scala.html`.

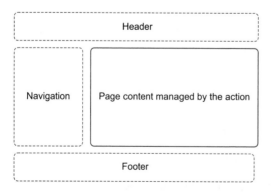

Figure 8.6   Web page composition

```
@()
<div class="navbar navbar-inverse " id="navigation">
<div class="navbar-inner">
  <div class="container">
   <a class="brand" href="@routes.Products.index()">
  Products Catalog</a>
   <ul class="nav">
     <li><a href="@routes.Products.index()">Home</a></li>
     <li><a href="@routes.Products.list()">Products</a></li>
     <li><a href="">Contact</a></li>
   </ul></div>
</div>
</div>
```

Now we can simply include this template from the main template, views/navigation
.scala.html, and include it with @navigation(). Because it lives in the same package
as the main template, views.html, we can use just the name of the template and omit
the views.html qualifier, as shown in the following listing.

> **Listing 8.10 Catalog page with navigation extracted**

```
@(currentPage: com.avaje.ebean.Page[Product])
<!DOCTYPE html>

<html>
  <head>
    <title>paperclips.example.com</title>
    <link href="@routes.Assets.at("bootstrap/css/bootstrap.min.css")"
     rel="stylesheet" media="screen">
    <link href="@routes.Assets.at("stylesheets/main.css")"
     rel="stylesheet" media="screen">
    <link rel="shortcut icon" type="image/png"
     href="@routes.Assets.at("images/favicon.png")">
    <script src="@routes.Assets.at("javascripts/jquery-1.9.0.min.js")"
     type="text/javascript"></script>
  </head>
  <body>
    @navigation()

    <div class="container">
      @if(flash.containsKey("success")){
        <div class="alert alert-success">
        @flash.get("success")
        </div>
      }

      @if(flash.containsKey("error")){
        <div class="alert alert-error">
        @flash.get("error")
        </div>
      }

    <h2>All products</h2>
    <script>
      function del(urlToDelete) {
        $.ajax({
```

```
          url: urlToDelete,
          type: 'DELETE',
          success: function(results) {
            // Refresh the page
            location.reload();
          }
        });
      }
  </script>
  <table class="table table-striped">
   <thead>
     <tr>
       <th>EAN</th>
       <th>Name</th>
       <th>Description</th>
       <th>Date</th>
       <th></th>
     </tr>
   </thead>
   <tbody>
   @for(product <- currentPage.getList()) {

   <tr>
     <td><a href="@routes.Products.details(product)">
         @product.ean
     </a></td>
      <td><a href="@routes.Products.details(product)">
         @product.name</a></td>
       <td><a href="@routes.Products.details(product)">
          @product.name</a></td>
       <td>@product.date.format("dd-MM-yyyy")</td>
         <td>
          <a href="@routes.Products.details(product)">
            <i class="icon icon-pencil"></i></a>
<a onclick="javascript:del('@routes.Products.delete(product.ean)')">
            <i class="icon icon-trash"></i></a>
       </td>
     </tr>
     }

   </tbody>
  </table>
  <div id="pagination" class="pagination">
         <ul>
             @if(currentPage.hasPrev) {
                 <li class="prev">
  <a href="@routes.Products.list(currentPage.getPageIndex - 1)">
&larr; </a>
                 </li>
             } else {
                 <li class="prev disabled">
                     <a>&larr;</a>
                 </li>
             }
             <li class="current">
  <a>@currentPage.getDisplayXtoYofZ(" - "," / ")</a>
```

```
                    </li>
                    @if(currentPage.hasNext) {
                        <li class="next">
    <a href="@routes.Products.list(currentPage.getPageIndex + 1)">
&rarr;</a>
                        </li>
                    } else {
                        <li class="next disabled">
                            <a>&rarr;</a>
                        </li>
                    }
                </ul>
            </div>
    <a href="@routes.Products.newProduct()" class="btn">
      <i class="icon-plus"></i> New product</a>
      </div>
      <footer class="footer">
        <div class="container">
          <p>Copyright ©2012 paperclips.example.com</p>
        </div>
      </footer>
    </body>
</html>
```

This improves our template, because the catalog template now no longer needs to know how to render the navigation. This pattern of extracting parts of a template into a separate template that is reusable is called *includes*, where the extracted template is called the *include*.

8.4.2   *Layouts*

The include that we used in the previous section made our template better, but it isn't very good yet. As it stands, the catalog page still renders a whole lot of HTML that it shouldn't need to, such as the HTML DOCTYPE declaration, the head element, and the header and the footer (which are on every page).

In fact, in listing 8.10, only the part between the <h2>All products</h2> and the footer is the responsibility of the catalog action:

```
<h2>All products</h2>
    <script>
      function del(urlToDelete) {
          $.ajax({
            url: urlToDelete,
            type: 'DELETE',
            success: function(results) {
              // Refresh the page
              location.reload();
            }
          });
      }
    </script>
    <table class="table table-striped">
     <thead>
```

```
  <tr>
    <th>EAN</th>
    <th>Name</th>
    <th>Description</th>
    <th>Date</th>
    <th></th>
  </tr>
</thead>
<tbody>
@for(product <- currentPage.getList()) {

  <tr>
    <td><a href="@routes.Products.details(product)">
      @product.ean
    </a></td>
    <td><a href="@routes.Products.details(product)">
     @product.name</a></td>
    <td><a href="@routes.Products.details(product)">
      @product.name</a></td>
    <td>@product.date.format("dd-MM-yyyy")</td>
    <td>
      <a href="@routes.Products.details(product)">
        <i class="icon icon-pencil"></i></a>
<a onclick="javascript:del('@routes.Products.delete(product.ean)')">
        <i class="icon icon-trash"></i></a>
    </td>
  </tr>
  }

</tbody>
</table>
<div id="pagination" class="pagination">
        <ul>
            @if(currentPage.hasPrev) {
                <li class="prev">
<a href="@routes.Products.list(currentPage.getPageIndex - 1)">
&larr; </a>
                </li>
            } else {
                <li class="prev disabled">
                    <a>&larr;</a>
                </li>
            }
            <li class="current">
<a>@currentPage.getDisplayXtoYofZ(" - "," / ")</a>
            </li>
            @if(currentPage.hasNext) {
                <li class="next">
<a href="@routes.Products.list(currentPage.getPageIndex + 1)">
&rarr;</a>
                </li>
            } else {
                <li class="next disabled">
                    <a>&rarr;</a>
                </li>
            }
```

```
      </ul>
    </div>
  <a href="@routes.Products.newProduct()" class="btn">
    <i class="icon-plus"></i> New product</a>
```

Everything else should be factored out of the template for the `catalog` action. We could of course use the *includes* technique, but it isn't ideal here because we need to extract some HTML that's above the content and some HTML that's below the content. If we use includes, we'd need to extract two new templates. One would contain all the HTML before the content, and the other one would contain everything after the content. This isn't good, because that HTML belongs together. We want to avoid having an HTML start tag in one template and the corresponding end tag in another. That would break coherence in our template.

Luckily, the Scala template engine offers some compositional features that allow us to extract all this code into a single, coherent template. From the `catalog` `.scala.html` template, we extract all HTML that shouldn't be the responsibility of the `catalog` template, as in the following listing.

Listing 8.11 Extracted page layout

```
<!DOCTYPE html>

<html>
  <head>
    <title>paperclips.example.com</title>
    <link href="@routes.Assets.at("bootstrap/css/bootstrap.min.css")"
      rel="stylesheet" media="screen">
    <link href="@routes.Assets.at("stylesheets/main.css")"
      rel="stylesheet" media="screen">
    <link rel="shortcut icon" type="image/png"
      href="@routes.Assets.at("images/favicon.png")">
    <script src="@routes.Assets.at("javascripts/jquery-1.9.0.min.js")"
      type="text/javascript"></script>
  </head>
  <body>
    @navigation()
    <div class="container">

      @if(flash.containsKey("success")){
        <div class="alert alert-success">
        @flash.get("success")
        </div>
      }

      @if(flash.containsKey("error")){
        <div class="alert alert-error">
        @flash.get("error")
        </div>
      }

      // Content here                      ⏎ Page content must
                                             be inserted here
    </div>
    <footer class="footer">
```

```
      <div class="container">
        <p>Copyright ©2012 paperclips.example.com</p>
      </div>
    </footer>
  </body>
</html>
```

What we extracted is a fragment of HTML that just needs the body of the `<div id="content">` to become a complete page. If that sounds exactly like a template, that's because it is exactly like a regular template. What we do is make a new template and store it in app/views/main.scala.html, with a single parameter named content of type Html, as in the following listing.

Listing 8.12   The extracted main template

```
@(content: Html)                      ⟵── New parameter "content"
 <!DOCTYPE html>
<<html>
  <head>
    <title>paperclips.example.com</title>
    <link href="@routes.Assets.at("bootstrap/css/bootstrap.min.css")"
      rel="stylesheet" media="screen">
    <link href="@routes.Assets.at("stylesheets/main.css")"
      rel="stylesheet" media="screen">
    <link rel="shortcut icon" type="image/png"
      href="@routes.Assets.at("images/favicon.png")">
    <script src="@routes.Assets.at("javascripts/jquery-1.9.0.min.js")"
      type="text/javascript"></script>
  </head>
  <body>
    @navigation()
    <div class="container">

      @if(flash.containsKey("success")){
        <div class="alert alert-success">
        @flash.get("success")
        </div>
      }

      @if(flash.containsKey("error")){
        <div class="alert alert-error">
        @flash.get("error")
        </div>
      }
      @content                    ⟵── Display the content
    </div>
    <footer class="footer">
      <div class="container">
        <p>Copyright ©2012 paperclips.example.com</p>
      </div>
    </footer>
  </body>
</html>
```

Now we have a new template that we can call, such as `views.html.main.render` `(content)`. At first, this may not seem very usable. How would we call this from the catalog template? We don't have a `content` value available that we can just pass in. Instead, our catalog template is rendering the content we want to include in the main template.

We can solve this problem with a Scala trick. In Scala you can also use curly braces for a parameter block, so this is also valid: `views.html.main { content }`. By wrapping our template in this function call, we actually render the `main` template and pass it the contents of our `catalog` template. This is demonstrated in the following listing.

Listing 8.13 Refactored catalog template

```
@(currentPage: com.avaje.ebean.Page[Product])
@main("Products catalogue") {

  <h2>All products</h2>

    <script>
     function del(urlToDelete) {
        $.ajax({
          url: urlToDelete,
          type: 'DELETE',
          success: function(results) {
            // Refresh the page
            location.reload();
          }
        });
      }
    </script>

    <table class="table table-striped">
     <thead>
       <tr>
         <th>EAN</th>
         <th>Name</th>
         <th>Description</th>
         <th>Date</th>
         <th></th>
       </tr>
     </thead>
     <tbody>
     @for(product <- currentPage.getList()) {

       <tr>
         <td><a href="@routes.Products.details(product)">
           @product.ean
         </a></td>
         <td>
<a href="@routes.Products.details(product)">@product.name</a></td>
         <td>
<a href="@routes.Products.details(product)">@product.name</a></td>
         <td>@product.date.format("dd-MM-yyyy")</td>
         <td>
<a href="@routes.Products.details(product)">
<i class="icon icon-pencil"></i></a>
```

```
<a onclick="javascript:del('@routes.Products.delete(product.ean)')">
<i class="icon icon-trash"></i></a>
        </td>
      </tr>
      }

    </tbody>
  </table>

  <div id="pagination" class="pagination">
          <ul>
              @if(currentPage.hasPrev) {
                  <li class="prev">
<a href="@routes.Products.list(currentPage.getPageIndex - 1)">
&larr; </a>
                  </li>
              } else {
                  <li class="prev disabled">
                      <a>&larr;</a>
                  </li>
              }
              <li class="current">
      <a>@currentPage.getDisplayXtoYofZ(" - "," / ")</a>
              </li>
              @if(currentPage.hasNext) {
                  <li class="next">
<a href="@routes.Products.list(currentPage.getPageIndex + 1)">
 &rarr;</a>
                  </li>
              } else {
                  <li class="next disabled">
                      <a>&rarr;</a>
                  </li>
              }
          </ul>
      </div>


  <a href="@routes.Products.newProduct()" class="btn">
    <i class="icon-plus"></i> New product</a>
}
```

We wrapped all the HTML that this template constructed in a call to the main template! Now the only thing that this template does is call the main template, passing in the proper content parameter. This is called the *layout* pattern in Play.

We can add more than just the content parameter to the main.scala.html template, but we'll add a new parameter list for the next parameter, because you can only use curly braces around a parameter list with a single parameter. Suppose that we also want to make the title of the page a parameter. Then we could update the first part of the main template from:

```
@(content: Html)
<html>
  <head>
    <title>Paper-clip web shop</title>
```

to:

```
@(title: String)(content: Html)
<html>
  <head>
    <title>@title</title>
```

Now we can call this template from another template with:

```
@main("Products") {
  // Content here
}
```

It's useful to give the title parameter of the `main.scala.html` a default value so that we can chose to skip it when we call the method:

```
@(title: String ="Paperclips!")(content: Html)
```

If we want to call this template and are happy with the default title, we can simply call it using:

```
@main() {
  // Content here
}
```

Note that we still need the empty parentheses for the first parameter list; we can't skip it altogether.

A web page doesn't consist solely of HTML. Styling is provided by CSS, and additional interaction can be defined in JavaScript. Play makes writing CSS and JavaScript easier, by supporting tools that improve on the existing technology.

8.5 *Using LESS and CoffeeScript: the asset pipeline*

Browsers process HTML with CSS and JavaScript, so your web application must output these formats for browsers to understand them. These languages are not always the choice of developers, however. Many developers prefer technologies like LESS and CoffeeScript over CSS and JavaScript. LESS is a stylesheet language that is transformed into CSS by a LESS interpreter or compiler, whereas CoffeeScript is a scripting language that is transformed into JavaScript by a CoffeeScript compiler.

As we mentioned in chapter 2, Play integrates LESS and CoffeeScript compilers. Although we won't teach you these technologies, we will show you how you can use them in a Play application.

8.5.1 *LESS*

LESS gives you many advantages over plain CSS. LESS supports variables, mixins, nesting, and some other constructs that make a web developer's life easier. Consider the following example of plain CSS, in which we set the background color of a header and a footer element to a shade of green. Additionally, we use a bold font for link elements in the footer.

```
.header {
  background-color: #0b5c20;
}

.footer {
  background-color: #0b5c20;
}

.footer a {
  font-weight: bold;
}
```

This example shows some of the weaknesses of CSS. We have to repeat the color code, and we have to repeat the .footer selector if we want to select an a element inside a footer. With LESS, you can write the following instead:

```
@green: #0b5c20;

.header {
  background-color: @green;
}

.footer {
  background-color: @green;

  a {
    font-weight: bold;
  }

}
```

We have declared a variable to hold the color using a descriptive name, so the value can now be changed in one place. We have also used nesting for the .footer a selector by moving the a selector inside the .footer selector. This makes the code easier to read and maintain.

8.5.2   *CoffeeScript*

CoffeeScript is a language that compiles to JavaScript, consisting mainly of syntactic improvements over JavaScript. Instead of curly braces, CoffeeScript uses indentation and has a very short function literal notation. Consider the following example in JavaScript:

```
math = {
  root: Math.sqrt,
  square: square,
  cube: function(x) {
    return x * square(x);
  }
};
```

In CoffeeScript, you would write this as:

```
math =
  root:   Math.sqrt
  square: square
  cube:   (x) -> x * square x
```

No curly braces are used around the object, and the function definition is more concise.

8.5.3 *The asset pipeline*

There are various ways to use CoffeeScript or LESS. For both languages, command-line tools are available that transform files to their regular JavaScript or CSS equivalents. For both there are also JavaScript interpreters that allow you to use these files in a browser directly.

Play supports automatic build-time CoffeeScript and LESS compilation, and shows compilation errors in the familiar Play error page. This highlights the offending lines of code when you have syntactical errors in your CoffeeScript or LESS code.

Using LESS or CoffeeScript is trivial. You simply place the files in the `app/assets` directory or a subdirectory of the same. Give CoffeeScript files a `.coffee` extension and LESS files a `.less` extension, and Play will automatically compile them to JavaScript and CSS files and make them available in the `public` folder.

For example, if you place a CoffeeScript file in `app/assets/javascript /application.coffee`, you can reference it from a template using

```
<script src="@routes.Assets.at("javascripts/application.js")"></script>
```

You can also use an automatically generated minified version of your JavaScript file by changing `application.js` to `application.min.js`.

> **COMPILED FILE LOCATION** Although you can reference the compiled files as if they reside in the `public` directory, Play actually keeps them in the `resources_managed` directory in the `target` directory. The assets controller will look there too when it receives a request for a file.

Apart from LESS and CoffeeScript, Play has also support for the Google Closure compiler. This is a JavaScript compiler that compiles JavaScript to better, faster JavaScript. Any file that ends in `.js` is automatically compiled by the Closure compiler.

There are occasions when you don't want a file to be automatically compiled. Suppose that you have a LESS file `a.less` that defines a variable `@x` and includes `b.less`, which references the variable. On its own, `b.less` won't compile, because `@x` is undefined. Even though you never intended to call `b.less` directly, Play tries to compile it and throws an error. To avoid this, rename `b.less` to `_b.less`. Any `.less`, `.coffee`, or `.js` file that starts with an underscore is not compiled.

> **CONFIGURE COMPILATION INCLUDES AND EXCLUDES** Sometimes it isn't convenient to only exclude files that start with an underscore: for example, when you use an existing LESS library that isn't designed that way. Luckily, it's possible to configure the behavior of Play regarding which files it should compile. See the Play documentation for more details.

Now that we've shown you how to use the asset pipeline, we'll continue in the next section with adapting your application for multiple languages.

8.6   *Internationalization*

Users of your application may come from different countries and use different languages, as well as have different rules for properly formatting numbers, dates, and times. The combination of language and formatting rules is called a *locale*. The adaptation of a program to different locales is called *internationalization* and *localization*. Because these words are so insanely long and often used together—which makes it even worse—they're often abbreviated as *i18N* and *l10N* respectively, where the number between the first and last letter is the number of replaced letters. In this section, we'll demonstrate the tools Play provides to help you with internationalization.

> **Internationalization versus localization**
>
> Although it's easy to mix them up, internationalization and localization are two different things. Internationalization is a *refactoring* to remove locale-specific code from your application. Localization is making a locale-specific version of an application. In an internationalized web application, this means having one or more selectable locale-specific versions. In practice, the two steps go together; you usually both internationalize and localize one part of an application at a time.

In this section we only discuss internationalizing the static parts of your application: things that you'd normally hard-code in your templates or your error messages, for example. We won't cover internationalizing your dynamic content, so having the content of your web application in multiple languages isn't included.

8.6.1   *Configuration and message files*

Building a localized application in Play is mostly about text and involves writing *message* files. Instead of putting literal strings like "Log in," "Thank you for your order," or "Email is required" in your application, you create a file in which message keys are mapped to these strings.

For each language that your application supports, write a messages file that looks like this:

```
welcome = Welcome!
users.login = Log in
shop.thanks = Thank you for your order
validation.required = {0} is required
```

Here you can see how the message keys are mapped to the actual messages. In the last example, there's a placeholder that will be replaced by a value when this message is used. The dots in the keys have no meaning, but you can use them for logical grouping.

To get started, you must configure Play so that it knows which languages are supported. In the application.conf file, list the languages that you support:

```
application.langs="en,en-US,nl"
```

This is a comma-separated list of languages, in which each language consists of an ISO 639-2 language code, optionally followed by a hyphen and an ISO 3166-1 alpha-2 country code.

Then, for each of these languages, you must create a messages file in the `conf` directory, with the filename `messages.LANG`, where `LANG` should be replaced by the language. A French messages file would be stored in `conf/messages.fr`, with the following content:

```
welcome=Bienvenue!
```

Additionally, you can create a `messages` file without an extension, which serves as the default and fallback language. If a message is not translated in the `messages` file for the language you're using, the message from this `messages` file will be used.

To deal with messages in your application, it's recommended that you start with a `messages` file and make sure that it's complete. If you later decide to add more languages, you can easily create additional `messages` files. When you forget to add a key to another language's messages file, or when you don't have the translation for that message, then the default messages file will be used instead.

8.6.2 *Using messages in your application*

To use messages in your application, you can use the `get()` method on the `play.i18n.Messages` class:

```
Messages.get("welcome")
```

By default, Play will use the language specified in the current request's `Accept-Language` header, or default to the first language defined in your application's configuration. If you want to, you can override the language that you want to use, like so:

```
Messages.get(new Lang("fr"), "welcome")
```

In a template, you can use the `Messages` class as follows:

```
@()

<h1>@Messages.get("welcome")</h1>
```

Prior to Play 2.1, in order for the automatic language selection to work in templates, you need to add an *implicit parameter* so that the request is available. You can do that as follows:

```
@(title:String = "Paperclips!")(implicit request: Request)

<h1>@Messages.get("welcome")</h1>
```

Messages aren't just simple strings; they're patterns formatted using `java.text.MessageFormat`. This means that you can use parameters in your messages:

```
validation.required={0} is required
```

You can substitute these by specifying more parameters in the call to `Messages.get()`:

```
Messages.get("validation.required", "email")
```

This will result in the string `email is required`. `MessageFormat` gives you more options. Suppose that we want to vary our message slightly, depending on the parameters. Suppose that we're showing the number of items in our shopping cart, and we want to display "Your cart is empty," "Your cart has one item," or "Your cart has 42 items" depending on the number of items in the cart. We can use the following pattern for that:

```
shop.basketcount=Your cart {0,choice,0#is empty|1#has one item
   |1< has {0} items}.
```

Now if we use the following in a template

```
<p>@Messages("shop.basketcount", 0)</p>
<p>@Messages("shop.basketcount", 1)</p>
<p>@Messages("shop.basketcount", 42)</p>
```

we get the following output:

```
Your cart is empty.
Your cart has one item.
Your cart has 42 items.
```

Using this, you can achieve advanced formatting that can be different for each language, decoupled from your application logic. For more possibilities with `Message-Format`, consult the Java SE API documentation.

8.7   *Summary*

In this chapter, we've seen that Play ships a type-safe template engine, based on Scala. This type-safe template engine helps you write more robust templates that give you more confidence that everything will still work as intended after you refactor. On top of that, the template engine is faster than conventional, non-type-safe alternatives.

The template syntax is very concise: The @ character is the only special character. Any value referenced in the template actually resolves to an object, and you can call methods on it. If you attempt to use a value or method that does not exist, Play will tell you exactly what and where the mistake is.

Templates are compiled to classes, and we have seen how to compose complex pages from reusable smaller pieces, by making use of composition.

With the asset pipeline, we can effortlessly use LESS and CoffeeScript instead of CSS and JavaScript, and it can also compile JavaScript into better JavaScript with the Google Closure compiler.

Finally, the internationalization functionality of Play is powerful and allows you to make your application available in multiple languages.

In the next chapter, we'll take a closer look at the advanced asynchronous features Play 2 provides.

Part 3

Advanced topics

Part 3 covers advanced functionality in Play. The techniques covered here are generally not required to create a basic web application with Play, but they can make your application better.

Chapter 9 is about one of Play's more powerful features: asynchronous request handling. It explains why long-running tasks are better performed "in the background," and how to achieve that easily. It also shows how you can have a web application with streaming data, using WebSockets or Comet.

Chapter 10 explains how to build a secure application in Play. It explains how you can avoid common security problems, and how you can use filters to implement authentication.

Chapter 11 covers the build process of Play. It explains the configuration files, and shows you how to package your code in reusable modules. Finally, it shows you what's involved with taking your application to production.

Chapter 12 introduces the tools that Play has for testing your application. It explains what different kinds of automated tests there are, and how you can write them for your application.

Asynchronous data

This chapter covers

- Handling data asynchronously
- Scheduling asynchronous tasks
- Streaming HTTP responses
- Unidirectional communication with Comet
- Bidirectional communication with WebSockets

In this chapter, we'll learn how to process data *asynchronously* and how to schedule asynchronous jobs. First, we'll get familiar with the principle behind asynchronous data handling and why it's useful. One of the goals of handling data asynchronously is allowing our application to scale to thousands of concurrent connections, while responding to clients immediately. Then we'll learn about an older but widely used protocol to handle data asynchronously between servers and clients: *Comet*. We'll finish with the *WebSocket* protocol, which is a standard way to communicate data asynchronously between servers and clients.

This is a long chapter, as we're going to try to cover most of the aspects of Play 2's asynchronous feature. But because this is an essential Play 2 feature, it's worth it.

Before we start, a little introduction to asynchronous data is useful.

9.1   *What do we mean by asynchronous data?*

Traditional web frameworks use "call-and-return," also known as *synchronous* processing. It means that the client of a service calls the service and then stops; it waits for the service to complete its task before the client code continues. If the client code has nothing else to do, this places a burden on the system running the client, since it has to keep the code hanging around in memory with nothing going on. For example, let's imagine you're requesting a report to be displayed on the page. Generating the report is a pretty intensive computation. Using synchronous processing means that every client will have to wait for this intensive computation to finish, as illustrated in figure 9.1.

In contrast, if we were to delegate the intensive processing to another subsystem, our framework would have more time to answer the other clients or do other things. For example, we could call one of the services to compute the report and another one to calculate a second report. Those two reports could be executed in parallel instead of sequentially. In these cases, what's called for is *asynchronous* processing. You can think of this as the client firing off a request message to a service and then doing some other work. The service does its work and, when it's done, it fires a response message back to the client.

To accomplish this kind of functionality, Play uses an event-driven middleware framework called *Akka*[1] to process every client request. This means that every time a request is sent, the processing of the request is delegated to the Akka event-driven framework, making Play asynchronous by nature. Once the Akka subsystem finishes processing the request, Akka calls back to Play, and Play issues a response to the client. Figure 9.2 illustrates precisely that.

By default, Play is intended to work with short requests. That means that if a request's processing time is long (for example, waiting for a long computation), it'll

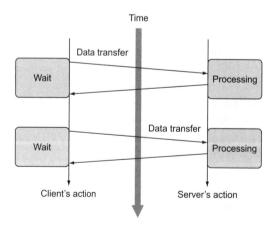

Figure 9.1   Web framework with synchronous architecture

---

[1]   Akka is also part of the type-safe stack. If you want to know more about Akka, visit http://akka.io and read *Akka in Action*: http://www.manning.com/roestenburg/.

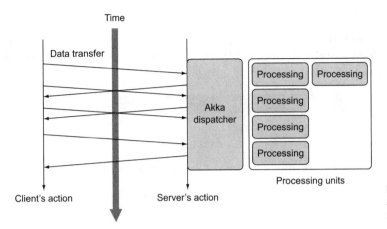

Figure 9.2 Play's asynchronous architecture

block the Akka component of the Play application (the Akka thread pool is saturating) and hinder your application's responsiveness. We therefore need to make sure we're programming using Play's asynchronous special features, explained in the next section.

9.2 *Handling asynchronous data*

Let's see an example of how asynchronous programming actually works in a Play application. Our warehouse application needs a dashboard. The dashboard contains several reports indicating the current warehouse performance (also known as *key performance indicators* or *KPI*). These reports are quite heavy to compute. Therefore it would be much better to execute them in parallel. Figure 9.3 shows what we want to achieve.

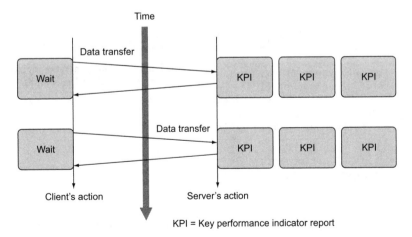

Figure 9.3 Parallel execution in Play

9.2.1   *Handling asynchronous requests*

Let's see how we can compute two reports in parallel from a request. Let's create a `Reports` controller and a `Report` model in our project. The following listing shows where to create our file.

Listing 9.1   Project directory structure

```
warehouse
    ├── app
    │    ├── controllers
    │    │    └── Reports.java        ◄── Our new controller
    │    ├── models
    │    │    └── Report.java         ◄── Our new model
    │    ├── views
    ├── conf
    │    └── routes
    ├── public
    └── test
```

The `Report` model is simple and consists of faking some computation. The following listing shows how the report generation is simulated.

Listing 9.2   Model that simulates a report generation

```java
package models;
import play.Logger;

public class Report {
    String name;

    public Report(String name) {
        this.name = name;
    }

    public void execute() {
        long start = System.currentTimeMillis();
        Logger.info("starting intensive " + name + " report at " + start);
        try {
            Thread.sleep(5000);        ◄─┤ Simulate report generation by suspending
        } catch(Exception e) {}           current thread for five seconds
        Logger.info("done with intensive " + name + " report ");
        Logger.info("took "
            + ((System.currentTimeMillis() - start) / 1000) + "s");
    }

    public String toString() {
        return name;
    }
}
```

The report model is straightforward and consists of a report name and the `execute()` method to simulate the report generation.

As you know, an action method must return a `Result`. In order to be asynchronous, we need to return a `Promise` of a `Result` (`Promise<Result>`) instead. A `Promise` is a commitment to do or not do something. A `Promise<Result>` will eventually be redeemed with a value of type `Result`. By giving a `Promise<Result>` instead of a regular `Result`, we are able to compute the result without blocking anything. Play will then serve this result as soon as the promise is redeemed.

A simple way to execute a block of code asynchronously and to get a `Promise` is to use the `play.libs.Akka` helpers, as listing 9.3 shows. To run code asynchronously, all that is needed is to implement the `Callable` interface. You can look at Akka helpers as helpers that execute code snippets in another thread. Akka allows you to distribute those "threads" on other servers as well, but that's a different subject. You can find more information on the subject in the excellent book[2] published by Manning.

Listing 9.3 Controller that executes report generation in parallel

```
package controllers;

import models.Report;
import java.util.List;

import java.util.concurrent.Callable;
import play.*;
import play.libs.F.Promise;
import play.libs.F.Function;
import play.mvc.*;
import views.html.*;

public class Reports extends Controller {

    public static Result index() {

        Promise<Report> promiseOfKPIReport =
        play.libs.Akka.future(
            new Callable<Report>() {
                public Report call() {
                    return intensiveKPIReport();
                }
            }
        );
        Promise<Report> promiseOfETAReport =
        play.libs.Akka.future(
            new Callable<Report>() {
                public Report call() {
                    return intensiveETAReport();
                }
            }
        );
        Promise<List<Report>> promises =
            Promise.waitAll(promiseOfKPIReport, promiseOfETAReport);
        return async(
```

Indicates that this report generation runs asynchronously

Indicates that we want to return a result that will be computed later on

Indicates that we want results of report generation to be on the Promise object

---

[2] *Akka in Action*, http://www.manning.com/roestenburg/, by Raymond Roestenburg, Rob Bakker, and Rob Williams.

Once we have
our result, we
are giving
back a Result

```
                    promises.map(
                        new Function<List<Report>, Result>() {
                            public Result apply(List<Report> reports) {
                                return ok(report.render(reports));
                            }
                        }
                    );
                }

    public static Report intensiveKPIReport() {
        Report r = new Report("KPI report");
        r.execute();
        return r;
    }

    public static Report intensiveETAReport() {
        Report r = new Report("ETA report");
        r.execute();
        return r;
    }
}
```

Render the
reports. The
view will be
created later on.

The preceding code needs careful explanation. First, we're wrapping each report gen-eration inside blocks of code that are run asynchronously (using the `Callable` imple-mentations). Then we tell our client that, before we can return a response, we need to wait for both reports to be generated. Using the `Promise` object allows Play not to wait for the reports to be processed, but to suspend the current request. You may have noticed also that we use the `async()` method to wrap our `Result` object. This tells Play that whatever we're doing, don't wait for it, because it's going to take some time. Instead, once the processing of the report is done, the `Promise` object will make sure Play knows when it's time to return a `Result`.

9.2.2 Returning the asynchronous result

You probably noticed that we returned a `Result` that is in fact a `Promise` of a result. This is done using the `async()` method, as shown in the following code sample:

```
Promise<List<Report>> promises =
        Promise.waitAll(promiseOfKPIReport, promiseOfETAReport);
return async(
                promises.map(
                    new Function<List<Report>, Result>() {
                        public Result apply(List<Report> reports) {
                            return ok(index.render(reports));
                        }
                    }
                )
            );
```

The apply
method is
acting as a
constructor
here

This is
effectively an
inner class that
we implement;
it simulates a
function given
as parameter

The `async()` method itself takes a `Promise` object. The `Promise` object is nothing more than a holder that indicates when the report's processing is finished. This is called *redeeming* the promise.

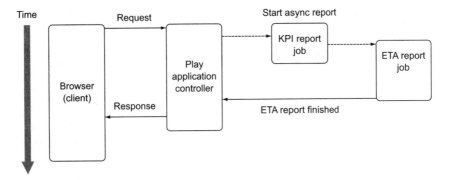

Figure 9.4 Sequence events generated reports

Once the `Promise` is redeemed, we execute a function that takes the `List` of newly generated reports and returns a `Result`. The `Result` is then sent back to our client. Figure 9.4 shows the sequence of events.

It's important to realize that generating the reports doesn't block the code in our controller's action method. We are effectively suspending the current client request so that Play can spend time on other clients. The actual report generation is handled by the Akka helpers (that is, other threads), and Play won't block at any point, allowing it to serve a large number of requests simultaneously. This is also rather useful when you need to process multiple sources of information in order to compute a response for your clients.

Let's create the `views/report.scala.html` file to perform the computation and display our simulated generated reports. The following listing shows the `views /report .scala.html` file content.

Listing 9.4 `views/report.scala.html` view file

```
@(reports: List[models.Report])

@main("Reports") {
<h2>Reports</h2>
  <ul>
     @for(report <- reports) {
 <li><b>@report</b> ready to be downloaded
 <a href="#">here</a></li>
     }
</ul>
}
```

We now need to add a new entry to our routes file.

```
GET /reports/  controllers.Reports.index()
```

Now, if you point your browser to http://localhost:9000/reports/ you should see the following in your log:

```
[info] play - database [default] connected at jdbc:h2:mem:play

play - Application started (Dev)

application - starting intensive KPI report report at 1381609106439

application - starting intensive ETA report report at 1381609106439

application - done with intensive ETA report report at 1381609111444

application - done with intensive KPI report report at 1381609111444

application - took 5s application - took 5s
```

Report ETA starts

Report KPI ends

Report KPI starts

Report ETA ends

It's interesting to note that report generation starts at the same time and finishes at the same time. They're executed in parallel instead of sequentially. Figure 9.5 shows the application's screen after report generation.

We're now able to execute jobs in an asynchronous way and in parallel. Let's see how we can schedule those jobs.

9.3   *Scheduling asynchronous tasks*

In Play, you can schedule repetitive tasks using Akka, either by using an actor or by passing a Runnable class. For example, to send an order to the default actor every five seconds:

```
Akka.system().scheduler().schedule(
        Duration.create(4, SECONDS),
        Duration.create(5, SECONDS),
        defaultActor,
        new Order(),
        Akka.system().dispatcher(),
        null
    );
```

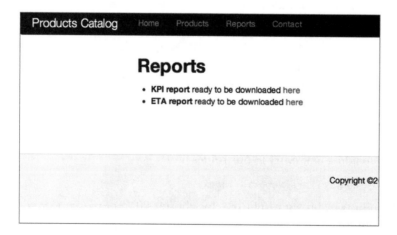

Figure 9.5   Screenshot of our application once the reports are generated

The `Akka.system.scheduler` allows us to schedule a background job; the job starts four seconds after initialization and occurs every five seconds. Every five seconds, we send a new `Order` to the default actor. Explaining an actor is outside the topic of this book, but actors are concurrent processes that communicate by exchanging messages. Actors can also be seen as a form of active objects for which invoking a method corresponds to sending a message. You can read more about actors and Akka in the excellent *Akka in Action* book[3] published by Manning.

Instead of an actor, you can use a class that implements `Runnable` and pass your business logic inside the `run()` method:

```
Akka.system().scheduler().schedule(
  Duration.create(10, TimeUnit.SECONDS),
  new Runnable() {
    public void run() {
      // Your business logic here.
    }
  }
);
```

Let's see how Play responds to clients, and how Play can stream large amounts of data back to its clients.

9.4 Streaming HTTP responses

As we've seen in the earlier chapters, after receiving and interpreting a request message, the Play server responds with an HTTP response message.

Sometimes we also want to *stream* information to the clients. This means that we want to continuously send data to our web clients. As an example for our application, we want to stream the expedited orders; we want to see our client orders on a screen as soon as they're entered. People in the warehouse can then pack and ship those orders as soon as they see them. Figure 9.6 shows our final application.

But before we start streaming our expedited orders, let's recap the different methods to return data with Play and, from there, see how streaming data is different from a technical point of view.

9.4.1 Standard responses and Content-Length header

When you send a standard (non-streaming) HTTP response, Play automatically sends the appropriate `Content-Length` HTTP header with the response, which lets the client know how many bytes are in the response, and the connection between client and server is closed as soon as all bytes have been transmitted. For this to work, Play needs to know the entire content of the response before it starts sending it.

---

[3] *Akka in Action*, http://www.manning.com/roestenburg/, by Raymond Roestenburg, Rob Bakker, and Rob Williams.

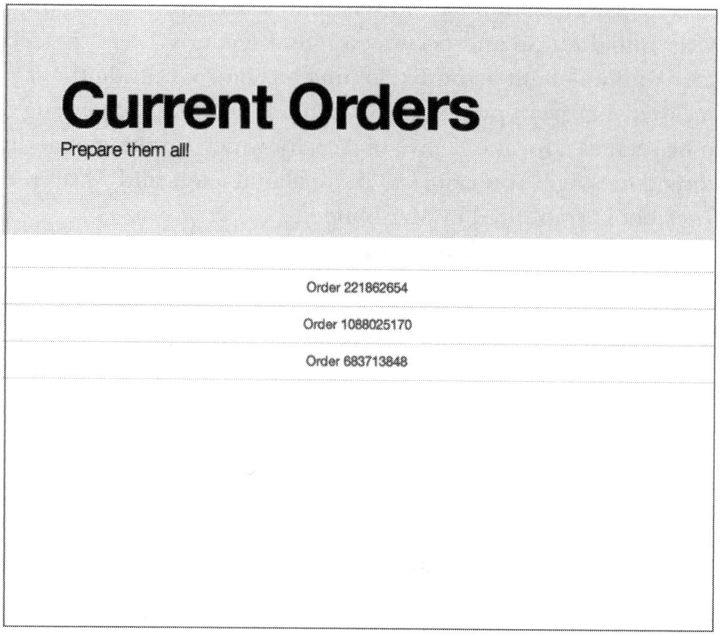

Current Orders
Prepare them all!

Order 221862654
Order 1088025170
Order 683713848

Figure 9.6   Screenshot of our future application

For example, the following code sends back the "Hello World" message to clients:

```
public static Result index() {
   return ok("Hello World")
}
```

Since Play knows the entire response body ("Hello World"), Play sets the appropriate `Content-Length` HTTP header, as well as any other mandatory headers. You don't have to specify anything yourself to make this happen.

This would be the appropriate method to use if the number of expedited orders was fixed. But for our use case, the number of expedited orders is unpredictable; we want to stream them as they arrive. Play can't calculate the length of the response, and we don't know if and when to close the connection. Therefore, this method of sending responses is not suitable in this case.

Another problem with this approach is that the entire response must be loaded into memory—which can be problematic if the response is very big, such as when transferring big files.

9.4.2   *Serving files*

Play is able to stream a file to web clients without loading the file's content into memory. That is useful if you want to send back larger files to web clients. If we take our previous report example, once the report computation is done, we can easily send back the computed report as a PDF file:

```
public static Result retrievePdf(String reportId) {
   return ok(new java.io.File(report.asPdfFile());
}
```

Again, Play will set the appropriate `Content-Length` HTTP header. It can do this because it can tell how big the file is before it starts sending out the response. Additionally, this helper will determine the `Content-Type` header from the filename and set the `Content-Disposition` header to specify how the web browser should handle this response. Once the response is consumed, the connection is again closed.

Like the previous approach, this approach only works because the size of the response is known beforehand. We're still no closer to sending content that is computed on the fly, without knowing how big the content will be.

We just saw how to stream large files to our web clients with a fixed-size response. Let's see how we can stream arbitrarily sized data back to our clients.

9.4.3 *Chunked responses*

Our application example needs to stream expedited orders. There is no predefined content length; it could really be an infinite number. For this kind of response we have to use *chunked* transfer encoding, and Play provides full support for that.

As the name suggests, chunked transfer encoding sends the response in multiple *chunks*. The way this works is that these chunks of data are sent out as soon as a reasonable number of bytes becomes available. The server first sends out the size of the next chunk, and then the chunk itself. This is repeated until the response is complete.

The advantage of this approach is that we can serve live data as it becomes available. The drawback is that since the web browser doesn't know the content size, it isn't able to display a proper download progress bar, which isn't an issue for our expedited orders.

Let's say we have a service that provides our expedited orders from another system as soon as they are entered. We can ask Play to stream this content directly using a chunked response:

```
public static Result index() {
   InputStream is = getExpeditedOrders(); return ok(is);
}
```

This requires us to implement the expedited-orders service to return an `InputStream`. Expedited orders are written to the input stream as soon as they are entered.

Another (simpler) alternative is to implement your own chunked response builder. The Play Java API supports both text and binary chunked streams (via `String` and `byte[]`). Listing 9.5 shows the `liveUpdate()` action method of our `Application .java` controller file.

> **Listing 9.5 Streaming expedited orders: Application controller**

```
public static Result liveUpdate() {
   // Prepare a chunked text stream Chunks<String>
   chunks = new StringChunks() {

      // Called when the stream is ready
      public void onReady(Chunks.Out<String> out) {           Method called when the
         ExpeditedOrders.registerChunkOut(out);               connection is established
                                                              with the client
```

```
    }
  }
  response().setContentType("text/html;charset=UTF-8");
  ok(chunks);
}
```

Indicates to client that we're sending back HTML

The `onReady()` method is called whenever Play is ready to send out data, and it's therefore safe to write to the output stream. It gives you a `Chunks.Out` channel to write to. Let's say we have an asynchronous process somewhere pushing to this stream; you can safely use that channel to push information to the web client. Listing 9.6 shows a simple example of such a service. This service should live in the `models` package.

Listing 9.6 The `ExpeditedOrders` service

Sockets as a list that we want to write to

Default actor uses ExpeditedOrders object

ExpeditedOrders object is an actor, allowing us to schedule it at regular intervals

```
public class ExpeditedOrders extends UntypedActor {
    static List<Chunks.Out<String>> outs =
                    new ArrayList<Chunks.Out<String>>();
    static ActorRef defaultActor =
        Akka.system().actorOf(new Props(ExpeditedOrders.class));

    static {
        Akka.system().scheduler().schedule(
            Duration.create(4, SECONDS),
            Duration.create(5, SECONDS),
            defaultActor,
            new Order(),
            Akka.system().dispatcher()
        );
    }

    public static void registerChunkOut(
      Chunks.Out<String> out) {
        ExpeditedOrders.outs.add(out);
    }

    public void onReceive(Object message)
      throws Exception {
        Order order = (Order)message;
        // Writing to our channel
    for(Chunks.Out<String> out: outs) {
        // Send enough data to be displayed
        char[] buffer = new char[1024 * 5];
        Arrays.fill(buffer, ' ');
        out.write(new String(buffer));
          out.write("<li>" +
            order.toString() + "</li>");
        }
    }
}
```

Schedule ExpeditedOrders to call its onReceive method every five seconds with a new Order object

Register socket from clients we want to write on

Every five seconds, this method is executed and a new order is passed as an argument

Fill in empty data so the chunk size is reached. This allows us to display the line without waiting for extra data.

Send back a script with the order to display it on the page; we append the order to the html element with id container.

The class `ExpeditedOrders` might look cryptic, but with a bit of explanation it's quite straightforward. As seen in section 9.3, the `Akka.system.scheduler` allows us to schedule a background job; the job starts four seconds after initialization and occurs every five seconds. The container for this job is the `ExpeditedOrder` object, and we send to the container a new `Order`.

Every five seconds, a new order is created and sent to the `ExpeditedOrder` object. Upon receipt, the `ExpeditedOrders` onchange method writes to all the channel outputs (the `Chunks.outs` list object) and sends a chunk to every connected web client, streaming the orders. Once the data is received, the client executes the script element and adds the order to the current page.

We now need to create our `Order` model class. The following listing shows the `Order` class.

> **Listing 9.7 The `Order` model class**

```
public class Order {

    public Order() {}

    public String toString() {
        return "Order " + nextId() + " date " + new Date();
    }

    private static String nextId() {
        Random random = new Random();            Generate a random
        return new BigInteger(30, random).toString(9);   ◁┘ unique ID
    }

}
```

To see the orders streamed, we need to edit the `index.scala.html` view with the following:

```
@(message: String)
@main("live streaming") {
    <p>
     <iframe id="messages" style="width:100%;height:100%"
         src="@routes.Application.liveUpdate()"></iframe>
    </p>
}
```

We need to update our routes file with the following:

```
GET  /live       controllers.Application.index()
GET  /live-update    controllers.Application.liveUpdate()
```

If you point your browser to http://localhost:9000/live you should now see live orders appearing on your screen.

As you can see, streaming data is straightforward with a bit of explanation. But this doesn't do much by itself. Let's go a step further and see how we can use the chunks mechanism from our views.

9.5   Unidirectional communication with Comet

Comet sockets are a useful application of chunked transfer encoding. *Comet* is a web application model in which a long-held HTTP request allows a web server to push data to a browser, without the browser explicitly requesting it. Figure 9.7 illustrates how Comet works.

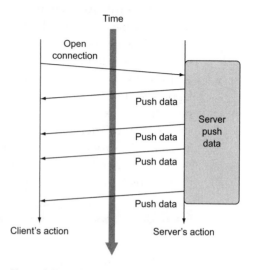

With Comet, the browser starts a request, and the server keeps the connection open until it has something to send. It's more efficient than traditional long polling, in which a web client queries the server at regular intervals to see if there are new messages. But it only allows for receiving messages from the server: it's a unidirectional communication protocol.

Figure 9.7   Unidirectional communication with Comet

Comet is an umbrella term, encompassing multiple techniques for achieving this interaction. All these methods rely on features included by default in browsers, such as JavaScript, rather than on nondefault plugins. The Comet approach differs from the original model of the web, in which a browser requests one complete web page at a time.

A Comet socket is just a chunked text/HTML response (see the previous section about chunks) containing only HTML <script> elements. In each chunk, we write a <script> tag containing JavaScript that is immediately executed by the web browser upon receipt. This way we can send events live to the web browser from the server; for each message, wrap it in a <script> tag that calls a JavaScript callback function, and write it to the chunked response.

To illustrate how Comet works, let's extend our previous example with the concepts we just mentioned. Listing 9.8 shows how to send back script commands from the server.

Listing 9.8   The scheduler `onReceive` method

```
public void onReceive(Object message) throws Exception {
        Order order = (Order)message;
        for(Chunks.Out<String> out: outs) {
    out.write("<script type=\"text/javascript\">" +
      "parent.jQuery('#container').append('<li><a href=\"#\">" +
      order.toString() + "</a></li>');</script>");
    }
    }
```

Write to all registered clients a JavaScript command to be executed by the client; append order to the html element with id container

We now need to change our view to reflect our new Comet implementation. Let's edit our `comet.html` file. Listing 9.9 shows the new view.

Listing 9.9   Comet client-side implementation (our view)

```
@main("COMET") {
    <iframe style="display:none" id="messages"                          The iframe that
      src="@routes.Application.liveUpdate.unique"></iframe>    ◁       sets up a
                                                                        permanent
    <ul id="container" style=" text-align:center"                       connection to
      class="nav nav-tabs nav-stacked"></ul>                            our server
}
```

For each chunk we receive, we add the order to the div with the ID `container`. The chunk we're receiving evaluates the script tag. The script tag refers to the parent jQuery functions. Because the iframe receives the orders through the `liveUpdate` action method, the end user sees the current page as a normal web page. We now only need to update our route file with the following routes:

```
                                                        This route displays the web page that
                                                      ┐ shows the orders' IDs
GET   /live    controllers.Application.index()      ◁─┘

GET   /live-update    controllers.Application.liveUpdate()    ◁┐  This route streams
                                                               │  the orders
```

If you run this action from a web browser (http://localhost:9000/live), you'll see live orders getting displayed on the web page.

Play provides a Comet helper to handle these Comet-chunked streams that does almost the same as what we just wrote. Actually it does more, such as pushing initial blank buffer data for browser compatibility and supporting both `String` and JSON messages. Let's rewrite the previous example to use Comet (see listing 9.10).

Listing 9.10   `liveUpdate`

```
public static Result liveUpdate() {
  Comet comet = new Comet("parent.cometMessage") {    ◁┐   Indicates we are using
    public void onConnected() {                       ◁    Comet protocol;
      ExpeditedOrders.registerChunkOut(this);              parent.cometMessage
    }                                                       refers to the JavaScript
  };                            Upon web client            client code to be
  return ok(comet);             connection,               executed
}                               register client
```

We need to slightly change the `ExpeditedOrders` class as well. Listing 9.11 shows our new `ExpeditedOrders` implementation.

Listing 9.11   `ExpeditedOrders` listing with Comet implementation

```
public class ExpeditedOrders extends UntypedActor {

  static List<Comet> comets = new ArrayList<Comet>();    ◁──  Comet client registry
```

```
...

    public static void registerChunkOut(Comet out) {
      ExpeditedOrders.comets.add(out);                    ◁──  Add a new client to registry
    }

    public void onReceive(Object message) throws Exception {
      Order order = (Order)message;
      for(Comet comet: comets) {
        comet.sendMessage(order.toString());              ◁┐  Send message to client; note
        }                                                   │  that we don't need to pass
    }                                                       │  script instructions anymore
  }
```

The standard technique for writing a Comet socket is to load an infinite, chunked
Comet response in an iframe and specify a callback calling the parent frame with an
HTML page. Let's rewrite our `comet.html` view, as in the following listing.

Listing 9.12   Client-side Comet implementation (our view)

```
@(message: String)
@main("COMET") {
<script type="text/javascript">                           │  JavaScript function invoked
var cometMessage = function(event) {                       │  when a chunked response is
    console.log('Received event: ' + event)        ◁─┘    │  sent by server
   $("#container").append("<li><a href='#'>" +      ◁┐  Append response to
  event + "</a></li>")                                  │  container element
}
</script>
<div class="hero-unit">
<h1>Current Orders</h1>
<p>Prepare them all!</p>
</div>                                                     │  iframe that opens
<iframe style="display:none" id="messages"                │  permanent connection
src="@routes.Application.liveUpdate.unique"></iframe>  ◁─┘  with server
 <ul id="container" style=" text-align:center"
class="nav nav-tabs nav-stacked"></ul>
}
```

Comet essentially consists of opening a permanent connection to the server through
an iframe HTML element. The server can then decide when to send chunked
responses to the web client. Each time a response is sent, the JavaScript callback function `cometMessage` is called. The response is passed as a function argument. In our
case, the web client then updates the web page and appends the response. Due to the
nature of Play, it allows a lot of connections to be open concurrently without saturating the server. In fact, as we previously explained, for each connection open there is
no matching thread. This allows the Play server to scale to thousands of concurrent
open connections. But you'll still have one socket open per connection.

   This solution allows us to push data from the server to the client. To send data
from the web client to the server, you might want to use AJAX requests in combination
with Comet. But this is out of scope for this book. The protocol doesn't allow you to

push data from web clients to the server; it's a one-way, live communication. You can read more on this subject in the excellent Manning book *Single Page Web Applications* by Michael S. Mikowski and Josh C. Powell (www.manning.com/mikowski/). This brings us to the next section, about WebSocket: a protocol that makes bidirectional communication possible.

9.6 *Bidirectional communication with WebSockets*

Until now, we've only seen that the web supports one-way communication: the web client issues a request to the server, and the server sends a response. We've also seen how to stream data from the server to web clients, effectively making a permanent connection between web clients and the server and allowing us to push data to web clients. We could stop right here, as it's a long chapter already, but we think it might be worthwhile to know about the use cases for which you really need to have a bidirectional means of communication—such as whenever you need real-time interactions with your users.

Let's try to extend our previous example. We're now able to display an order's list in real time. Each order needs to be processed by the warehouse operators. In the warehouse, different people will prepare different orders. If we don't allow operators to notify others that they're working on a particular order, chances are the same order will be prepared twice. What we want is to allow people to click on an order and notify all other operators that the order is being processed.

Figure 9.8 shows the resulting application.

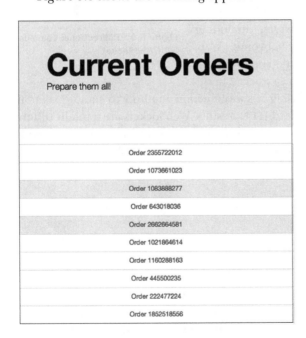

Figure 9.8   WebSocket pickup order application

We want to receive live data, but we also want to send back data over the same connection. Happily, modern web browsers natively support such two-way live communication via WebSockets. WebSocket is a web technology providing bidirectional, full-duplex communication channels over a single TCP connection.

9.6.1 *WebSockets explained*

The WebSocket API is being standardized by the W3C, and the WebSocket protocol has been standardized by the IETF as RFC 6455 (http://tools.ietf.org/html/rfc6455). WebSocket can be used by any client or server application, even if the primary focus is web clients and web servers. The protocol simply defines a standard way to enable bidirectional communication between servers and clients. It also defines a JavaScript API to be used from within web browsers. Figure 9.9 shows the bidirectional nature of the protocol.

In addition, the communication happens over the regular TCP port number 80, which is of benefit for those environments which block nonstandard internet connections using a firewall. The WebSocket protocol is currently supported in several browsers, including Safari, Firefox, and Google Chrome. WebSocket also requires server-side support from the web applications in order to work.

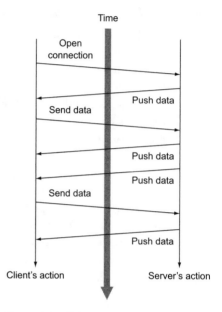

Figure 9.9   **Bidirectional communication with WebSocket**

Until now we've been using a simple action method to handle standard HTTP requests and send back standard HTTP results. WebSockets are a totally different beast and can't be handled via standard actions. To handle a WebSocket, your method must return a `WebSocket` instead of a `Result`. Play's server-side WebSocket support defines one method to interact with clients:

```
/**
 * Called when the WebSocket is ready
 *
 * @param in The Socket in.
 * @param out The Socket out.
 */
public abstract void onReady(In<A> in, Out<A> out);
```

This method is the entry point for our code. Our action method must return a Web-Socket result that must implement this method. How exactly do we interact with the clients, then? The answer is easy: we can interact through the `In` and `Out` objects.

The `In` object allows you to add handlers to incoming events. To handle client messages, you can use the following two methods by providing a callback handler:

- `onMessage()`—This method calls the provided handler when a client sends a message.
- `onClose()`—This method calls the provided handler when a client closes its connection with the server.

To send messages to clients, two methods need to be implemented:

- `write`—Send a message to clients.
- `close`—Close the connection with clients.

Messages are either of type `String` or type `byte[]`. A WebSocket has access to the request headers (from the HTTP request that initiates the WebSocket connection), allowing you to retrieve standard headers and session data. But it doesn't have access to any request body, nor to the HTTP response. Once the WebSocket is ready, you get both in and out channels.

At first glance, it's surprising, since all action handling must happen in a callback method. To interact with WebSocket, our action must return a WebSocket result and implement the `WebSocket Result` class. Listing 9.13 shows a basic example that sends `hello` to our clients and prints any client messages to the console.

Listing 9.13   Basic WebSocket example

```
public static WebSocket<String> hello() {        ◁── Return WebSocket Result instance
    return new WebSocket<String>() {

        public void onReady(WebSocket.In<String> in,   ◁┐ Implement onReady
            WebSocket.Out<String> out) {                  │ method, giving access
                                                          │ to incoming and
            in.onMessage(new Callback<String>() {         │ outgoing channels
                public void invoke(String event) {        │ (can read and write
                    System.out.println(event);            │ from/to clients)
                }
            });

            in.onClose(new Callback0() {               ◁─ Add callback
                public void invoke() {                      handler to
                    System.out.println("Disconnected");     process any
                }                                           closed
            });                                             connections

            out.write("Hello client!");                ◁─ Send "hello"
                                                          message to
        }                                                 clients
    };
}
```

Add callback handler to process any incoming messages

The Play server-side implementation is straightforward. The only tricky part consists of adding the `Callback` handlers: they're the interfaces that you need to implement. Listing 9.14 shows the client-side implementation. Edit the new `index.html` view, and add the listing content to the view.

Listing 9.14   Basic WebSocket example, client-side view

Print incoming message data to browser console

Send back "hello" to server

The reverse routing notation, asking for the WebSocket version; translates to ws://localhost:9000/hello

Client-side handler to process any incoming messages from server

```
@main(message) {
    <script type="text/javascript" charset="utf-8">
    $(function() {
    var WS = window['MozWebSocket'] ? MozWebSocket : WebSocket
    var socket =
     new WS("@routes.Application.hello.webSocketURL(request)")

        var receiveEvent = function(event) {
            console.log(event.data)
            socket.send("hello server")
        }
        socket.onmessage = receiveEvent
    });
    </script>
}
```

Last but not least, to make our example work, we need to add a rule to our `hello()` action method. Add the following line to the routes file:

```
GET  /hello  controllers.Application.hello()
```

Now if you point your browser to http://localhost:9000/, you should see the same output as shown in figure 9.10 in your console.

Looking at your browser console, you should see the same output as figure 9.11.

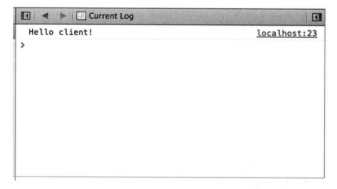

```
[info] Loading global plugins from /Users/nicolasleroux/.sbt/plugins
[info] Loading project definition from /Users/nicolasleroux/Projects/Personal/sa
[info] Set current project to ch08-5-websocket-simple (in build file:/Users/nico

--- (Running the application from SBT, auto-reloading is enabled) ---

[info] play - Listening for HTTP on /0:0:0:0:0:0:0:0:9000

(Server started, use Ctrl+D to stop and go back to the console...)

[info] play - Application started (Dev)
hello server
```

Figure 9.10 Output server side

Current Log

Hello client!   localhost:23

>

Figure 9.11   Output client side

What just happened? The web client made the request. The server set up the Web-Socket connection and sent out a "Hello client!" message. The client then received the message, logged it, and sent back "Hello server."

9.6.2 *A more advanced application with WebSockets*

We now have the elements to finish building our example application. Let's use Web-Sockets to display live orders and notify all warehouse operators when an order is being processed. If we remove our previous Comet implementation and substitute our new WebSocket implementation, we end up with listings 9.15 and 9.16 on the server side.

Listing 9.15 Server-side listing of our WebSocket application

```
public static WebSocket<String> liveUpdate() {
        return new WebSocket<String>() {

            // Called when the WebSocket Handshake is done.
            public void onReady(final WebSocket.In<String> in,
                final WebSocket.Out<String> out) {          ◁─┐ The connection
                                                               is established

                // For each event received on the socket,
                in.onMessage(new Callback<String>() {
                    public void invoke(String event) {
                        ExpeditedOrders.notifyOthers(out, event
    + " is being processed");
                    }
                });

                // When the socket is closed.             ┌─ A client
                in.onClose(new Callback0() {               │  disconnects
                    public void invoke() {            ◁────┘
                        ExpeditedOrders.unregister(out);
                    }                                      ┌─ Register
                });                                        │  WebSocket to
                                                           │  expedited
                ExpeditedOrders.register(out);        ◁───┘  order object

            }
        };
    }
```

Listen to any incoming message ▷ (annotation pointing to `in.onMessage` block)

This code is really close to what we saw before; when our socket is ready, we start listening for incoming events. For each incoming event, we use our `ExpeditedOrders` object to notify any other clients that someone picked up a shipment in order to prepare it.

In order to keep track of the client's connection, register its `WebSocket.Out` object with a registry on the `ExpeditedOrders` object.

Let's now look at the `ExpeditedOrders` object to see how to notify other clients, as listing 9.16 shows.

Listing 9.16 The server-side component that notifies our clients

```
public class ExpeditedOrders extends UntypedActor {
    static List<WebSocket.Out<String>> members
    = new ArrayList<WebSocket.Out<String>>();

    static ActorRef defaultActor
    = Akka.system().actorOf(new Props(ExpeditedOrders.class));

    static {
        Akka.system().scheduler().schedule(
            Duration.create(4, SECONDS),
            Duration.create(5, SECONDS),
            defaultActor,
            new Order(),
            Akka.system().dispatcher()
        );
    }

    public static void register(WebSocket.Out<String> out) {
        members.add(out);
    }

    public static void unregister(WebSocket.Out<String> out) {
        members.remove(out);
    }

public static void notifyOthers(WebSocket.Out<String> me,
                                    String event) {
    for(WebSocket.Out<String> out: members) {
        if (!out.equals(me))
        out.write(event);
    }
}

public static void notifyAll(String event) {
    for(WebSocket.Out<String> out: members) {
    out.write(event);
    }
}

public void onReceive(Object message)
                    throws Exception {
        Order order = (Order)message; notifyAll(order.toString());
    }
}
```

The registry, a list of open sockets to web clients

The default actor/scheduler; it'll be scheduled every five seconds

Initialize scheduler

Send message to all the web clients other than the one specified in parameter

Send message to all web clients

This method called every five seconds by actor/scheduler

You'll notice that listing 9.16 is similar to the Comet `ExpeditedOrders` implementation. We have two methods: one to notify all web clients (`notifyAll()`) and another one to notify only other clients (`notifyOthers()`). The latter is used whenever we are notified of a client picking up an order. After all, we only need to notify other clients that the order is being taken care of.

Every five seconds, the `onReceived()` method is called with a new `Order` as a parameter. We then notify all web clients that a new order has been sent, using the `notifyAll()` method.

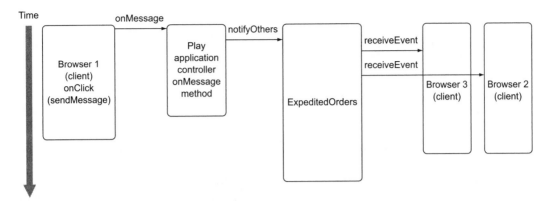

Figure 9.12 Sequence diagram of a client clicking on an order

The `notifyOthers()` method is called whenever a user clicks on an order, signalling the server that a particular client is taking care of an order. The `onMessage()` controller's method is then called. In turn, it calls the `notifyOthers()` method on the `ExpeditedOrders` object. Figure 9.12 illustrates the sequence of events.

It's important to note that the WebSocket protocol is bidirectional and allows for a client to send messages to the web server (unlike the Comet protocol). The following listing shows the client-side implementation, in order to send and receive messages on the client.

Listing 9.17 Client-side WebSocket part of our application

```
@(message: String)


@main(message) {                                            Set up
  <script type="text/javascript" charset="utf-8">         WebSocket
  $(function() {                                           connection
    var WS = window['MozWebSocket'] ? MozWebSocket : WebSocket
    var socket
      = new WS("@routes.Application.liveUpdate.webSocketURL(request)")

    var sendMessage = function() {
      socket.send($(this).text())
      $(this).css("background-color", "#EEE")
    }
    var receiveEvent = function(event) {
      var a = $("<li><a href='#'>" + event.data + "</a></li>")
      $("#container").append(a)
      if (event.data.match(/processed/g)) {
        a.css("background-color", "#EEE")
      } else {
        a.click(sendMessage)
      }
    }
    socket.onmessage = receiveEvent
```

Function to send message to web server → (annotation for `var sendMessage` block)

On receipt of message from server, create new HTML element with order information (annotation for `var receiveEvent` block)

Add listener on the mouse click that sends message to server if order wasn't already processed (annotation for `a.click(sendMessage)`)

```
  });
</script>

<div class="hero-unit">
  <h1>Current Orders</h1>
  <p>Prepare them all!</p>
</div>
<ul id="container" class="nav nav-tabs nav-stacked">
</ul>
}
```

This client-side implementation is straightforward. We have two functions: the `socket.onMessage` that is triggered every time a message is received, and `socket.send`, which allows us to send a message to the web server.

Now open two different browsers, navigate to http://localhost:9000/live in each of them, and click on an order in one of the browsers. You'll then see a message in the other browser indicating the order has been picked up and is being processed, as shown in figure 9.13.

As you can see, WebSockets are easy to use, and they facilitate real-time communication between clients and servers, making it easier to build interactive web applications.

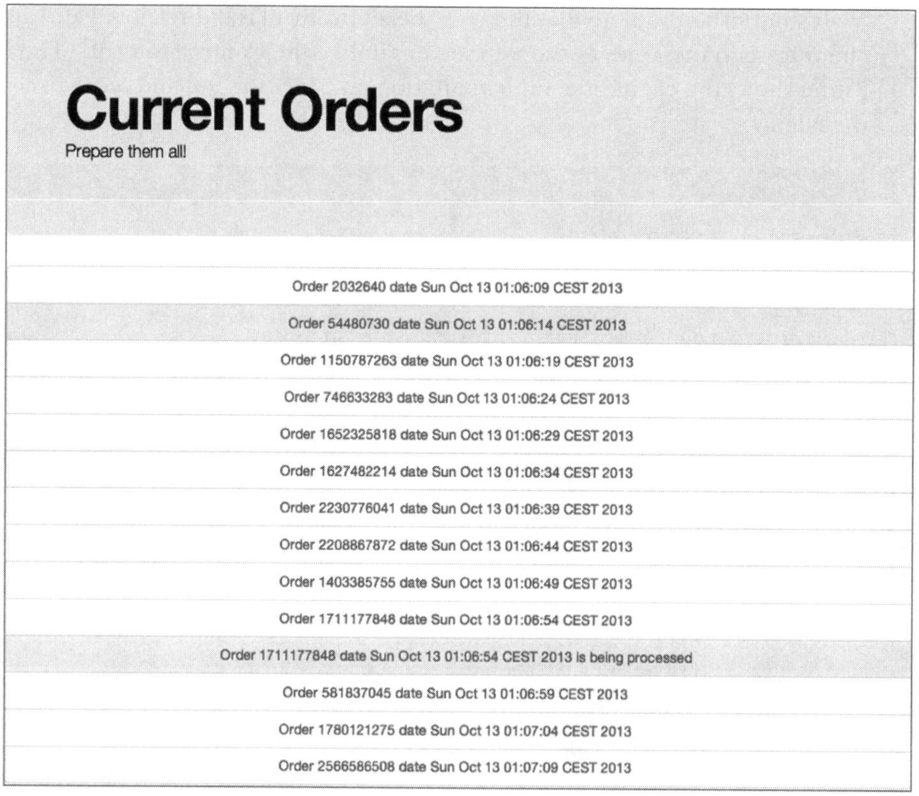

Current Orders
Prepare them all!

Order 2032640 date Sun Oct 13 01:06:09 CEST 2013

Order 54480730 date Sun Oct 13 01:06:14 CEST 2013

Order 1150787263 date Sun Oct 13 01:06:19 CEST 2013

Order 746633283 date Sun Oct 13 01:06:24 CEST 2013

Order 1652325818 date Sun Oct 13 01:06:29 CEST 2013

Order 1627482214 date Sun Oct 13 01:06:34 CEST 2013

Order 2230776041 date Sun Oct 13 01:06:39 CEST 2013

Order 2208867872 date Sun Oct 13 01:06:44 CEST 2013

Order 1403385755 date Sun Oct 13 01:06:49 CEST 2013

Order 1711177848 date Sun Oct 13 01:06:54 CEST 2013

Order 1711177848 date Sun Oct 13 01:06:54 CEST 2013 is being processed

Order 581837045 date Sun Oct 13 01:06:59 CEST 2013

Order 1780121275 date Sun Oct 13 01:07:04 CEST 2013

Order 2566586508 date Sun Oct 13 01:07:09 CEST 2013

Figure 9.13 Order being processed

9.7 *Summary*

In this chapter, you learned advanced techniques for manipulating asynchronous data. This has been a long chapter, but you've learned a lot. You saw how to process requests asynchronously and how to return an asynchronous result. Asynchronous results allow you to process a large number of requests concurrently. This is important when you have to deal with multiple data sources.

You also saw how to stream data, from fixed-size data such as a file to arbitrary-length responses. From there, you learned about the concept of chunked responses. To better understand how chunked responses can be put to use, you saw a demonstration of how they're used within the Comet protocol. The chapter ended by explaining the newer WebSocket protocol and how to use it from Play applications.

In the next chapter, you're going to find out about Play's security mechanisms and see how to secure your application.

10

Security

This chapter covers

- Play security concepts
- Adding basic authentication with filters
- Fine-grained authentication with action composition

In this chapter, we'll first look at Play 2 security concepts to understand what it means from a developer's point of view to secure your application. We'll review the different types of attacks our application can be exposed to and the tools Play 2 provides to secure our application. We'll then move forward to actually implement security in our application, with basic authentication as an example, using filters. This section shows a low-level framework security implementation, but of course Play provides built-in helpers for authentication and authorization. Last, we'll see how to use those helpers together with action composition to add more fine-grained security constraints to our application.

10.1 Play security concepts

Web application frameworks are made to help developers building web applications. Some of them also help secure the web application. One framework is not more secure than another: if you use them correctly, you'll be able to build secure apps with many frameworks. Some frameworks have some clever helper methods, for example against SQL injection, which makes it easier to build secure web applications.

In general there's no such thing as plug-and-play security. Security depends on the people using the framework, and sometimes on the development method. And it depends on all layers of a web application environment: the back-end storage, the web server, and the web application itself (and possibly other layers or applications).

It's estimated that about 75% of attacks are at the web application layer. In 2004, a study found "that out of 97% of the over 300 Web sites audited were found vulnerable to web application attack."[1] Web applications are relatively easy to attack, as they're simple to understand and manipulate. The threats against web applications include user account hijacking, bypassing access control, reading or modifying sensitive data, or presenting fraudulent content. Or an attacker might be able to steal users' personal information, steal money, or cause brand name damage by modifying company resources.

In order to prevent attacks, minimize their impact, and remove points of attack, you first have to fully understand the attack methods in order to find the correct countermeasures. That's the aim of this section, which will expose some of the most common web application security issues.

10.1.1 *Play 2 session*

Often you need to keep information associated with a user, in particular the user's login status. Without a session, the user would need to pass credentials with each request. That's what sessions are for: a set of cookies stored in the user's browser that identify the user to the website, and provide other information your web application may choose to store there rather than in the data layer (for example, the user's locale).

With Play 2, a session is a cookie that lives on the client side. So it's important to understand the implications of this. You can't store large objects in the session; instead you should store them in the database and save their IDs in the session.

This will eliminate synchronization headaches and it won't fill up your session storage space. This will also be a good idea if you modify the structure of an object while old versions of it are still in some user's cookies. Critical data shouldn't be stored in session. If the user clears his cookies or closes the browser, they'll be lost. And with client-side session storage, the user can read the data.

The cookie session is a hash of key/values, signed but not encrypted. It's signed against a secret key stored in the file `conf/application.conf`. The property `application.secret` defines the hash the cookie is signed against. The cookie is signed using the keyed-hash message authentication code SHA1 algorithm. It means that nobody can tamper with the cookie content. Every time a request is received, Play 2 verifies that the cookie hasn't been tampered with. Here's what the `application.secret` key looks like:

```
application.secret="6uU34sXWd:vm/...19]6H4omJ0pvNgQOIw"
```

---

[1] http://www.blackhat.com/presentations/win-usa-04/bh-win-04-grossman/bh-win-04-grossman-up.pdf

As your secret is safe, it's not possible for a third party to forge sessions. It's important to keep it private: don't commit it in a public repository, and when you install an application written by someone else, change the secret key to your own.

Don't store critical data: since it's not encrypted, you shouldn't store critical data in the session. The cookie's content (your session) can be seen by looking at the user cookie, or by sniffing the connection on a local network or over WiFi. As we said previously, the session is stored in a cookie, and cookies are limited to 4 KB. In addition to this limit, only strings can be stored.

10.1.2 *Cross-site scripting*

Cross-site scripting is one of the most common vulnerabilities in web applications. It consists of injecting malicious JavaScript into web pages using forms that your application provides. Using JavaScript, one can easily redirect users to another website, asking them for personal information.

For example, in our application, when adding a product, the user is asked to fill in a description for the product, as shown in figure 10.1. If you blindly include what commenters have written into your HTML page, you're opening your site to attacks.

Using this technique, an attacker could:

- Show a pop-up to your visitors
- Redirect your visitors to a site controlled by the attacker
- Steal information that's supposed to be visible only to the current user, and send it back to the attacker's site

Product form
Product (New)

ean

name

description

Submit

Figure 10.1   New product form

Consequently it's crucial to protect yourself from those attacks. That's why, by default, Play 2 will escape any content entered by the user. For example, if the user enters

```
<script>alert("hello user");</script>
```

in the description field, Play 2, when displaying the content, will escape it so the JavaScript won't be executed. Instead, it'll render the following HTML code:

```
&lt;script&gt;alert(&quot;hello user&quot;);&lt;/script&gt;
```

Figure 10.2   Pop-up window hello user

By default, Play 2 is protecting you against the cross-site scripting attack. If for some reason you want to allow the raw data to be rendered, you can use the @Html directive in your template. So, following our previous example:

```
@Html(product.description)
```

The user will see the pop-up in figure 10.2. This is why you have to be extra careful when using the @Html directive in the templates.

10.1.3 SQL injection

SQL injection is an exploit that consists of using user input to execute an SQL query that wasn't intended by the developer. This can be used to destroy data, or to get access to data that shouldn't be visible to the current user. For example, when you're using high-level "find" methods, you should be covered against SQL injection. When you build your own queries manually, you need to be careful not to concatenate strings with + but instead use question marks (?) and let the underlying persistence service correctly escape the data.

For example, using JPA style, the following is subject to SQL injection:

```
JPA.em().createQuery("select * from product where name=" + name);
```

This means that someone could insert the following name:

```
'nicolas';drop table users;
```

Obviously this is not desirable.

Instead you should use the following:

```
JPA.em().createQuery("SELECT * from product where name= ?1")
                                    .setParameter(1, name);
```

10.1.4 Cross-site request forgery

This attack method works by including malicious code or a link that accesses a web application into a page that the authenticated user is viewing. If the session for that web application hasn't timed out, an attacker may execute unauthorized commands.

In our case, this might be a link to our warehouse application. For example, a user might be browsing a chat forum where another user, Bob, has posted a message. Suppose that Bob has crafted an HTML image element that references an action on our warehouse website (rather than an image file).

Bob's post might look like this:

```
Hello! Look here:
<img src="http://paperclips.example.com/transfer/productId=1&to=Bob">
```

Because our warehouse application keeps authentication information in a cookie, if the cookie hasn't expired, then the attempt by the browser to load the image will submit the product transfer form with the cookie, thus authorizing a transaction without the original user's approval. Play 2 provides a simple mechanism that prevents cross-site request forgery attacks: the only way to secure critical actions properly is to issue an authenticity token. The idea is to generate a unique token on the form for a given user and check that this same token is submitted with the form. Happily, Play 2 provides all the tools to do so.

We're going to secure our new product form against cross-site request forgery. In order to do that, we have to enable a special filter. We're going to explain everything about filters in the next section. For now, to enable the filter, we need to import the `filters` module into our application project.

This is done by editing the file `build.sbt`. The following shows where to locate the `build.sbt` file:

```
warehouse
      ├─ app
      ├─ conf
      ├─ public
      ├─ project
      │          └─ test
      └─ build.sbt
```

We then need to add the `filter` module to our `build.sbt` file. This is easily done in the `libraryDependencies` section of the `ApplicationBuild` project class.

Listing 10.1   build.sbt

```
name := "warehouse"

version := "1.0-SNAPSHOT"

libraryDependencies ++= Seq(
  javaJdbc,
  javaEbean,
  cache,
  "com.google.guava" % "guava" % "14.0",
  filters                                    ⟵─── The filters module
)

play.Project.playJavaSettings
```

We also need to create a new class called `Global.java` that extends `GlobalSettings`. The following shows where to create the new `Global` class.

```
warehouse
      ├─ app
      │    └─ Global.java
```

```
├── conf
├── public
├── project
└── test
```

The following listing shows the new `filters()` method of our `Global.java` class.

Listing 10.2   Global.java

```
import play.*;
import play.api.mvc.EssentialFilter;      Global class is our
import play.filters.csrf.CSRFFilter;      application entry point

public class Global extends GlobalSettings {      ◁

    ...                                      Override filter methods to
                                             provide our custom filters
    @Override
    public <T extends EssentialFilter> Class<T>[] filters() {      ◁
        Class[] filters = {CSRFFilter.class};      ◁   CSRFFilter that takes
        return filters;                                care of cross-site
    }                                                  request forgery attack

    ...

}
```

The `Global` class extends the `GlobalSettings` class. This class calls methods during your application lifecycle, namely `onStart`, `onStop`, `onError`, and so forth. You can look at the javadoc class for more information. In our case, we want to provide a filter that allows us to counter the cross-site request forgery attack.

We now need to change our product form to include the generated token. Let's change our `details.scala.html` form located in the `app/views/products` directory as shown in the following:

```
warehouse
     ├── app
     │      ├── controllers
     │      ├── models
     │      └── views
     │             └── products
     │                    └── details.scala.html
     ├── conf
     ├── public
     ├── project
     └── test
```

We now need to change our form to use the specific CSRF helper. In the `details.scala.html` file, we need to replace the following line:

```
@helper.form(action = routes.Products.save(),
            'enctype -> "multipart/form-data") {
```

With the following:

```
@helper.form(action = helper.CSRF(routes.Products.save()),

    'enctype -> "multipart/form-data") {
```

Now, if you refresh your page and point your browser to http://localhost:9000
/products/new, in the HTML source code you should see the following:

```
<form action="/products/?csrfToken=d671e4ba123be8408bb6"
    method="POST" enctype="multipart/form-data">
```

The `csrfToken` is automatically generated and Play 2 will automatically check that this
is a valid CSRF token for the given `POST` request. If someone tampers with it, you'll
receive an invalid CSRF token error message like the following:

```
Invalid CSRF Token
```

You can fine-tune the CSRF filter using the following properties in your `application`
`.conf`:

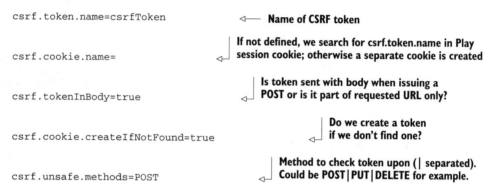

csrf.token.name=csrfToken   ◁—— **Name of CSRF token**

csrf.cookie.name=   ◁┛ **If not defined, we search for csrf.token.name in Play**
session cookie; otherwise a separate cookie is created

csrf.tokenInBody=true   ◁┛ **Is token sent with body when issuing a**
POST or is it part of requested URL only?

csrf.cookie.createIfNotFound=true   ◁┛ **Do we create a token**
if we don't find one?

csrf.unsafe.methods=POST   ◁┛ **Method to check token upon (| separated).**
Could be POST|PUT|DELETE for example.

We just used a filter, but it's important to understand exactly how filters work in Play 2,
as you might need to code some.

10.2 *Adding basic authentication with filters*

In this section we're going to discuss filters, an advanced Play 2 feature. In the next
section, we'll see how we can use more out-of-the-box Play authentication features,
but it's important to understand the more advanced features as well. It's time to
secure our warehouse application and to only let selected users access it. For this,
we're going to implement basic authentication. Basic authentication is simple and is
supported by all browsers. When the server wants the user agent to authenticate
itself, it can send a request for authentication. This request should be sent using the
HTTP 401 Not Authorized response code containing a `WWW-Authenticate` HTTP
header. The `WWW-Authenticate` header for basic authentication (used most often) is
constructed as follows:

```
WWW-Authenticate: Basic realm="warehouse app"
```

On the client side, when the user agent wants to send the server authentication credentials, it may use the `Authorization` header. The `Authorization` header is constructed
as follows: Username and password are combined into a string: `username:password`.

The resulting string literal is then encoded using Base64. The authorization method and a space are then placed before the encoded string (for example, "Basic"). So if the user agent uses *Nicolas* as the username and *secret* as the password then the header is formed as follows:

```
Authorization: Basic bmljb2xhczpzZWNyZXQ===
```

Figure 10.3 summarizes the basic authentication protocol we just explained.

To implement the basic authentication protocol, we need to check every incoming request for the `Authorization` header to see if the client is authorized. If there's a value for the `Authorization` header, we need to decode it and to check the username and password. We could do that for *every* action method we implement, but this isn't handy, as we really want the authentication to be applied over the whole application. This is where filters come in handy.

Filters are essentially pieces of code that are applied to every incoming request and/or response. Filters are also reusable from project to project. This is actually different from implementing custom code in the `Global` class and overriding the `onRequest` method (this method is called at the same moment as filters, actually).

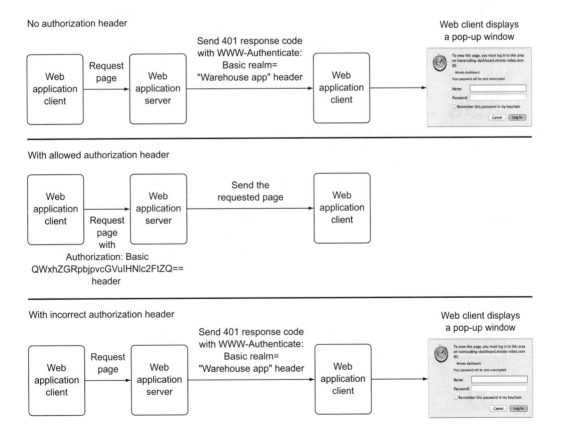

Figure 10.3   Basic authentication

As a reminder, when an HTTP request is made, Play 2 parses the request header. Then the request body is received. Next Play 2 parses the body, as explained in chapter 9. The next thing is to send the HTTP response. An HTTP response is a set of response headers, followed by a response body. Filters act just after Play 2 parses the HTTP request headers of an incoming request and before the body is parsed.

In Play 2, a filter is more of a Scala feature than a Java one. But it's still possible to create a filter in Java, even if some parts might be strange to a normal Java developer. Let's see in detail how we can create our basic authentication filter.

First, we need to create a new `BasicAuthenticationFilter` Java class in the `utils` package:

```
warehouse
     ├── app
     │     └── utils
     │              └── BasicAuthenticationFilter.java
     ├── conf
     ├── public
     ├── project
     └── test
```

A filter always implements the `EssentialFilter` interface. This interface only has one method, `apply`, that takes an `EssentialAction` and returns an `EssentialAction`. An `EssentialAction` is an interface that essentially represents what needs to be sent back to the web client: HTTP headers and a body. For example, an OK response is an `EssentialAction` with an HTTP header response code 200 and a body text `ok`. So basically, a filter allows you to chain `EssentialActions` to apply a piece of code to them. In our case, we want to check for an `Authorization` header, and if the username and password included in this header are valid, proceed with the next `EssentialAction`. `EssentialActions` are chained one after another—all we need to implement is our own `EssentialAction`.

Because we're using Scala code from Java, we need to slightly adapt our code. We're going to dive into the advanced Play 2 mechanism. The first thing to do is to create an abstract class that will allow us to reuse Scala functions property and that extends the `EssentialAction` interface. This is easily done with the following code. We won't go into details, but the `AbstractFunction1` is a Scala-Java bridge provided by the Scala library.

```
public abstract class JavaEssentialAction extends
    AbstractFunction1<RequestHeader, Iteratee<byte[], Result>>
                                implements EssentialAction
```

We're now ready to implement our `BasicAuthenticationFilter`. The following listing shows the complete source code of our basic authentication filter.

Listing 10.3   BasicAuthenticationFilter.java

```java
package utils;

import static play.mvc.Results.*;
import play.api.libs.iteratee.*;
import play.api.libs.iteratee.Done;
import play.api.mvc.*;
import play.libs.Scala;
import scala.Option;
import scala.Tuple2;
import scala.collection.Seq;
import scala.runtime.AbstractFunction1;
import sun.misc.BASE64Decoder;

import java.util.ArrayList;
import java.util.List;

public class BasicAuthenticationFilter implements EssentialFilter {

  public BasicAuthenticationFilter() {
    // Left empty
  }

  public EssentialAction apply(final EssentialAction next) {

    return new JavaEssentialAction() {

      @Override
      public EssentialAction apply() {
        return next.apply();
      }

      @Override
      public Iteratee<byte[], SimpleResult> apply(RequestHeader rh) {
        Option<String> authorization=rh.headers().get("Authorization");
        if (!authorization.isEmpty()) {
          String auth = authorization.get();
          BASE64Decoder decoder = new BASE64Decoder();
          String passanduser = auth.split(" ")[1];
          try {
            String[] pass = new String(decoder.decodeBuffer(passanduser))
                                                 .split(":");
            String username = pass[0];
            String password = pass[1];
            if ("nicolas".equals(username)&&"nicolas".equals(password)){
              return next.apply(rh);
            }
          } catch(Exception e) {
            // Nothing
          }
        }
```

Implement
EssentialFilter
interface

Empty constructor needed by Play 2

Implement the only method from
EssentialFilter interface. The next parameter
lets us continue with next action (chaining).

Implement EssentialAction
(a JavaEssentialAction that's
Scala compatible)

Apply method from EssentialAction.
Forward to next essential action.

Apply method that takes RequestHeader as
parameter and return response in form of a body
and a Result (Iteratee<byte[], Result>)

Extract
Authorization
header. It's
either empty
or contains
our header.

If we have an Authorization
header, proceed with
decoding this content

Decode
username
and
password

If username and password
match, proceed with next
EssentialAction

```
         List<Tuple2<String, String>> list
            = new ArrayList<Tuple2<String, String>>();
         Tuple2<String, String> t =
                           new Tuple2<String, String>("WWW-Authenticate",
                                      "Basic realm=\"warehouse app\"");
         list.add(t);
         Seq<Tuple2<String, String>> seq = Scala.toSeq(list);
         return Done.apply(
            unauthorized("Forbidden access to the warehouse app").
            getWrappedSimpleResult().withHeaders(seq), null);
      }
   };
}
```

Convert our list to a Scala sequence (Scala's own list type) to pass it on to the withHeaders Scala method

Return response with Result forbidden, content "Forbidden access to ..." and a WWW-Authenticate header. Again we are getting the Scala object type.

```
public abstract class JavaEssentialAction extends
AbstractFunction1<RequestHeader, Iteratee<byte[], SimpleResult>>
                          implements EssentialAction {}
   }
```

Implement our Java essential action by extending the Scala abstractFunction. This is required as we can't directly implement the Scala EssentialAction trait (a more powerful Scala interface).

The preceding listing might seem complicated at first, but it's not that complex. It has two distinct parts: the `EssentialFilter` implementation and the `EssentialAction` implementation. The `EssentialFilter` part consists of implementing the `apply` method. It allows us to apply the next filter or action if the authentication is successful. The `EssentialAction` implementation mainly consists of implementing its own `apply` method. This implementation extracts the `Authorization` header and performs the authentication check. If successful, we pass it on to the next `EssentialAction`; otherwise we send a response with a forbidden result.

The only thing left to do is to enable our `BasicAuthentication` filter. As we've seen in section 10.1.4, we need to enable it in the `Global` Java class. Here's where to locate the class:

```
warehouse
      ├── app
      │    └── Global.java
      ├── conf
      ├── public
      ├── project
      └── test
```

We just need to include our new filter inside the `filters` method. The following listing shows how to do that.

Listing 10.4   `Global.java`

```
import play.*;
import play.api.mvc.*;
import play.filters.csrf.CSRFFilter;
import utils.BasicAuthenticationFilter;
```

```
public class Global extends GlobalSettings {
...
public <T extends EssentialFilter> Class<T>[] filters() {
  Class[] filters={CSRFFilter.class,BasicAuthenticationFilter.class};
  return filters;
}
...
}
```

Our new
BasicAuthenticatorFilter

Now that our filter is activated, if we point our browser to http://localhost:9000/, we should see a pop-up window as in figure 10.4.

Our application has now basic security!

It's important to note that filters have a broad range of application: compression, caching, authentication, logging, and so on. Filters aren't confined to authentication mechanisms. Filters apply to all incoming requests and can be chained one to another. Note that for basic authentication, we could have used the Global class as seen in section 6.2.3 and implemented the onRequest() method. It would've been really straightforward: check the headers for basic authentication, and if it's valid, call the super.onRouteRequest() method; otherwise return a not-authorized status code. But that would've been way too easy for this advanced section, and not as much fun. In this section, we're giving conceptual background to help you understand how security works, but of course Play provides built-in helpers for authentication and authorization. The next chapter details those.

We're now going to see how to add authentication for part of our application using action composition.

10.3　Fine-grained authentication with action composition

We already presented action composition in section 5.4.3. We're now going to see how to use action composition to implement fine-grained authentication. The first step is probably to present our users with a login screen. For that we need to create a simple form that contains username and password.

We'll add a simple Java form to our application controller. The following shows the Application.java file we need to edit.

Figure 10.4　Basic authentication pop up

```
warehouse
       ├─ app
       │    └─ controllers
       │            └─ Application.java
       ├─ conf
       ├─ public
       ├─ project
       └─ test
```

For our purposes, we need to declare a static inner class called Login at the end of it:

```
public static class Login {

    public String email;
    public String password;

}
```

This class will hold our user information. For now, the authenticate action that processes the user information does nothing. We now need an action to render our login form and an action to process the login form. This is easily done by adding listing 10.5 to our application controller.

Listing 10.5 Displaying the login form

```
import static play.data.Form.form;
...

public static Result login() {
    return ok(
        login.render(form(Login.class))
    );
}

public static Result authenticate() {
 return ok();
}
```

All that's left to do is to create the login form. We need to create a new view as shown in the following:

```
warehouse
       ├─ app
       │    └─ views
       │            └─ login.scala.html
       ├─ conf
       ├─ public
       ├─ project
       └─ test
```

Listing 10.6 shows the content of our view. It should now be easy for you to understand.

Listing 10.6 login.scala.html

```
@(loginForm: Form[Application.Login])
@import helper._
@import helper.twitterBootstrap._

@main("Please sign in to the warehouse application") {
  @helper.form(helper.CSRF(routes.Application.authenticate)) {
    <h1>Sign in</h1>
    <p>
        <input type="email" name="email" placeholder="Email"
                           value="@loginForm("email").value">
    </p>
    <p>
        <input type="password" name="password"
                                    placeholder="Password">
    </p>
    <p>
        <button type="submit">Sign in</button>
    </p>
}

}
```

Last, we need to modify our conf/routes file to include the following routes:

```
GET  /login        controllers.Application.login()
POST /authenticate controllers.Application.authenticate()
```

If you now point your browser to http://localhost:9000/login you should see the same form as figure 10.5.

We're now ready to implement the core authentication methods. Before we can start, we need a simple model object that represents our users. Let's create a file in app/models/ called User.java. Listing 10.7 shows the content of the class.

Figure 10.5   Login form

Listing 10.7   `User.java`

```java
@Entity
public class User extends Model {

  @Id
  public Long id;
  @Constraints.Required
  public String email;
  @Constraints.Required
  public String password;

  public User() {
  }

  public User(String email, String password) {
    this.email = email;
    this.password = password;
  }

  public static User authenticate(String email,
                                  String password) {
// Should be something like
// return finder.where().eq("email", email)
//    .eq("password", password).findUnique();
if ("nicolas".equals(email)
            && "nicolas".equals(password))
      return new User("nicolas", "nicolas");
    else
      return null;
  }

  public static Finder<Long, User> finder
    = new Finder<Long, User>(Long.class, User.class);

}
```

User authentication method always returns nicolas for this example. It's trivial to perform a database search.

We now only need to slightly modify our application controller to call the User authenticate method. The following listing shows the content of our authenticate method.

Listing 10.8   The authenticate method

```java
public static Result authenticate() {
  Form<Login> loginForm = form(Login.class)
                  .bindFromRequest();
  String email = loginForm.get().email;
  String password = loginForm.get().email;
  if (User.authenticate(email, password) == null){
    return forbidden("invalid password");
  }
  session().clear();
  session("email", email);
```

Bind our login form parameters

Extract email and password

Perform actual authentication against DB; in our case we always return nicolas for simplicity

Login failed, return "Forbidden"

Clear session

Add user's email to session. This indicates user is logged in.

```
    return redirect(
       routes.Products.index()          <--- Redirect user to product page
    );
}
```

The implementation of the `authenticate` method is trivial, and the annotations in listing 10.8 should be clear enough. The important thing to remember is that we'll use the `email` session attribute later to find the currently logged-in user.

> **NOTE** We could've used the login form's `validate` method as we saw in section 6.4.3, but to simplify the explanation we chose not to.

Now that we're able to log in, we can start protecting actions with authentication. Play allows us to do this using *action composition*. Action composition is the ability to compose multiple actions together in a chain. Each action can do something to the request before delegating to the next action, and can also modify the result. An action can also decide not to pass the request on to the next action, and instead generate the result itself. We already explained how action composition works in section 5.4.3, so in this section, we'll put our knowledge into practice. We're also going to see how Play 2 provides action composition helpers, making it even easier.

In our case, Play 2 comes with a built-in authenticator action, `Security.Authenticator`, which we'll extend to add our logic. We'll call this authenticator `Secured`. We'll create a `Secured` class in our app/controllers directory. The following listing shows the `Secured` class content.

Listing 10.9 Secured.java

```java
package controllers;

import play.mvc.Http.Context;
import play.mvc.Result;
import play.mvc.Security;

public class Secured extends Security.Authenticator {

    @Override
    public String getUsername(Context ctx) {
        return ctx.session().get("email");
    }

    @Override
    public Result onUnauthorized(Context ctx) {
        return redirect(routes.Application.login());
    }
}
```

We need to implement two methods. `getUsername` is used to get the username of the current logged-in user. In our case this is the email address that we set in the `email` attribute in the session when the user logged in (the application's `authenticate` method). If this method returns a value, then the authenticator considers the user to be logged in and lets the request proceed. If the method returns `null`, then the authenticator will block the request and instead invoke `onUnauthorized`, which we've implemented to redirect to our login screen.

The only thing left to do is to use the `Secured` authenticator. Again, this is trivial. All we need to do is to annotate the controller or the methods we want to be secured using the following notation:

```
@Security.Authenticated(Secured.class)
```

In our case, we want to secure the product controller but not the application controller (because we need to call the `authenticate` and `login` methods without being logged in). Open the `app/controller/Products.java` file and add the `Authenticated` annotation to the class declaration.

```
...
import play.mvc.Security;
...
@Security.Authenticated(Secured.class)
public class Products extends Controller {
```

Play 2's action composition mechanism makes sure that when the `@Security.Authenticated` annotation is encountered, the cookie session is checked for the user's email. This is basically a helper for what you learned about action composition in chapter 5.

Now, try to access the product page—http://localhost:9000/products/. If you're not already logged in, you'll be redirected to the login page. Same thing if you try to access the product form—http://localhost:9000/product/new. Our application is no longer public. The `@Security.Authenticated` method can also be applied at the action method level.

10.4   Summary

In this chapter, you learned how Play 2 deals with web application security concerns. We first saw the general security concepts and the common security breaches. As an example, we added protection against cross-site request forgery to our application. From there, we learned what filters are and how to implement basic authentication using them. We also saw that filters apply to all requests, so they're a potential tool for securing the whole web application. We saw how to use action composition to implement fine-grained authentication. We then put our knowledge into practice: using Play 2 helpers, we secured our warehouse web application, allowing only selected users to access it.

Our application is almost done, and in the next chapter, we're going to learn how to deploy it.

Modules and deployment

This chapter covers

- Using modules and creating your own
- Publishing your modules
- Splitting your application into multiple sub-applications
- Deploying your application
- Configuring the production environment

Now that we've seen how to do a lot of things for ourselves in Play, it's time to see how to use code that others have made. This chapter explains how to use Play modules, but also how to create your own and publish them so that others can use them. The second half of the chapter deals with how to deploy your application to production on your own machines or in the cloud. It also explains how to set up a front-end proxy and use SSL.

11.1 Modules

Any kind of serious software development project will use libraries to decrease the effort required from developers. JVM developers have access to a large body of libraries that can save them a lot of time and stop them re-inventing the wheel. In chapter 2, we saw how we could use `build.sbt` to add a dependency on any library to use any Java library, just as you normally would. But Play provides an additional form of code reuse in the form of modules. Currently available modules for Play 2 provide anything from alternate template engines to NoSQL-database layers. This section will explain how to use a commonly used module and, later on, how to build one yourself.

We'll show you how to use the SecureSocial module. Another module that is frequently used is the Mailer[1] module, which, as you might guess from the name, allows you to send email.

11.1.1 Using modules

Play modules are, just like any other library, a collection of files in a JAR. The difference is that there will be some Play-specific non-class files in this JAR and that the code depends on Play. This means that you add a module to your project the same way you add any other library: you add it to `libraryDependencies` in `build.sbt`.

Let's say we want our application's users to log in and, later, possibly allow them to log in with OAuth. If we can find a module that allows us to do this, we won't have to waste time writing our own code. You can find a comprehensive list of modules that are available in the Play 2 modules directory.[2]

If we search for "social" on that page, we'll find a module named SecureSocial which seems to fit the bill.[3] Each module's entry shows a URL and a short description. We can now follow the URL to find out how to use the module. The entry for Secure-Social points you to the module's website.[4] Once you navigate to the installation instructions, you'll have to add a dependency and a resolver. A resolver is how we tell SBT where to look for libraries that can't be found in the default repositories.

Let's get started. Open `build.sbt` and add the new dependency to `library-Dependencies` and the resolver in the project settings. Your `build.sbt` should now look like the following listing:

Listing 11.1 The build properties—`build.sbt`

```
ame := "warehouse"

version := "1.0-SNAPSHOT"

libraryDependencies ++= Seq(
  javaJdbc,
  javaEbean,
  cache,
  "com.google.guava" % "guava" % "14.0",
  filters,
```

---

[1] https://github.com/typesafehub/play-plugins
[2] http://www.playframework.com/documentation/2.1.1/Modules
[3] SecureSocial is for *authentication* (logging in). It works well in combination with the *Deadbolt 2* module, which does *authorization* (permission checking).
[4] http://securesocial.ws/

```
    "securesocial" %% "securesocial" % "master-SNAPSHOT"
)

resolvers += Resolver.url("sbt-plugin-snapshots",
    url("http://repo.scala-sbt.org/scalasbt/sbt-plugin-snapshots/")
    )(Resolver.ivyStylePatterns)
```

```
play.Project.playJavaSettings
```

If you were already in the Play console, you'll want to let SBT know about your changes by running the `reload` command. This will make SBT reread all the files that make up the project's configuration. If you're using an IDE with a Play-generated project, you should also regenerate the project (using `idea` for IDEA, `eclipse` for Eclipse) so that your IDE knows about the module.

To use SecureSocial, we need to disable the CSRF filter we added in chapter 10. This is easily done by commenting out the following *filters* line in our `Global.java` file:

```
public <T extends EssentialFilter> Class<T>[] filters() {
//Class[] filters={CSRFFilter.class,BasicAuthenticationFilter.class};
  Class[] filters={};
  return filters;
}
```

Now we can start using the module in our application. According to the documentation, SecureSocial provides an annotation `@SecureSocial.SecuredAction` that we can use to secure our action methods. It also adds a `user` to the current context, which tells us the current user.

Changing our application so that the user has to log in via OAuth is now a simple matter of annotating our actions in all the relevant places. This would be all the actions in the `Products` controller. For example:

```
import import securesocial.core.java.SecureSocial;
....

public class Products extends Controller {
...
  @SecureSocial.SecuredAction
  public static Result newProduct() {
    return ok(details.render(productForm));
  }
...
}
```

Running the application after this change would probably fail, since there are still a couple of things we need to provide. First, SecureSocial requires us to provide an implementation of `UserService`; this is what SecureSocial delegates to in order to store and retrieve users. Listing 11.2 shows a simple implementation that stores everything in memory.

Listing 11.2   Simple `UserService`—`app/utils/SimpleUserService.java`

```java
package utils;

import play.Application;
import securesocial.core.Identity;
import securesocial.core.identityId;
import securesocial.core.java.BaseUserService;
import securesocial.core.java.Token;

import java.util.HashMap;
import java.util.Map;

public class SimpleUserService extends BaseUserService {
  private HashMap<String, Identity> users
     = new HashMap<String, Identity>();                    ◄─── Stores users
  private HashMap<String, Token> tokens
     = new HashMap<String, Identity>();                    ◄─── Stores login tokens

  public SimpleUserService(Application application) {
    super(application);
  }

  @Override
  public Identity doSave(Identity user) {                  ◄─── Saves a user
    users.put(user.identityId().userId() +
      user.identityId().providerId(), user);
    return user;
  }

  @Override
  public void doSave(Token token) {                        ◄─── Saves a token
    tokens.put(token.uuid, token);
  }

  @Override                                                    Looks up
  public Identity doFind(IdentityId identityId) {          ◄─── users by ID
    return users.get(identityId.userId() + identityId.providerId());
  }

  @Override
  public Token doFindToken(String tokenId) {               ◄─── Looks up a token
    return tokens.get(tokenId);
  }
                                                               Looks up
  @Override                                                    users by
  public Identity doFindByEmailAndProvider(String email,       email
                              String providerId) {  ◄───       address
    for (Identity user : users.values()) {
      if(user.identityId().providerId().equals(providerId) &&
          user.email().isDefined() && user.email().get()
          .equalsIgnoreCase(email)) {
        return user;
      }
    }
    return null;
  }
```

```
  @Override
  public void doDeleteToken(String uuid) {          <--- Deletes a token
    tokens.remove(uuid);
  }

  @Override
  public void doDeleteExpiredTokens() {             <--- Deletes expired tokens
    for (Map.Entry<String, Token> entry : tokens.entrySet()) {
      if(entry.getValue().isExpired()) {
        tokens.remove(entry.getKey());
      }
    }
  }
}
```

Second, we have to provide some configuration to tell SecureSocial what we want it to do. Since SecureSocial comes with a bunch of optional plugins that help it do its job, we'll have to create a conf/play.plugins with the following contents.

```
9994:securesocial.core.DefaultAuthenticatorStore
9995:securesocial.core.DefaultIdGenerator
9996:securesocial.core.providers.utils.DefaultPasswordValidator
9997:securesocial.controllers.DefaultTemplatesPlugin
9998:utils.SimpleUserService                      <--- The plugin we just wrote
9999:securesocial.core.providers.utils.BCryptPasswordHasher
10004:securesocial.core.providers.UsernamePasswordProvider
```

For now we'll just set up SecureSocial to use email and password for logins; this is why we're only enabling a couple of the available plugins. When you're building your own applications, you can follow SecureSocial's instructions to set up OAuth with one or more of the OAuth providers it supports. Now we can create the file conf/securesocial .conf with the following contents:

```
userpass {
    withUserNameSupport=false
    sendWelcomeEmail=false
    enableGravatarSupport=false
    tokenDuration=60
    tokenDeleteInterval=5
    minimumPasswordLength=8
    enableTokenJob=true
    hasher=bcrypt
}

securesocial {
    onLoginGoTo=/
    onLogoutGoTo=/signin
    ssl=false
}
```

To fully use SecureSocial, you'll need to configure some provider such as Twitter. We'll skip this step but feel free to refer to the SecureSocial documentation to add your tokens against Twitter, for example.

In order for Play to load the settings in this file, it needs to be included from the regular configuration file. Put the following line in `conf/application.conf`:

```
include "securesocial.conf"
```

Now we need to add some routes so that our users can actually log in. For this example we'll just add the login and logout routes:

```
GET /signin  securesocial.controllers.LoginPage.login
GET /logout securesocial.controllers.LoginPage.logout
GET /authenticate/:provider
 securesocial.controllers.
   ProviderController.authenticate(provider)
POST /authenticate/:provider
 securesocial.controllers.
    ProviderController.authenticateByPost(provider)
GET /not-authorized
 securesocial.controllers.ProviderController.notAuthorized
# User Registration and password handling
# (only needed if you are using UsernamePasswordProvider)
GET /signup
 securesocial.controllers.Registration.startSignUp
POST /signup
 securesocial.controllers.Registration.handleStartSignUp
GET /signup/:token
 securesocial.controllers.Registration.signUp(token)
POST /signup/:token
 securesocial.controllers.Registration.handleSignUp(token)
GET /reset
 securesocial.controllers.Registration.startResetPassword
POST /reset
 securesocial.controllers.Registration.handleStartResetPassword
GET /reset/:token
 securesocial.controllers.Registration.resetPassword(token)
POST /reset/:token
 securesocial.controllers.Registration.handleResetPassword(token)
GET /password
securesocial.controllers.PasswordChange.page
POST /password
 securesocial.controllers.PasswordChange.handlePasswordChange
```

If you point your browser to http://localhost:9000/products/new or if you click on the New Product button, you should now see a login page.

We now have a complete working example that shows how to use just one of a large number of useful modules. Unfortunately, you'll have to figure out for yourself how to use any of the other available modules, if you need them. Now that we know what a module looks like from an application developer's perspective, let's look at how to build one for yourself.

11.1.2 Creating modules

Creating a Play module is as easy as making a Play application. In fact, that's how you start a new module—you create a new Play application as the starting point. Let's create a bar code module. This module will allow a user of this module to add bar code images to any page by simply including a tag. Run the following command:

```
play new barcode
```

Now that you have a new application, can now remove everything in `public` and the sample controller and view. You should also remove `application.conf` since configuration, if any, will be done from the application using our module.

WRITE THE CODE

We said we wanted our user[5] to be able to add a bar code image by including a tag in a page. This means our module will need a tag (that renders an HTML `img` element), a controller (that renders a bar code), and a route that will connect the tag's `img` element with the bar code controller.

But first, we'll need something to create our bar code images for us. We'll use a library aptly named `barcode4j`. Go ahead and add the dependency to `build.sbt`:

```
libraryDependencies ++= Seq(
  javaJdbc,
  javaEbean,
  cache,
  "net.sf.barcode4j" % "barcode4j" % "2.1"
)
```

Now, let's create the controller. Though a controller for a module is just like a controller in a regular application, putting it in the `controllers` package isn't a good idea: it might clash with our users' controllers. Therefore, let's make a package: `com.github.playforjava.controllers`.

Let's start with the view. Create a file `barcode.scala.html` in `app/views/tags` and add the following:

```
@(ean: String)
<img class="barcode" alt="@ean" src="@routes.Barcodes.barcode(ean)">
```

Including the controller part is less straightforward; were we to put our controller in `app/controllers`, like we've been doing until now, things might break, because someone might add the same controller name. Let's make a package `com.github.playforjava.barcodes.controllers` for our controller that's unlikely to clash with anything in a regular Play application, and put the controller there. Create the directory structure for the package, and create the class shown in the following listing there.

Listing 11.3 `app/com/github/playforjava/barcodes/Barcodes.java`

```
package com.github.playforjava.barcodes;

import org.krysalis.barcode4j.impl.upcean.EAN13Bean;
import org.krysalis.barcode4j.output.bitmap.BitmapCanvasProvider;
import play.mvc.Controller;
import play.mvc.Result;
```

---

[5] Our user, in this case, is another developer who will add this module as a dependency to their project.

```
import java.awt.image.BufferedImage;
import java.io.ByteArrayOutputStream;
import java.io.IOException;

public class Barcodes extends Controller {

   public static Result barcode(String ean) {
      ByteArrayOutputStream out = new ByteArrayOutputStream();
      BitmapCanvasProvider provider = new BitmapCanvasProvider(out,
         "image/png", 144, BufferedImage.TYPE_BYTE_BINARY, false, 0);
      try {
         new EAN13Bean().generateBarcode(provider, ean);
         provider.finish();
         return ok(out.toByteArray());
      } catch (IOException e) {
         return badRequest("Could not render barcode. " + e.getMessage());
      } finally {
         try { out.close(); } catch(Exception e) {}
      }
   }
}
```

Bitmap object represents a bar code

Send back the bar code as image bytes

Generate bar code ◁—

Clashing package names

Play encourages the use of short package names, like `controllers` and `models`. This is perfectly fine if the source code you're writing never leaves your premises. But this becomes a problem when you write code to be used by other developers—especially if you stick to Play's default package names like `controllers` and `models`. Not only do you run the risk of causing name clashes with the developer's code, but in Play particularly, they can end up with two different `controllers.routes` classes, which will definitely break things in ways that make it difficult to figure out what's wrong.

For modules, our advice is to name your packages like we've always done in the JVM world: use the reverse notation of a domain (and path, if necessary) that you control. This way you won't leave your users confused or worse—annoyed with you because you made them waste their time.

The `Barcodes` controller contains a single action, `barcodes()`, that utilizes barcode4j to generate a bar code image. Of course, we need to provide a route to it. Because we provide the routes through a module, we need to create a new routes file called `barcode.routes` in the `config` directory. This will allows us to identify the routes file and import the routes from another application. We're going to remove the "/barcode" prefix from the route, since the importing application can provide its own prefix when it imports the route. The route will therefore look like this:

```
GET  /:ean
  com.github.playforjava.barcodes.Barcodes.barcode(ean: String)
```

That's it: we have a module that provides bar code rendering functionality for any Play application that needs it. We can now have a look at how to publish our module.

PUBLISH

Since Play uses Maven/Ivy repositories to get its dependencies, that's what we'll have to publish to. Fortunately SBT can produce the necessary files for us. It uses `appName` in `build.sbt` as the `artifactId` and `groupId`. This isn't usually what we want, so we'll add an `organization` property to the build settings in the same file.

```
...

    organization := "playforjava"

...
```

Now we just need a place to publish to. If you already have a repository that you want to publish to, you can tell SBT where it is by setting the `publishTo` key and, if necessary, your credentials with the `credentials` key. Assuming your repository is at `http://maven.example.com/releases` and you call it "My Maven repository", this is how you'd set it up:

```
...

publishTo := Some("My Maven repository" at
      "http://maven.example.com/releases"),
credentials += Credentials(Path.userHome / ".repo-credentials")

...
```

In this example, `~/.repo-credentials` is a properties file with the following properties: `realm`, `host`, `user`, and `password`. Another way of adding your credentials is to do it directly in a `.sbt` file with the following syntax:

```
credentials += Credentials("Repository Realm",
  "maven.example.com", "username",
  "hashed-password")
```

Replace the credentials in the example as appropriate.

You might not have a publicly accessible Maven or Ivy repository to publish to. That's okay; we can use something like GitHub. Apart from providing a place to host your Git repositories, GitHub makes it easy for anyone to have their own website, and if you don't need anything fancy, it only takes a few steps.

SETTING UP A REPOSITORY

GitHub has a feature that allows you to publish a website as a sub-domain of github.com, called Pages. Their documentation[6] explains how to set up either a User/Organization Pages site or a Project Pages site. Which one you choose doesn't matter for the purposes of this book, since how we'll be using it doesn't change much. Which one you choose for the modules you'll be publishing (very soon, no doubt) is wholly up to you and depends on the particulars of your situation.

Let's get started with a User/Organization Pages site. According to GitHub's instructions, we're supposed to create a new repo and give it the same name as the user

---

[6] http://pages.github.com

or organization (depending on the type of account the site is for) with `.github.io`
appended. For this book's Pages site, that would be `playforjava.github.io`. Once
you've pushed something to your new repo—an `index.html` for instance—you'll be
able to point your browser to "your" site, `http://playforjava.github.io/` in our
example, and see the result. You might have to wait a couple of minutes, according to
GitHub's instructions, before your site is actually up and running.

If you want to create a Project Pages site, you have to create a new branch called
`gh-pages` in the corresponding Git repo and put your site's files in that branch. These
pages will show up as a new subdirectory under your .github.com site; for example,
`http://playforjava.github.io/some-repo` if the repo is called `some-repo`. Since
this new branch has nothing to do with your other branches, you'll want to start the
`gh-pages` branch with an *orphan commit.* An orphan commit is a commit with no par-
ents—you won't see anything connected to this commit below it in the commit log.
Furthermore, there'll be no connections between this branch and the other branches:
there won't be any shared history between them. You can make this commit with the
following command:

```
git checkout --orphan gh-pages
```

Since `git` creates the new branch with the current checkout as its basis and puts its
contents in the index, you'll want to remove everything by issuing the following:

```
git rm -f .
```

Everything we commit to the `gh-pages` branch and push to GitHub will show up on
the Pages site. Now that we have a place to publish our module, we need to start thinking about testing the module in its intended environment, another Play application.
We wouldn't want to publish a buggy module, would we?

TESTING THE MODULE

It's probably a good idea to test our module, in the environment of a Play application,
before we release it to the world. Fortunately, this is easy to do. If you run the `publish-
local` command, SBT will publish the module to your local Ivy cache. Now it's simple
to create a new project and include our module. Let's quickly create this project and
test our module:

```
play new module-test
```

Add a dependency to the module in `build.sbt`:

```
...

libraryDependencies ++= Seq(
  javaJdbc,
  javaEbean,
  cache,
  "playforjava" %% "barcode" % "1.0-SNAPSHOT"
)
...
```

Import the module's route by adding the following line at the end of your `conf/routes.conf` file:

```
-> /barcode barcode.Routes
```

The following listing shows the template `index.scala.html`, which uses the `tags/barcode` template that we created earlier.

Listing 11.4 Bar code template—`app/views/index.scala.html`

```
@(message: String)

@main("Welcome to Play") {

    @tags.barcode("1234567890128")

}
```

Figure 11.1 Generated bar code

If we run our test application and point our browser to it, we can see that our module does what it's supposed to do. Figure 11.1 shows a bar code generated by our application.

Now that we know our module works, we can finally publish it.

PUBLISHING THE MODULE

We've made a module, tested it, and set up a repository where we can publish it. The next step is actually publishing the module. Since, in our example, we have to publish to a Git repository, the process will consist of generating the necessary files, copying them to the repository, committing the changes, and pushing them to GitHub. The Play console (or SBT, if you prefer) can generate the files for us and if we configure it correctly, it can put the files in the right place for us. If we add the right `publishTo` setting in our project's settings, Play will write the files to our Pages repo clone and we'll just need to commit and push. The following listing shows what the final version of `build.sbt` looks like.

Listing 11.5 `build.sbt`

```
name := "barcode"

version := "1.0-SNAPSHOT"

organization := "playforjava"

publishTo := Some(Resolver.file("Our repository",
        new File("/Users/sietse/playforjava.github.com")))

libraryDependencies ++= Seq(
  javaJdbc,
  javaEbean,
  cache,
  "net.sf.barcode4j" % "barcode4j" % "2.1"
)

play.Project.playJavaSettings
```

Be sure to replace the path of the publishing repo with your own. Now, if we issue the `publish` command in the Play console, commit, and push the changes in the Pages repo, we'll have published our module. Note that, since we never updated the version number, we've published a snapshot version. This has a specific meaning in the world of Maven artifacts and no sane project will rely on snapshot versions other than for development and testing. If you're happy with the state of your module, update the version to 1.0 or any version number you like (without the `-SNAPSHOT` part) and publish that. Don't forget to increment the version number and add `-SNAPSHOT` back afterward, lest you release a development version with an already existing production version number.

11.2 Splitting your application into multiple sub-applications

When projects grow, or if the application scope requires a large team, it's better to split your application up into several smaller applications. Having several small applications allows you to distribute the work better and helps to ensure that each single application stays simple and manageable. This is where Play sub-applications come in handy.

A *sub-application* is a Play application within a Play application. It's time to give you an overview on how this works and how you can structure your project. Let's pretend that our application needs to be handled by two different teams: Team A will take care of the product details while Team B will handle the reports. We therefore need two sub-applications inside our application: the report application and the product application.

Application dependencies are declared in the `build.sbt` file at the root of the project. A sub-application is also called a *sub-project*. Our current main application is going to be shared by both sub-applications. Both the report and product applications depend on some common libraries as well. The common libraries include the model classes that are shared between all the sub-applications. The `build.sbt` file with the two sub-projects and the common library have extra lines, as shown in the followng listing.

Listing 11.6 Directory structure of our application and sub-applications

```
lazy val common = project          ⟵── Common libraries such as utils and models packages
    .settings(playJavaSettings: _*)    ⟵┐

lazy val report = project
    .settings(playJavaSettings: _*)    ⟵┤  Tell the build system
    .dependsOn(common)                      it's a Play application
                                            structure
lazy val product = project
    .settings(playJavaSettings: _*)    ⟵┤
    .dependsOn(common)                 ⟵┐  Product sub-application
                                          depends on common
lazy val root = project.in(file("."))
    .dependsOn(common)
```

Report sub-application depends on common ⊢▷

```
.dependsOn(product)
.dependsOn(report)
.aggregate(common, product, report)
```

Main play application depends on all sub-applications and needs to compile all the sub-applications (aggregate)

The `aggregate()` function is important, as it tells the build system to automatically recompile a sub-application if one changes. The `depends()` function indicates that one project depends on another project and thus compilation of the other project must happen first. Also, the classes from the other project are made available after compilation.

Our directory structure looks like the following listing.

Listing 11.7 Directory structure of our application and sub-applications

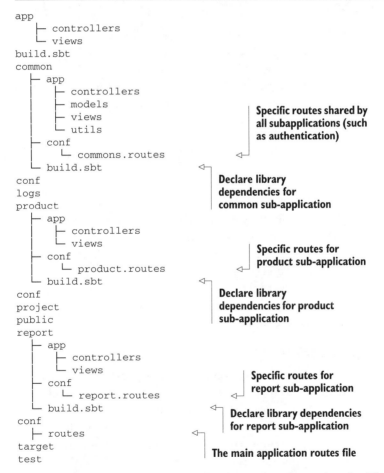

```
app
    ├─ controllers
    └─ views
build.sbt
common
    ├─ app
    │   ├─ controllers
    │   ├─ models
    │   ├─ views
    │   └─ utils
    ├─ conf
    │   └─ commons.routes
    └─ build.sbt
conf
logs
product
    ├─ app
    │   ├─ controllers
    │   └─ views
    ├─ conf
    │   └─ product.routes
    └─ build.sbt
conf
project
public
report
    ├─ app
    │   ├─ controllers
    │   └─ views
    ├─ conf
    │   └─ report.routes
    └─ build.sbt
conf
    ├─ routes
target
test
```

Specific routes shared by all subapplications (such as authentication)

Declare library dependencies for common sub-application

Specific routes for product sub-application

Declare library dependencies for product sub-application

Specific routes for report sub-application

Declare library dependencies for report sub-application

The main application routes file

You can switch from one sub-application to another using the Play console. For example, `project report` allows you to switch to the report project:

```
$ play
[info] Loading project definition from /ch11.2/project
[info] Set current project to warehouse (in build file:/ch11.2/)

       _
 _ __ | | __ _ _  _
| '_ \| |/ _' | || |
|  __/|_|\___|\__ /
|_|            |__/

play 2.2.0 built with Scala 2.10.2 (running Java 1.6.0_65),
http://www.playframework.com

> Type "help play" or "license" for more information.
> Type "exit" or use Ctrl+D to leave this console.

[warehouse] $ project report
[info] Set current project to report (in build file:/ch11.2/)
```

To list all the sub-applications, use the `projects` command. You can then select a project using the `project [name]` command. Then use the normal Play commands to compile, test, or start the project (`test`, `run`, and so on).

Each sub-project contains a `build.sbt` file that can contain its own dependencies, as explained in chapter 2. More interesting, you can also import all the routes from your sub-applications into the main application. This works in exactly the same way as for modules, as explained in section 11.1.2.

For example, to add all the routes from the report sub-application, you'd add the following line your main routes file:

```
-> /report     report.Routes
```

This means that the sub-application routes are made available at http://localhost :9000/report from the main application. It's also important to notice that the reversed route will be `controllers.report.routes.Report.index()`. The assets—the public folder from the sub-application—can also be accessed using the same pattern: `controllers.report.routes.Assets.at("...")`.

We now have a complete overview on how we could split up our applications to satisfy larger team or application complexity.

11.3 *Deploying to production*

Finally you're done. Your Play application is done, it's great, and it'll rule the world. That's when you realize you're not done yet. Your application still needs to be deployed to production. There are various ways to do that. You might want to deploy your application standalone on your own server, or maybe on the infrastructure of a cloud provider. If you're in an enterprise Java environment, chances are that you want or need to deploy on an application server.

In this section we'll go through the various options and help you decide which way is best for you.

11.3.1 *Packing up your application*

When you use `play run`, your application is started in development mode. This is unsuitable for running your application in production, because at each request Play checks whether any files are changed, greatly slowing down your application.

As a better alternative, you can use `play start`. This will start play in *production mode.* In production mode, a new JVM is forked for your application, and it runs separately from SBT. You can still see your application's logging output to verify that it started correctly. When you've seen enough, type `Ctrl-D`, and the SBT process will terminate but leave your application running. You can stop this application with `play stop`.

Though `play start` starts your application in the proper mode, it's often still not a suitable way of starting your app. It requires interaction to detach and end the SBT process from your application. Generally, you'll want your application to start without human intervention. Also, you may not always have the `play` command available on the machine where you want to deploy.

For this, Play provides the `stage` and `dist` tasks. When running `play stage`, Play compiles your application to a JAR file, and—together with all the dependency JARs— puts it in the `target/staged` directory. It also creates a start script in `target/start`.

With this script, you can start your application without the `play` command. Just running `target/start` will start your application.

> **PLAY DOESN'T SUPPORT WINDOWS IN DIST MODE** Unfortunately, Play doesn't support Windows while working in production mode. This is because running a Windows service is not at all comparable to running a background process on a Unix-based environment. For this reason, the `stage` and `dist` tasks won't work on Windows.

The `dist` task does something similar, and zips up the start script and dependencies into a file. After running `play dist`, you get a directory `dist`, which contains a zip file with your application. You can transfer this zip file to the server where you want to deploy, unzip it, and run the `start` script that's contained in the zip file. You might need to make the start script executable first with `chmod +x start`.

The `stage` and `dist` commands make particularly nice distributions. All your dependencies are packed with your application, including Play and Scala! This means that the only thing you need on the target machine is a Java installation. This makes an application packaged with the `dist` command extremely portable.

11.3.2 *Working with multiple configurations*

During development, you only need a single application configuration in the file `conf/application.conf`. But when you deploy to production, you need to be able to use different configuration settings. This applies to settings that are either machine- or environment-specific, such as directory paths, and to sensitive information such as database passwords. In this section, we'll see how we can configure the production environment separately.

At first you expect to avoid this issue by deploying the application and then editing the configuration by hand. This doesn't work, or is at least inconvenient, because the application is packaged in a JAR file. Besides, modifying the distributed application is error-prone and less convenient to automate.

Don't use the same credentials for your production database

You might not be the first person to consider the "pragmatic" solution of using the same settings for development, test, and production environments, to avoid the need for separate configurations. This seems like a good idea right up until the moment when a team member mistakenly thinks he's logged into a development environment and deletes the entire production database.

If you use different database credentials for each environment, perhaps adding *test* or *dev* to user names, then you have to try a lot harder to make this kind of mistake.

What you need is a default application configuration that's "safe" for the test environment. A safe configuration is one that won't cause unwanted side effects when you do things like running tests.

Suppose your application sends email notifications to users. In the test environment, it would be useful to configure the application to override the recipient email address, and use a safe email address like `info@example.com` instead. Put the following in `conf/application.conf`:

```
mail.override.enabled = true
mail.override.address = "info@example.org"

include "development.conf"
```

The first two lines of this configuration override email recipient addresses, making the application send all notifications to one address, `info@example.org`, so that continuous integration doesn't mean continuous spam for your system's real users.

The last line includes settings from another configuration file in the same directory called `development.conf`. This allows each developer to override the default test configuration in their development environment, perhaps to send all email notifications to their own email address. Developers can create their own `conf/development.conf` and override the email address—be sure to add this file to `.gitignore` or your source control system's equivalent.

```
mail.override.address = "code.monkey@paperclip-logistics.com"
```

This configuration overrides the earlier test environment configuration in `application.conf`. This works because if the application configuration contains the same setting twice, the second value overrides the first. Note that the developer doesn't have to override the `email.override.enabled` setting, because it's already set to `true` in the default test environment configuration.

A nice thing about the configuration library is that the configuration doesn't break if the `development.conf` file doesn't exist; the library silently ignores it. This means developers don't have to provide their own overrides if they don't need to, perhaps because they're not working on email notifications.

Make sure to add `conf/development.conf` to the `.gitignore` file, or whatever your version control system uses to specify files that aren't under version control, so that one developer's configuration doesn't affect anyone else's development environment.

Finally, we have to set up the production environment configuration. In this case, including a file that overrides the default settings, like we just did with `development.conf`, isn't such a good idea because there will be no error if the file is missing. In addition, the file location might not be known in advance, often because the production configuration file is in a different directory on the server (keeping production database passwords safe from developers).

For production, then, we can use a separate `/etc/paperclips/production.conf` configuration file:

```
include "application.conf"

email.override.enabled=false
```

This time, the file starts by loading the default configuration in `application.conf` as a resource from the deployment archive, which is followed by the production environment settings. To use the production configuration instead of the default configuration, specify the file as a system property when starting the application:

```
play "start -Dconfig.file=/etc/paperclips/production.conf"
```

In this case, you'll get an error if the file is missing.

```
(Starting server.
Type Ctrl+D to exit logs, the server will remain in background)

Play server process ID is 61819
Oops, cannot start the server.
Configuration error:
Configuration error[/etc/paperclips/production.conf:
/etc/paperclips/production.conf (No such file or directory)]
```

Alternatively, instead of `-Dconfig.file`, you can use `-Dconfig.url` to load the configuration file from a remote location.

11.3.3 *Creating native packages for a package manager*

A zip file may be pretty universal, but the operating system you intend to deploy on likely has a more advanced package management tool. If you're using Debian or Ubuntu or a derivative, an `apt` package is more appropriate, whereas many other Linux distributions use `rpm` packages.

You can package up your application as one of these packages. The SBT plugin sbt-native-packager helps you create these `deb` and `rpm` packages as well as Homebrew packages that can be used on Mac OS X and MSI packages for Windows. This plugin is powerful, but it's a plugin for SBT and not specific for Play. So it'll require some thought and effort to make packages for your Play application.

There are also somewhat more specialized plugins built upon the sbt-native-packager plugin. The play2-native-packager plugin builds deb packages for Debian or Ubuntu, and the play2-ubuntu-package plugin builds lightweight deb packages designed specifically for recent versions of Ubuntu.

11.3.4 *Setting up a front-end proxy*

Generally, web applications are run on port 80. This is a *privileged port* on Unix machines, which means that programs running under a regular user account can't bind to such a port. This explains why Play doesn't use port 80 as the default port number, but something else.

Of course, you can tweak the permissions so that it's possible to run your Play application on port 80, and let it serve web traffic directly. But the common way to let your application be available on port 80 is to set up a front-end proxy, like HAProxy, nginx, or even Apache. This proxy will bind to port 80 and redirect all traffic intended for your Play application, which listens to an unprivileged port.

The use of a proxy isn't limited to making the application available on a specific port. It can also provide load balancing between multiple instances of your application. You can, for example, run two instances of your application and let the front-end proxy divide traffic between the two instances. This means you're not bound to a single machine; you can utilize multiple machines for your application.

It also gives you the ability to do upgrades without downtime. If you have a front-end proxy do load balancing between two application instances, you can take one instance down, upgrade it, and bring it back up, all without downtime. When the upgraded instance is up, you can do the same to the other one. When done, you've upgraded your application with zero downtime for your clients.

HAProxy is a powerful and reliable proxy that has a plethora of advanced options, but is still easy to get started with.

Suppose that we want to set up HAProxy to listen on port 80 and redirect traffic to two instances of our Play application. We'll also use WebSockets in this application (these are explained in chapter 9), so we must make sure that these connections are properly proxied as well.

This can be accomplished with a configuration file as shown in the following listing:

Listing 11.8 HAProxy configuration

```
global
    daemon
    maxconn 256

defaults
    mode http
    timeout connect 5s
    timeout client 50s
```

```
    timeout server 50s                          ❶ Add X-Forwarded-For header
    option forwardfor            ◁
                                                 ❷ Don't keep connections open
    option http-server-close     ◁

frontend http-in                                 ❸ Bind to port 80
    bind *:80                    ◁
                                                    ❹ Configure back end
    default_backend playapp      ◁

backend playapp                                  ❺ Configure back-
    server s1 127.0.0.1:9000 maxconn 32 check  ◁    end servers
    server s2 127.0.0.1:9001 maxconn 32 check
```

Here we set up HAProxy to listen to port 80 ❸ and use the `playapp` back end as the default back end for incoming traffic ❹. The `playapp` back end is configured to contain two servers: one listening on port 9000 ❺, and the second one on port 9001. The `check` option in the server lines causes HAProxy to periodically try to establish a TCP connection to the back-end server to see if it's up. If it's not up, no requests will be sent to that server.

HAProxy creates the connection to the Play applications, so from the Play application's perspective, HAProxy is the client. It's often useful to have the original client's IP address as well in the Play application, for example for logging purposes. That's why we set the `forwardfor` option ❶, which makes HAProxy add a header `X-Forwarded-For` that contains the original client's IP address to the request.

Finally, because we want to use WebSockets, we set the `http-server-close` option ❷, which makes HAProxy close the connection to Play after each request. This prevents a new WebSocket connection from being sent to the server over an existing TCP connection, which doesn't work.

Apache is the most commonly used web server, and it also has proxy capabilities. It doesn't support WebSockets, but that's not a problem if your application doesn't use them. If you're already using Apache, it might be interesting to stick to using Apache as a proxy, to reduce the number of different components in your architecture. The following listing shows a typical Apache configuration.

Listing 11.9 Apache front-end proxy configuration

```
<VirtualHost example.com:80>
  ServerName example.com
  ServerAdmin webmaster@example.com

  ErrorLog /var/log/apache2/example.com-error.log
  CustomLog /var/log/apache2/example.com-access.log combined

  ProxyRequests     Off
  ProxyPreserveHost On
  ProxyPass         / http://localhost:9000/
  ProxyPassReverse  / http://localhost:9000/

  <Proxy http://localhost:9000/*>
    Order deny,allow
```

```
    Allow from all
  </Proxy>

</VirtualHost>
```

This example sets up a front-end proxy for the site example.com, and proxies requests to localhost, on port 9000.

Apache, like HAProxy, is also capable of load balancing between multiple back-end servers. For this, we slightly change the configuration, as shown in the following listing.

Listing 11.10   Apache front-end proxy and load-balancing configuration

```
<VirtualHost example.com:80>
  ServerName example.com
  ServerAdmin webmaster@example.com

  ErrorLog /var/log/apache2/example.com-error.log
  CustomLog /var/log/apache2/example.com-access.log combined

  ProxyRequests     Off
  ProxyPreserveHost On
  ProxyPass         / balancer://playapps/
  ProxyPassReverse  / http://localhost:9000/        ┐ Make proxy load
  ProxyPassReverse  / http://localhost:9001/        │ balance between
                                                  ◁─┘ the two instances
  <Proxy balancer://playapps>
    BalancerMember http://localhost:9000
    BalancerMember http://localhost:9001
    Order deny, allow
    Allow From all
  </Proxy>
</VirtualHost>
```

If you're trying to run multiple instances of your application from the same directory, you'll get an error: *This application is already running (Or delete /path/to/RUNNING_PID file)*. This is caused by each instance wanting to store its own process ID in the RUNNING_PID file.

You can change the file where Play stores its process ID with the pidfile.path setting. So for example:

```
target/start -Dhttp.port=9001 -Dpidfile.path=PID_9001
```

If you set the pidfile.path to /dev/null, no PID file will be created.

11.3.5 *Using SSL*

Starting with version 2.1, Play supports SSL. It uses the libraries in java.security to read a private key and certificates from a *key store*.

Play can automatically generate a key store for you with a self-signed certificate. This is useful in development mode. All you need to start experimenting with SSL is to set the https.port system property:

```
play -Dhttps.port=9001 run
```

This will start your application, and it will listen on port 9000 for HTTP traffic, as well as on port 9001 for HTTPS traffic. If you point your browser to `https://localhost:9001/`, you should get a warning that the certificate is not trusted. This is expected because you don't have a certificate signed by a trusted certificate authority yet. But during development it's safe to ignore this, and allow this certificate in your browser.

The generated key store is saved in `conf/generated.keystore`, and Play will reuse it if you restart your application so you don't get the certificate warning again and again.

If you want to use SSL in production, you need to get a certificate that's either trusted by your organization if it's for an internal application, or one signed by an authority that's trusted by major browser vendors if it's to be used for a public application. These certificates can be bought from commercial vendors.

The process likely involves generating a private key, creating a *certificate signing request* (or *CSR*), and sending the CSR to the certificate vendor. They will create a certificate and send it back to you, together with root and intermediate certificates. Finally, you need to create a Java key store containing your private key, your generated certificate, and the root and intermediate certificates. Your certificate vendor should have instructions on how to do this.

Once you have a key store file with your key and certificates, you need to point Play to it. You need to set `https.keyStore` to point to your key store, and set `https.keyStorePassword` to your password:

```
play -Dhttps.port=9001 -Dhttps.keyStore=mykeystore.jks
  -Dhttp.keyStorePassword=mypassword run
```

Even though Play supports SSL, the recommended way to use SSL with Play in production is to let the front end—like HAProxy or Apache—handle it.

> **Configuration settings versus system properties**
> Note that `http.port`, `https.port`, `https.keyStore`, and `https.keyStore-Password` are not configuration settings but Java system properties.

11.3.6 *Deploying to a cloud provider*

Deploying a Play application isn't hard. The `target` and `dist` commands package your application with all dependencies, and to run it you only need Java. But you'll still need to set up a front-end proxy. You'll also need scripts to start your application when the machine reboots, and a place to store the logs.

There are service providers that take even these concerns away. *Platform as a service* providers like Heroku, Cloudbees, or Cloud Foundry allow you to upload your Play application to them, and their system will manage starting it and upgrading it without downtime. Those platforms have a web interface to manage basic application properties like domain name, and they provide a range of additional services like database instances or logging systems. Finally, they can easily spawn more instances of your application when there's a lot of traffic, and scale down when it gets quieter.

In short, if you want to minimize the effort of running and scaling your application, these providers are an excellent choice.

Each of these providers works a little differently from the others, but the main idea is the same. You install a command-line tool from the provider, and you use this to upload your application to the platform. The command-line tool also allows you to check the status of your application, restart it, retrieve the logs, and so on.

11.3.7 *Deploying to an application server*

Play is a full-stack framework; a Play application can be deployed without the need of an application server or servlet container, unlike most other Java web frameworks.

If you work in a big organization that uses JVM technologies, chances are that all web applications are deployed on an application server, and that the only way that your precious Play 2 application will ever be allowed to hook up to the internet is through an application server.

This poses a problem, because Play doesn't use the servlet API, which makes it impossible to run on an application server that expects web applications to use it.

Luckily, there's a plugin for Play 2, *play2-war-plugin*, that can package your application as a WAR. It provides a layer between the servlet API and your Play application.

Some of the more advanced features of Play, like WebSockets, don't work with all servlet API versions, and there are also differences in the capabilities of Play 2.0 and Play 2.1. So make sure you check the compatibility matrix on the plugin's web page to determine whether your application and server will match.

11.4 *Summary*

In this chapter we've learned how to include a module in an application and how to use one popular module. We've extracted generic functionality from our original application and turned it into a module of our own. Furthermore, we now know how to publish a module so that others can use it.

In the second half of this chapter we learned the different strategies for deploying our applications to production and how to configure front-end proxies and use SSL. Finally we've looked at several cloud providers that support Play and seen that we can run our Play 2 application on an application server if necessary.

In the next chapter, we'll see how we can test our modules and applications.

Testing your application

12

This chapter covers

- An introduction to testing with Play
- Explaining the different levels of testing
- Unit, functional, and integration testing with Play and JUnit
- Browser testing with Play and Selenium

Now that we have a complete application, we need to start thinking about further development and maintenance. But as you evolve your application, new bugs may creep into your code, and changes in external factors may introduce errors in your application even if you never touch it.

Automated testing is an invaluable tool when you want to make sure that your application still works like you expect it to. In addition, automated tests also help you during development—they allow you to verify that your code does what you think it does.

In this chapter, we'll show you different kinds of tests that help you test applications at different levels, and how Play helps you create and run these tests.

12.1   *Testing Play applications*

As we've seen in the previous chapters, a Play application consists of several core components—controllers, models, view templates, routes, forms, and so on. One of the nice things about Play is that they all result in runnable code. This means that for all these concepts, there's a class or method that you can access from your Java code. It also means that you can take any separate component and test it by executing its code and checking the result. This is the core principle of automated testing—run some code, compare the result against an expected value, and return the findings. This kind of testing is called *unit testing*. It's called unit testing because you take an individual *unit* of code and... well... test it.

Of course, you don't only want to check the internal behavior of your application. You also want to make sure that it interacts with the outside world—the browser or system that's calling your web app or API—correctly. This is called *integration testing*. Play offers a library to test your web service API and integration with a tool called *Selenium*. This will test how your application behaves in a browser.

Play has facilities to make it possible to test every part of your application and make running your tests easy. In this section, we'll create our first unit test, and learn how to run it. In the following sections, we'll show you how to test every aspect of your application.

But first things first. Let's see how to write and run tests in Play.

12.1.1   *Writing tests*

In Play 2, all tests are written using JUnit. JUnit is probably the most popular testing framework for Java. In JUnit, a test is a method annotated with the @org.junit.Test annotation. Inside a test method, you write some code and verify your assumptions about that code using *assertions*—methods that compare an expected and an actual situation. JUnit provides a lot of assertion methods to help you make comparisons and report exactly what's wrong when an assertion fails.

Let's write a simple test to see how this works in practice. Any test you write should go in your application's test folder, so create one now. If you're using an IDE, you might have to regenerate your IDE project files for it to show up properly. In this folder, create a new Java class called ApplicationTest, with the contents shown in the following listing.

> **Listing 12.1   ApplicationTest.java**

```
import org.junit.Test;
import static org.junit.Assert.*;

public class ApplicationTest {

  @Test
  public void passingTest() {
    String first = "OK";
    String second = "OK";
```

```
      assertEquals("This test will pass", first, second);
    }

    @Test
    public void failingTest() {
      String first = "OK";
      String second = "NOT OK";
      assertEquals("This test will fail", first, second);
    }
}
```

As you can see, this test is a simple Java class: it doesn't extend any classes or implement any interfaces. But we did create a static import of `org.junit.Assert.*`. The `Assert` class, part of JUnit, contains a lot of static assertion methods. We import them all statically, so that they're directly available from our code in our class.

The two methods in our class are the actual tests. To indicate that these are our test methods, they have to be annotated with `org.junit.Test`. Our two tests, `passingTest` and `failingTest`, compare two strings for equality. First we set up two strings, and then we call `assertEquals` to do the comparison. The first parameter is optional, but allows you to define a message about what you're testing. If this were a real test, you'd call some of your own code, and then compare the return value of some method calls, or the state of your objects.

Now that we have our tests, let's see what happens if we run them.

12.1.2 *Running tests*

In Play 2, all tests are run from the Play 2 console. To run them, simply run the `test` command. Play will run your tests. Go ahead and run the test we just wrote. You should get output as shown in listing 12.2. You can also use the `~test` (with a tilde) command. The command allows you to run the test as soon as the code changes. This is useful when using the test-driven development methodology. This method focuses on writing the test first that defines the desired improvement or new function, then producing the minimum amount of code to pass that test.

Listing 12.2 Running our test

```
[test-test] $ test
[info] ApplicationTest
[error] Test ApplicationTest.failingTest failed:
 These strings should be
    equal expected:<[]OK> but was:<[NOT ]OK>
[info] + ExampleTest.passingTest
[info] x ExampleTest.failingTest
[info]
[info]
[info] Total for test ApplicationTest
[info] Finished in 0.062 seconds
[info] 2 tests, 1 failures, 0 errors
[error] Failed: : Total 2, Failed 1, Errors 0, Passed 1,
    Skipped 0
```

```
[error] Failed tests:
[error]     ExampleTest
[error] test-test/test:test: Tests unsuccessful
[error] Total time: 0 s, completed Nov 10, 2012
  8:36:09 PM
```

Now, this way of running tests is fine if you only have one, or maybe even a few tests, but since the test command runs *all* the tests in your application, it'll eventually be too slow and there will be too much output to find what you're looking for. Therefore, if you ever want to focus on one test only, you can use the test-only command.

The test-only command takes one or more class names as parameters, and will execute only the tests in those classes. So, if you wanted to run our example test, you'd run test-only ApplicationTest. The output would in this case be the same as before, since it's currently the only test we have.

Unit tests are great for testing classes that are more or less standalone, and require no outside dependencies that aren't easily faked (we call that *mocking* the dependencies). Examples of such are model classes or utility classes and methods. But not every part of your application can exist in such a vacuum, as we'll see next.

Let's write a more useful test to test our Product model. We want to test that our findByEan() method introduced in chapter 3 works correctly. For this, we need to add the following test:

```
@Test
public void findByEan() {
  Product product = Product.findByEan("1111111111111");
  assertThat(product.name).isEqualTo("Paperclip 1111111111111");
}
```

For now, go ahead and run the test. You'll get the following output:

```
Test ApplicationTest.findByEan
failed: javax.persistence.PersistenceException:
java.sql.SQLException: Attempting to obtain a connection
 from a pool that has already been shutdown.
```

That's probably not what you expected. But what went wrong?

Not all classes and methods (and therefore templates) are completely standalone. Sometimes your code depends on objects and code from other methods and classes. In Play, some code may depend on a running Play application. For example, your code might need to read configuration, access the database, or just use one of Play's contexts (such as Session or Flash). When you try to run code like that outside the scope of your Play application, you'll encounter an error. That's exactly what happened in this case:

```
java.sql.SQLException: Attempting to obtain a connection
 from a pool that has already been shutdown
```

Our test tried to access the database, but Play isn't running, and therefore the configuration isn't loaded.

Now that we know what's wrong, how do we fix it? Of course, Play has the tools for you. Play allows you to use a *fake application*. By wrapping your test code in a fake application, the Global object that loads initial data and the database access you've defined are available by default. But things such as the session or request won't be available. You still need to pass those, as we'll see later in the chapter.

Play's facilities to make testing easier can be found in the play.test.Helpers class. Go ahead and add a static import for all its members:

```
import play.test.Helpers.*;
```

This will give us access to a bunch of things, but for now we're interested in the running() and fakeApplication() methods. The fakeApplication will give us our fake application, whereas running() allows us to run code in the context of that application. The running() method takes two parameters: Application to use as context, and a block of code to run, represented by an implementation of Runnable, which contains a run() method that will execute our code.[1] Wrap the test in these methods:

```
@Test
public void findByEan() {
 running(fakeApplication(), new Runnable() {
   public void run() {
 Product product = Product.findByEan("1111111111111");
 assertThat(product.name).isEqualTo("Paperclip 1111111111111");
   }
  });
}
```

Please note that the Product with EAN 1111111111111 exists and has been added to our evolution scripts as explained in section 7.5.3. We're also using some helpers that allow us to be more human when describing what we're testing. Indeed, we're asserting that product.name is equal to "Paperclip 1111111111111". In order to use those helpers, you need to import statically org.fest.assertions.Assertions.*:

```
import static org.fest.assertions.Assertions.*;
```

Rerunning the test gives us the expected results:

```
[error] Test ApplicationTest.failingTest failed:
This test will fail expected:<[]OK> but was:<[NOT ]OK>
[info] play - Starting application default Akka system.
[info] play - Shutdown application default Akka system.
[info] ApplicationTest
[info] x failingTest
[info] + findByEan
[info] + pagination
[info] + passingTest
[info]
[info]
[info] Total for test ApplicationTest
```

---

[1] This way of passing around runnable code is verbose, but will have to do until JDK 8 brings us lambdas, which provide a much nicer syntax to do this kind of thing.

```
[info] Finished in 0.019 seconds
[info] 4 tests, 1 failures, 0 errors
```

You can also observe that Play was bootstrapped correctly and made the database available to the tests. Let's quickly create a pagination test:

```
@Test
public void pagination() {
  running(fakeApplication(), new Runnable() {
   public void run() {
     Page<Product> products = Product.find(1);
     assertThat(products.getTotalRowCount()).isEqualTo(50);
     assertThat(products.getList().size()).isEqualTo(10);
    }
   });
}
```

Here we're testing that whenever we're performing pagination, the total number of results is 50 and then we get 10 results for the current page. Of course, we pre-filled our database with 50 products, as explained in section 7.5.3.

Using a different configuration for tests

By default, `fakeApplication()` instantiates a fake Play application based on your current `application.conf` file. But you might want to test a different setup sometimes, for example when you want to use a different database. For that reason, you can supply a `Map<String, String>` as a parameter to `fakeApplication()`. You can use that map to supply configuration key/value pairs, and they will override the configuration from your `application.conf`.

12.2 Functional testing

In this section we're going to test various functions of our application. The first test is to confirm that not every user can log in to our application.

12.2.1 Testing your controllers

In order to know if our application works correctly, we need to test that not everyone can access the application. As you may remember, in our application, before you can access the product listing, you need to show credentials. In plain English, the software function is: "only authenticated users can access the product listing." Let's verify that by writing the corresponding test.

Create a new class under the `test` directory called `FunctionalTest`, and create the test shown in the following listing.

Listing 12.3 `FunctionalTest.java`

```java
import org.junit.*;

import java.util.*;

import play.mvc.*;
import play.test.*;
import play.libs.F.*;

import static play.test.Helpers.*;
import static org.fest.assertions.Assertions.*;
import com.google.common.collect.ImmutableMap;

public class FunctionalTest {

@Test
public void authenticateFailure() {
 running(fakeApplication(), new Runnable() {
  public void run() {
   Result result = callAction(
   controllers.routes.ref.Products.index(),
   fakeRequest()
   );
   assertThat(status(result)).isEqualTo(SEE_OTHER);
   assertThat(redirectLocation(result)).isEqualTo("/login");
  }
 });
 }
}
```

1 Create a Play fakeApplication to bootstrap our application

2 callAction() allows us to call an action method via the generated routes file

3 Reference to the index() action method from the Products controller

4 fakeRequest() simulates an HTTP request

5 Asserts that the HTTP result code is a redirect

6 Asserts that we're redirected to the /login page

In our test, we first start a `fakeApplication` **1**, as seen in the previous section, to instantiate Play persistence and routing features. From there, we're calling our `index()` action method on the `Products` **3** controller through the generated routes Java file with the `callAction()` method. You can actually access all action methods from any controllers using the `callAction` method and passing a reference to an action method. The `callAction()` **2** method also requires a `Request` object as argument: we're passing a `fakeRequest()` **4** that mocks a Play request.

We then test that we're redirected. This is done by checking that the result status code is `SEE_OTHER` (HTTP Redirect—303 status code) **5**. And finally, we test that the redirect location is `/login` **6**.

If you run the test now, you'll see that it passes! Indeed, as long as we're not authenticated, we can't display the product listing. It's now time to test a successful authentication. Let's edit our `FunctionalTest.java` file and add the test shown in listing 12.4.

Listing 12.4 FunctionalTest.java—authenticateSuccess

```
@Test
public void authenticateSuccess() {
  running(fakeApplication(), new Runnable() {          ❶ Create Play fakeApplication
    public void run() {                                   to bootstrap our application
      Result result = callAction(                       ❷ callAction() allows us to call an action
        controllers.routes.ref.Application.authenticate(),  method via the generated routes file
        fakeRequest()                                     Reference to
          .withFormUrlEncodedBody(ImmutableMap.of(        authenticate()
          "email", "nicolas",                             action method from
          "password", "nicolas"))                         the Application
        );                                              ❸ controller
      assertThat(status(result))
        .isEqualTo(SEE_OTHER);                          Fake request with our
      assertThat(redirectLocation(result))             username and password
        .isEqualTo("/");                               ❹ as an encoded form
      assertThat(session(result).get("email"))
        .isEqualTo("nicolas");                          Asserts that the HTTP
    }                                                  ❺ result code is a redirect
  });
}                                                       Asserts that we are
                                                        successfully redirected to
                                                       ❻ the root (/) web page

                                                        Asserts that we are correctly
                                                        authenticated by checking that the
                                                       ❼ session contains our login email
```

The test first starts a fakeApplication ❶, as seen previously. We then call the authenticate() ❸ method from the application controller that we defined in section 10.3 using the callAction() method ❷. If you recall, the authenticate() ❸ method expects an email and a password through an HTTP form. We're creating a URL encoded form with the withFormUrlEncodedBody(ImmutableMap.of("email", "nicolas", "password", "nicolas")) ❹ method—the ImmutableMap isn't really relevant here; just consider it as a map. This is appended to our fakeRequest() that's given as a parameter to the callAction() method.

We then test that we're redirected ❺ to the root application page ❻. Finally, we make sure we're signed in to the application ❼.

Running the test shows that our application is working and that we can authenticate. It's now time to test our product listing web page.

12.2.2 Template testing

Let's write our first test for a template. As you may recall, templates get compiled to classes and methods, which means that they can be unit tested, just like any other bit of code. We'll create a test for the product list template. Figure 12.1 shows a reminder of our products list.

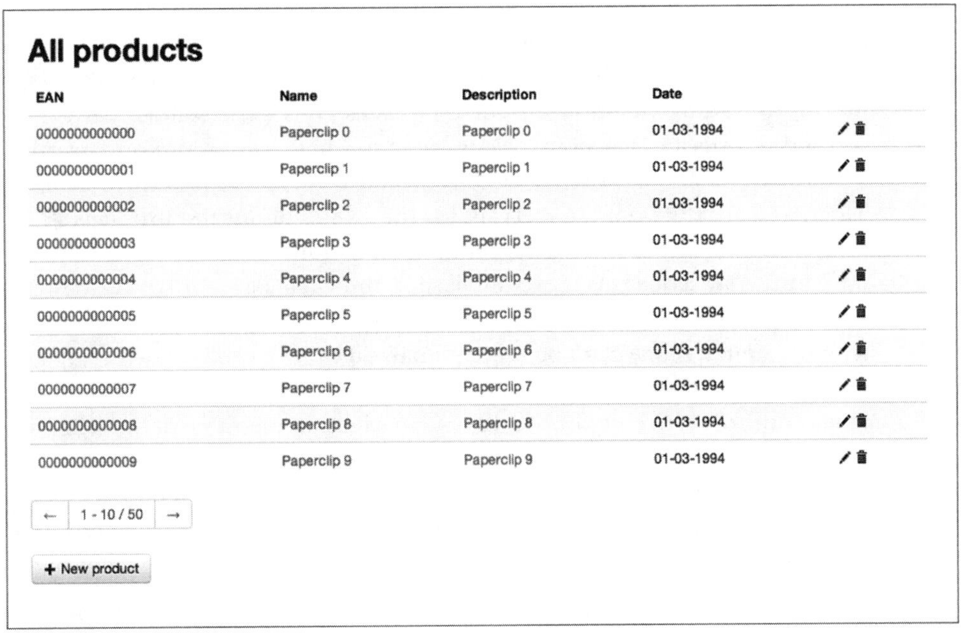

All products

EAN	Name	Description	Date	
0000000000000	Paperclip 0	Paperclip 0	01-03-1994	✏ 🗑
0000000000001	Paperclip 1	Paperclip 1	01-03-1994	✏ 🗑
0000000000002	Paperclip 2	Paperclip 2	01-03-1994	✏ 🗑
0000000000003	Paperclip 3	Paperclip 3	01-03-1994	✏ 🗑
0000000000004	Paperclip 4	Paperclip 4	01-03-1994	✏ 🗑
0000000000005	Paperclip 5	Paperclip 5	01-03-1994	✏ 🗑
0000000000006	Paperclip 6	Paperclip 6	01-03-1994	✏ 🗑
0000000000007	Paperclip 7	Paperclip 7	01-03-1994	✏ 🗑
0000000000008	Paperclip 8	Paperclip 8	01-03-1994	✏ 🗑
0000000000009	Paperclip 9	Paperclip 9	01-03-1994	✏ 🗑

← 1 - 10 / 50 →

\+ New product

Figure 12.1 The products list

So what can we test about this template? There are a few things:

- It should render HTML
- It should show products
- It should contain links
- It contains 10 products out of 50

We could use the render() method from our template and test the generated output. The following listing shows an example of such a test.

Listing 12.5 Not working `FunctionalTest.java`

```
@Test
public void displaysAllProducts() {
  running(fakeApplication(), new Runnable() {        ❶ Retrieve
    public void run() {                                  list of
      Page<Product> allProducts = Product.find(0);   ⟵   products
                                                       ❷ Render
      Content rendered = views.html.catalog.render(allProducts);  ⟵ template
      assertThat("text/html").isEqualTo(rendered.contentType());
      for(Product p : allProducts.getList()) {
        assertThat(rendered.body()).contains(p.name);
      }
    }
  });
}
```

Asserts on ❸ output

This test isn't going to work in our case because we can only use the `render()` method for simple use cases, but it's important to understand what's going on. In this test, we first need to retrieve a list of test products that we'll pass to the template ❶, and then we call the `render` method on our template's class (`views.html.catalog`) ❷. That method returns an object of type `Content`, on which we can run our assertions.

Now we assert that the `Content` returned is of the expected type: `text/html` ❸. Then, we check the rendered HTML for the names of our test products ❸.

We can only use the `render()` method for simple use cases, when we're not making use of the Play scopes. As we stated earlier, the `fakeApplication()` doesn't provide a session nor a request. This means that things like the flash scope, the session scope, and the request scope can't be used. Actually, if they're used by your template, Play will give you an error stating that it has no HTTP context available. This is useful for testing independent HTML components like the navigation menu we defined in section 8.4.1, and this is why we presented this test. But this isn't the case for the product listing page, because we're using the flash scope in our `main.scala.html` template.

Let's now see how to correctly implement our test for the product listing page. Let's edit our `FunctionalTest.java` file and add the test shown in the following listing.

Listing 12.6   FunctionalTest.java—listProductsOnTheFirstPage

```
@Test
public void listProductsOnTheFirstPage() {
    running(fakeApplication(), new Runnable() {
        public void run() {
            Result result = callAction(
    controllers.routes.ref.Products.list(0),
    fakeRequest().withSession("email", "nicolas"));
    assertThat(status(result)).isEqualTo(OK);
    assertThat("text/html").
                    isEqualTo(contentType(result));
    String content = contentAsString(result);
    assertThat(content).
                        contains("1 - 10 / 50");
    Page<Product> allProducts = Product.find(0);
    for(Product p : allProducts.getList()) {
      assertThat(content).contains(p.name);
    }
        }
    });
}
```

Asserts that we got an OK status back — points to `assertThat(status(result)).isEqualTo(OK);`

Call Products.list() action method (the /products in our routes file) with a session that authenticates user nicolas

Asserts that we got served text/html content

Asserts that we are at the first page and displaying the first 10 products out of 50

Find all the products for the first page (page 0)

Make sure the product coming out of the database is displayed on the page

This test is quite similar to the one we've seen previously using the `callAction` method. We're calling the `list()` action method from our `Products` controller. That's the action used to display the product listing. The `list(0)` indicates that we want to display the first page. As annotated in the code, we then assert that Play returns an OK status, Play is serving us HTML, and that we're displaying the first page. We then make sure that if we query the database directly for the first 10 products (page 0), the same products are displayed on the first page.

These tests are rudimentary, and string comparison is usually not the way to go to test an HTML page. These tests suffice as a basic smoke test, but aren't very good as a complete web page test. Later in the chapter we'll introduce browser testing, which is a nicer and more complete way to correct the behavior of your web pages in a browser.

12.2.3 *Testing the router*

We're now able to test three major components from our Play application: the model, the controller, and the template. It's time to consider testing another crucial part of our Play application: the router.

Until now, we've trusted that our routes were all correct and according to specification. For example, in the previous section, we trusted that calling the `list()` action method on the `Products` controller was the same as calling the `/products/` URL. Let's see how we can make sure our assumptions are correct and enforce that the product listing is served by the `/products/` URL. Edit the file `FunctionalTest.java` one more time and add the test shown in the following listing.

Listing 12.7 `listProductsOnTheFirstPageWithRouter`

```
@Test
public void
    listProductsOnTheFirstPageWithRouter() {
  running(fakeApplication(), new Runnable() {
    public void run() {
  Result result =
    routeAndCall(fakeRequest(GET, "/products/")        ◁─┐ routeAndCall() method
      .withSession("email", "nicolas"));                  │ is used to call the
                                                          ◁─┘ /products/ URL
  assertThat(status(result)).isEqualTo(OK);
  assertThat("text/html").isEqualTo(contentType(result));
  String content = contentAsString(result);
  assertThat(content).contains("1 - 10 / 50");

  Page<Product> allProducts = Product.find(0);
  for(Product p : allProducts.getList()) {
     assertThat(content).contains(p.name);
  }
    }
  });
}
```

This example is exactly the same as the previous one, except that this time we're testing the `/products/` URL directly. We're now using the `routeAndCall()` instead of the `callAction` method. The `routeAndCall()` method takes two parameters: the URL we want to test and the HTTP method it should call the URL with. The `routeAndCall()` method is useful to test the not found or error pages, for example.

Now that we've seen how we can test our application's internals, let's see how we can test its interaction with the outside world. This is also called *integration testing*.

12.3   *Integration testing*

Integration testing is all about testing your application's behavior when dealing with the "outside world." This can be anything from a user's web browser to the communication with another web service—whether you're calling it from your application, or it's calling your application.

Integration testing differs from the way we've been testing so far. Up to now, we've been testing our application's code directly by calling methods and checking the results. Integration testing tests your application as a whole, by verifying the behavior of its external interface (your UI or web service API).

12.3.1   *Testing your HTTP interface*

As we've seen throughout the book, any web application, whether it's a web service or meant to be used through a web browser, consists of a set of HTTP URLs as far as the outside world is concerned. When doing integration testing, you make these calls and inspect the results. Other than testing something completely different, the actual testing is the same—you run some code, and run assertions on the results. Play comes with helpers to make this easy.

The first step in writing an integration test is getting the application running. This time, a fake application like we saw in section 12.2 isn't enough—we need a running server. For that, we'll use the `testServer()` method, instead of the `fakeApplication()` method that we saw in section 12.2. The `testServer()` method takes one parameter: the port number on which the server will run.

Other than using a `TestServer` instead of a `FakeApplication`, the mechanism for testing with a test server is the same as when testing using a fake application: use the `running()` method, and pass it the `TestServer` instance and a `Runnable` that contains the test code. The following listing illustrates this.

> **Listing 12.8   Testing using a test server**

```
public void myIntegrationTest() {
  running(testServer(9001), new Runnable() {
    @Override
    public void run() {
      // Test code goes here
    }
  });
}
```

To actually make our HTTP calls, we can use the WS class. The WS class is part of the WS (WebService) library provided with Play and allows us to make web calls to remote systems from a client perspective. It's straightforward to use, as we'll see. We'll test that the products list URL returns status code 200 and has a non-empty body. Listing 12.9 shows the test. Go ahead and run it: it should pass.

Listing 12.9 A simple test for an HTTP call

```
public void myIntegrationTest() {
  running(testServer(9001), new Runnable() {
    @Override
    public void run() {
      final WS.Response response =
        WS.url("http://localhost:9001").get().get();
      assertEquals(200, response.getStatus());
      assertFalse(response.getBody().isEmpty());
    }
  });
}
```

Using the testing techniques we've seen so far, you can test a fair amount of your application. If your application has no UI, but is "just" a web service, you can test pretty much everything. But if you have a web application with an HTML/CSS/JavaScript user interface, that's a big part of your application that you can't test just by verifying the results of your Play code. You need a browser, and a way to automate testing your UI.

12.3.2 *Browser testing*

Play comes with integration for Selenium[2] and FluentLenium.[3] Selenium is a tool that allows automated browser testing. It has support for several browsers, as well as HtmlUnit, which is a way to do *headless* browser testing—browser testing without actually running a browser. FluentLenium is a test framework that allows you to write Selenium tests much like you would a unit test, rather than recording and playing back browser interaction, which is the "regular" way to create Selenium tests.

Play makes it easy to run Selenium/FluentLenium tests. The basic approach is the same as what we've seen with integration tests: use the running() method, and pass it a TestServer and an object that holds your actual test code. The difference is that we must now also pass it a browser configuration, and that our test code is contained in a Callback rather than a Runnable.[4]

Explaining all of Selenium and FluentLenium would require a whole book, so we won't attempt to do that here, but we'll show you a basic test to illustrate how you can use these tools with Play. If you'd like to know more, both Selenium and Fluent-Lenium have excellent documentation.

For our test, let's see if the product list page works like we expect. We're going to test that the page actually contains the product list, and that clicking on a product takes us to the product detail view. First, let's set up the basic test structure. Listing 12.10 shows how.

---

[2] http://seleniumhq.org
[3] https://github.com/FluentLenium/FluentLenium
[4] We use a Callback because it can take a parameter, and a Runnable can't.

Listing 12.10   `IntegrationTest.java`

```
import static play.test.Helpers.*;

import org.junit.Test;
import play.libs.F;
import play.test.TestBrowser;

import static org.junit.Assert.*;

public class IntegrationTest {

  @Test
  public void simpleProductsTest() {
    running(testServer(3333), HTMLUNIT,
      new F.Callback<TestBrowser>() {
        @Override
        public void invoke(TestBrowser browser)
          throws Throwable {
          // Test code here
        }
      });
  }
}
```

❶ We'll use the HtmlUnit browser

This method will hold our test code

We've configured our test to use the `HTMLUNIT TestBrowser` ❶, which instructs Play to use Selenium with the headless HtmlUnit test browser. Since this browser is often used, `play.test.Helpers.HTMLUNIT` makes this test browser conveniently available as a constant. There's also a `FIREFOX` constant that sets up the test to use Firefox, but we'll use HtmlUnit.

Now that we have the framework for our test, let's implement it. You might've noticed that the `invoke` method is passed a `browser` parameter. That object actually represents our test browser and allows us to interact with it using the FluentLenium API. We'll use it to create the following test:

1 **Go to** the URL for the product list page.
2 **Assert** that at least one link to a product is present on the page.
3 **Click** one of the products in the list.
4 **Assert** that the browser's location has changed to the URL of the product detail page.
5 **Assert** that the page displays the correct product name.

The bold verbs in our test steps highlight what kind of interaction we want with our test browser: we want to be able to control navigation (go to), simulate user interaction (click), and read information from the page so we can verify that it shows what we expect (assert).

The first step, navigating to the proper URL, is the easiest one to do, so let's do that first. We'll use the `goTo()` method on the `browser` object, passing it the URL we want to navigate to, like so:

```
browser.goTo("http://localhost:3333/products");
```

Now, presumably, our browser has opened the page at the URL we gave it. But how do we verify that we're actually where we want to be, and that the correct page is showing? That's step two of our test: "Assert that the product list is present on the page."

For assertions, we'll use JUnit, just like we've been doing all along. The only thing that's not immediately obvious is how to ask the browser for information about the page that is currently rendered. For that, we can use the FluentLenium API as well.

If you've ever used CSS or jQuery, you're probably familiar with *selectors*. Selectors allow you to select elements of an HTML page by specifying element names, classes, and IDs. FluentLenium allows you to use selectors for this purpose as well. Play's integration with FluentLenium borrows the $ syntax from jQuery to give us access—the `browser` object has a `$()` method that allows us to run selectors on the currently rendered page.

Now that we have the tools, let's assert that we have a product list on our page. First, we need to sign in to the application as an authorized user. We're using the `fill()` method to input our username and password in the login screen. The selector for our input element is simply `input[name='email']` and `input[name='password']`, as defined in our HTML. We then submit the sign-in form and are redirected to the product listing page, where we're looking for at least one a element contained in a `td` element. The selector for this is `"table td a"`. To assert that we have at least one result, we'll use the `isNotEmpty()` method. The next listing shows the corresponding code.

Listing 12.11 Testing the presence of the product list

```
import org.junit.*;

import play.mvc.*;
import play.test.*;
import play.libs.F.*;

import static play.test.Helpers.*;
import static org.fest.assertions.Assertions.*;

import static org.fluentlenium.core.filter.FilterConstructor.*;

public class IntegrationTest {

@Test
public void productListingTest() {
 running(testServer(3333,
  fakeApplication()),
  HTMLUNIT, new Callback<TestBrowser>() {
  public void invoke(TestBrowser browser) {
   browser.goTo("http://localhost:3333");
    // login
    browser.fill("input[name='email']").with("nicolas");
    browser.fill("input[name='password']").with("nicolas");
    browser.submit("button[type='submit']");
    assertThat(browser.$("table td a")).isNotEmpty();
   }
  });
 }
}
```

Now that we've verified that our product list page correctly shows up in a browser, let's test some interaction. When we click the link, we expect to be taken to the product's detail page. To verify this behavior, we need to click the link, and then check the state of the browser.

To click the link, we can select it and then call the `click()` method on it. To then check the location of the browser, we can call the `url()` method on the `browser` object. Of course, the URL isn't enough to convince us. To verify that this is the product detail page, we'll check its title for the product name. The final test is shown in the following listing.

Listing 12.12 Testing interaction

```
...
@Test
public void productListingTest() {
 running(testServer(3333,
 fakeApplication()),
 HTMLUNIT, new Callback<TestBrowser>() {
 public void invoke(TestBrowser browser) {
  browser.goTo("http://localhost:3333");
  // login
  browser.fill("input[name='email']").with("nicolas");
  browser.fill("input[name='password']").with("nicolas");
  browser.submit("button[type='submit']");
  assertThat(browser.$("table td a")).isNotEmpty();
  browser.$("table td a").first().click();
  assertThat("http://localhost:3333/products/0000000000000")
   .isEqualTo(browser.url());
  assertThat("Product (Paperclip 0)").isEqualTo(
  browser.$("legend").getText());
 }
 });
}
...
```

If you haven't yet, go ahead and run these tests—they should all pass fine. Now, these tests may seem simple—why test if a link works, when you could just as easily check the value of its `href` attribute? Well, though it's correct that, in this case, we're essentially testing if the browser works, consider a JavaScript-heavy web page. An event handler might actually break navigation functionality. There's no way to test that without actually running the code in the browser. That is why browser tests are incredibly useful—they test your web pages like a user would, without burdening an actual human with all sorts of tedious clicking. Now that we've automated this kind of testing as well, we can test our application at every level.

12.4 *Summary*

In this chapter, we've seen how Play helps you write automated tests. We've seen how we can run JUnit tests, and the difference between unit, integration, and browser tests. We've seen that we could test different parts of our Play application: the models, the controllers, the templates, and the router. Using `FakeApplication`, and the `running()` method found in the `play.test.Helpers` class, your entire application can be tested by calling the application code directly. The `TestServer` allows you to call your application's HTTP interface like a client application would, enabling you to run integration tests. Play's integration with Selenium and FluenLenium means that you can easily test your application as the user sees it, including the effects of JavaScript and user interaction.

You've now made it through Play and learned a lot; you have the knowledge to tackle modern web applications and can expand on that knowledge. As a final suggestion, try to keep in touch with the Play community. It's a busy and exciting place, and we'd love to hear from you there. Hope you've enjoyed the ride!

index

RELATED MANNING TITLES

Scala in Action
by Nilanjan Raychaudhuri

ISBN: 978-1-935182-75-7
416 pages, $44.99
April 2013

Scala in Depth
by Joshua D. Suereth

ISBN: 978-1-935182-70-2
304 pages, $49.99
May 2012

Play for Scala
Covers Play 2

by Peter Hilton, Erik Bakker,
  and Francisco Canedo

ISBN: 978-1-617290-79-4
328 pages, $49.99
October 2013

HTML5 in Action

by Rob Crowther, Joe Lennon, Ash Blue
  and Greg Wanish

ISBN: 978-1-617290-49-7
466 pages, $39.99
February 2014

For ordering information go to www.manning.com